FROM THE MILL
TO
MONTE CARLO

FROM THE MILL
TO
MONTE CARLO

THE WORKING-CLASS ENGLISHMAN
WHO BEAT THE MONACO CASINO
AND CHANGED GAMBLING FOREVER

ANNE FLETCHER

AMBERLEY

For my father Dr Clifford Malcolm Fletcher (1929–1999)
who told me this story but didn't live to see me write it.

First published 2018

Amberley Publishing
The Hill, Stroud
Gloucestershire, GL5 4EP

www.amberley-books.com

Copyright © Anne Fletcher, 2018

The right of Anne Fletcher to be identified as
the Author of this work has been asserted in
accordance with the Copyrights, Designs and
Patents Act 1988.

ISBN 978 1 4456 7139 0 (hardback)
ISBN 978 1 4456 7140 6 (ebook)

British Library Cataloguing in Publication Data.
A catalogue record for this book is available
from the British Library.

Typesetting and Origination by Amberley Publishing
Printed in the UK.

CONTENTS

PART 3: 'And I've now such lots of money, I'm a gent'

PROLOGUE

'*Faites vos jeux*!' The croupier's voice was the only sound in the high, vaulted hall. Play had long since ceased at the other tables; all eyes were on the Englishman, watching for his next move. Could this extraordinary run of luck continue? The crowd was silent as the *toureur* spun the roulette wheel and the ball clattered across the metal struts that divided the numbers. The wheel slowed. '*Rien ne va plus*!' There was a nervous cough from the croupier and then it was over. '*Vingt-huit*!' was the shout from the crowd, '*Encore une fois, il gagne* – bravo monsieur, bravo!' A black cloth was called for and the *chef de partie* draped the table in mourning. The bank had been broken. The Englishman, a large, cheerful, bearded man, rose from the table and, showing little sign of nervous strain, shook hands with the croupier, gathered up his winnings and left the building.

I grew up on this tale; Joseph Hobson Jagger was my great-great-great-uncle. My dad told me the story often. He was proud of his famous ancestor, who began life as a poor Yorkshire mill worker and became a millionaire after breaking the bank at Monte Carlo. I was told that the famous song 'The Man Who Broke the Bank at Monte Carlo' was written about him. I recounted the tale too, telling my friends about this working-class Victorian man who had done a most extraordinary thing. Only when I was an adult did I start to question what I had always been told. Joseph's story posed some problems for me; there seemed to be gaping holes in the narrative. Why did a man from a working-class family, employed in a mill in Bradford, go to Monte Carlo? It was the playground of Europe's rich. How could he afford to go, and why would he want to? How did he get there, and what happened to the money he was alleged to have won? My family was not rich, had never been rich; to the contrary, my father had grown up in poverty. A newspaper search revealed no coverage at all of Joseph winning a fortune at Monte Carlo, apart from an article my own father had written which had been published in Bradford's *Telegraph & Argus* in 1960. His will, I discovered, was not that of a multimillionaire. I began to doubt that Joseph Hobson Jagger had broken the bank at all.

Armed with my experience as a professional historian and with access through the internet to a wealth of resources, I became determined to uncover what really happened in a way that my father never could. I underestimated just how hard it would be to get to the truth behind the family story. So little of Joseph's life remains. There are of course the records of official milestones in his life revealed in the census, in marriage and birth certificates and in wills and deeds, but there is not much more. All I had at the start of my search was the newspaper article that my father wrote, which records the family's oral history, the words of the song 'The Man Who Broke the Bank at Monte Carlo' and a photograph of Joseph Hobson Jagger that I had inherited.

It's a small photograph set in an oval frame and mounted on a card approximately 6 centimetres by 11 centimetres. This photographic portrait shows an affable, slightly portly man with full moustache and greying beard, his receding hair parted to the side. His woollen three-piece lounge suit isn't excessively smart, and the jacket doesn't fit well. The striped tie is in a knot, probably a 'four in hand', which was popular at the time, but it sits under a relatively unstarched collar.[1] Not a wealthy man, then, and yet this photograph was not taken in Bradford. Turning it over, I found the photographer's details were printed on the back. Joseph had sat for this portrait not at home, nor even in London, but at the studio of Wilhelm Bienmüller on the Rue Gioffredo, in Nice. This was a lifeline, proof that our treasured family story might yet be founded in truth. My great-great-great-uncle had been to Nice, the key transit point for visitors travelling to Monte Carlo.

Looking at Joseph I wondered what he had been like, what sort of a man he was. The song, written ostensibly about him by Fred Gilbert, and first performed in 1892, was not very encouraging. Its main character is a money-loving trickster and womanising show-off, not really the sort of ancestor that I could be proud of:

I've just got here, through Paris, from the sunny southern shore;
I to Monte Carlo went, just to raise my winter's rent;
Dame Fortune smiled upon me as she'd never done before,
And I've now such lots of money, I'm a gent.
Yes I've now such lots of money, I'm a gent.

As I walk along the Bois Boulogne
With an independent aire
You can see the girls declare
'He must be a Millionaire.'
You can hear them sigh, and wish to die,
You can see them wink the other eye
At the man who broke the bank at Monte Carlo.

I stay indoors till after lunch, and then my daily walk
To the great Triumphal Arch is one grand triumphal march.
Observed by each observer – with the keenness of a hawk.
I'm a mass of money, linen, silk, and starch –
I'm a mass of money, linen, silk, and starch.

As I walk along the Bois Boulogne, etc.

I patronised the tables at the Monte Carlo hell
'Til they hadn't got a sou for a Christian or a Jew:
So I quickly went to Paris for the Charms of mad'moiselle,
Who's the lodestone of my heart – what can I do,
When with twenty tongues she swears that she'll be true?

As I walk along the Bois Boulogne, etc.

Gilbert wrote the song after seeing the headline 'The Man Who Broke the Bank at Monte Carlo' on a newspaper billboard in the street. The phrase grabbed his attention, as did the story behind it: the story of Charles Deville Wells, who had recently become famous worldwide for his amazing win in the casino, a bank-breaking escapade which brought him a well-publicised fortune. The song became the hit of its generation, known to everyone, and Charles Wells was cemented in the public imagination as the man who broke the bank at Monte Carlo. It was a relief to realise that Joseph wasn't the man described in the song, that he might not be the fraudster that I first presumed and that my ancestor could be the man to shatter the myth that all Monte Carlo winners must be rogues.

But, on the other hand, if the song wasn't about Joseph then it was another piece of evidence gone. It could also mean that my ancestor hadn't broken the bank at all, that the family story was simply false. I quickly discovered that, of course, Joseph had not been the only person to break the bank at Monte Carlo. To break the bank means that an individual's winnings are so great that the table cannot be restocked with money quickly enough to pay out and must cease play until more money can be brought to it. It didn't happen very often, but neither was it unique; others had achieved it. But why had Wells become so famous while no trace of Joseph's win survived? Again I wondered: what if he had not broken the bank at all? My search could so easily have ended there before it really began, but the photograph from Nice persuaded me that I must not give up just yet.

I uncovered a set of correspondence between my father and Joseph's great-grandson Derek Jagger in the papers that he bequeathed to me. Over thirty years these distant cousins had swapped family trees and information but had not managed to meet before my father died in 1999. I called Derek Jagger's phone number and was greeted by the voice of Alice Jagger – his widow. While bitterly disappointed that I would not be able to meet him and find out what he knew, I was hugely relieved to realise that Derek had been a fastidious curator of the family history. Alice told me that he had split his archive between the Bradford Local Studies Library and his younger brother David.

My meeting with David Jagger and his wife Joyce established a route by which I could begin my research in earnest. After a full Yorkshire tea, the sort of magnificent spread of cold meats, sandwiches and cakes that I hadn't enjoyed since my childhood, we chatted about the fascination with our shared ancestor that has led our two branches of the family to search out information about him over so many decades. David showed me his family tree, his photographs and notes and letters from Jaggers all over the world who had written to him, all hoping for a connection to Joseph. The most famous Jagger of them all is thought to be a distant cousin: Sir Mick Jagger's grandfather was born in Morley, Yorkshire, and genealogists have suggested a link between his family and ours. That afternoon with David and Joyce, when they showed such great generosity in sharing their archive with a complete stranger, inspired me not only to add to the archives but to complete Joseph's story and to record it for us all.

Before I left Bradford, I arranged access to the part of Derek's archive that he had not left with his brother but was bequeathed to the Bradford Local Studies Library. It contains the key elements of his research together with the notes and correspondence received from my father over the years. I'd seen duplicates of these in the papers that were left to me but it moved me to think how proud he would have been to know that his documents were preserved within the official archive of Joseph's life. Leafing through the folder it became clear that there was no new evidence here, but it was a consolidation of all of the research that had been done by that generation who had worked to discover the facts but never managed to share them in person. I discovered that there had been a third researcher too, not a blood relative but a woman with a keen interest and a link to another branch of the family, who had written to Derek just as my father had. Pam Hill's letter, dated 1991, showed that she had met Derek and was planning another visit before he died. I realised that in the early 1990s these three amateur family historians had come frustratingly close to meeting up and sharing what they knew. Derek and his brothers had compiled a two-page summary of their many years of research and had lodged it in the library's file. It describes their search for the truth behind the family legend and concludes with a plea for others to take over:

> It would be helpful if relatives/descendants of the above who know of information concerning Joseph or his offspring would write in and help solve a mystery ... Peter and David Jagger, sons of Arnold, grandsons of Walter, and great-grandsons of the famous Joseph have carried out some research of their own, but feel that there is nothing more their side of the family can add.[2]

Now there was a challenge. My search for the truth about Joseph Hobson Jagger has taken me from Yorkshire to Monte Carlo, from archives in Bradford to those in South Africa and to seek help from Sotheby's, Midland Railways and Thomas Cook to name but a few. I've discovered what we've all been searching for over so many decades. The key to the truth, the evidence that supports the story that I am about to tell, was in the family all along. First, however, we need to go back to the beginning.

PART 1

'I TO MONTE CARLO WENT, JUST TO RAISE MY WINTER'S RENT'

ANCESTORS: THE JAGGERS OF PEPPER HILL

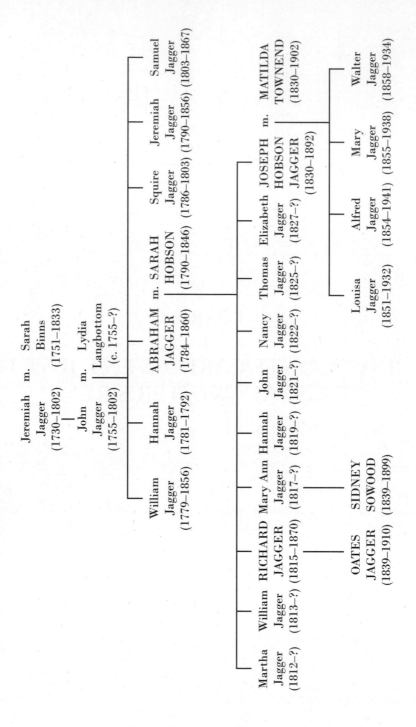

I

BRADFORD

Joseph Hobson Jagger was born on 2 September 1830, the eve of Queen Victoria's reign. To state that he was a Victorian may seem self-evident, but the time and place of his birth are crucial to his story. Being Victorian meant belonging to a generation that would see rapid change and a challenging of the accepted order of things. British explorers such as Livingstone, Burton and Speke were unlocking the mysteries of the wider world. Social and scientific advancements were improving and lengthening the lives of many: medical knowledge and midwifery practice were developing, public executions and floggings were put to an end, and Dr Barnardo created his eponymous home to provide care for orphaned children. Charles Darwin was challenging centuries-old beliefs about life on Earth. Dickens, Trollope, the Bröntes and Lewis Carroll were thrilling readers throughout the world while chronicling society's ills and pressing for change. The invention of the railway system, the automobile, photography, the steamship and the use of electricity for heat and light were transforming lives and their possibilities. Joseph's story would have been impossible before the Victorian era, a time that changed so much of society so quickly and with such dramatic effect.[3]

Nowhere was this sense of change and possibility felt more than in the industrial towns of the north of England. Joseph was born in Bradford in West Yorkshire. In 1830 Bradford was poised to undergo a startling change that would transform it from a small market town into one of the greatest industrial cities of Victorian Britain, if not the world. Since the Middle Ages it had thrived as part of the English wool trade. Graced with grassy hillsides where sheep could graze and abundant clean, fresh water flowing down from the Pennines, the town had the natural prerequisites to sustain a textile industry: almost limitless supplies of raw wool and water to wash it in. Families made a living washing, spinning and weaving woollen cloth, very often in their own homes or together in communities as piece workers. The arrival of steam power, the catalyst for the Industrial Revolution of the eighteenth century, brought about radical change in Bradford as it did everywhere else. By the end of the century the majority of the population of England would be living in towns, and most goods would be made by machine. The centuries-old textile industry was revolutionised as machines were invented that could perform all the necessary tasks quicker and more efficiently than people. Now Bradford had another huge advantage over the textile towns of East Anglia, which had been the market leaders since medieval times: it had vast coal fields on its doorstep. The new steam-powered machines devoured coal, and Bradford could refuel them quickly and cheaply.

Mills were built to house the new steam-powered technology that could create yarn from wool or cotton then spin it and weave it more quickly and more cheaply than ever before. Cities like Bradford and Manchester became global powerhouses of production, producing textiles more efficiently and competitively than anywhere else, and taking full advantage of the strength and reach of the British Empire to export its products all over the world. Bradford's textile industry boomed, driven by these new centres of mass production; the town now did it all, no longer relying on Leeds and Halifax to dye, finish and sell its fabrics.

By 1800 it had taken over as the national centre for worsted production.[4] Worsted, sometimes called 'stuff', is a woollen fabric with its fibres combed parallel to each other to make a smooth and very strong cloth which is used to make tailored garments such as suits. It became the mainstay of Bradford's textile industry and its dominance in this market earned Bradford the soubriquet 'Worstedopolis'.[5] From 1837 until 1874 Bradford ruled supreme over the English worsted industry as the principal centre of production and it developed an international reputation for excellence as a result. This marked the beginning of a period of exceptional growth and profit for the town and its textile industry.[6]

Victorian Bradford was a place where, through hard work and ingenuity, men could rise to positions of power and great wealth. 'Fortunes have been made in Bradford with a rapidity almost unequalled in the manufacturing districts. In half a dozen years, men have risen to possess mills and villas...'[7] These entrepreneurs benefitted from the economic boom and played a key part in sustaining it. Opportunities to speed production and create new products were the incentive for these great industrialists to innovate and push the industry's success to even greater heights. The Bradford textile entrepreneur Samuel Cunliffe Lister introduced his 'nip' machine in 1845, which mechanised the wool combing process, increasing its speed dramatically. Each 'nip' machine could do the work of a hundred men.[8] The speed of spinning and weaving also increased. In 1856, the West Yorkshire firm Hattersley and Company, based in Keighley, perfected the revolving box loom, which allowed more than one shuttle to be used in weaving. This innovation accelerated the development of completely new textiles in Bradford, created by weaving cotton or silk thread into wool, alpaca or mohair. New fancy worsteds such as Orleans cloth, coburgs, crapes,[9] mousselaines and lustres were launched into the market as well as cloth that interwove coloured threads to make stripes and checks. Stylish, vibrant and exciting, these new textiles were cheap to produce and became hugely fashionable, driving up their price as customers clamoured for them. Bradford manufacturers enjoyed huge profit margins and a golden era of enormous wealth between 1860 and 1874.[10]

The population of the northern textile towns and cities swelled as men, women and children relocated to work in the mills. Thousands of people were employed, bringing rapid urban growth. Bradford was essentially a new town. In the first half of the nineteenth century the town's population grew more than fifteen times from 6,393 in 1801 to 103,778 by 1851.[11] In 1849, the *Morning Chronicle*, where Charles Dickens had once been the parliamentary correspondent, carried out an investigation into the social and economic impact of industrialisation on the urban working classes. The journalist Angus Reach was sent to the northern manufacturing towns and his findings were published by the paper. His first impressions were of a new and very different world developing in this part of the country:

> The traveller by railway is made aware of his approach to the great northern seats of industry by the leaden-coloured sky, tainted by thousands of ever smoking chimneys, which broods over the distance. The stations along the line are more closely planted, showing that the country is more and more thickly peopled. Then small manufacturing villages begin to appear, each consisting of two or three irregular streets clustered around the mill, as in former times cottages were clustered round the castle ... They have all similar features ... Huge, shapeless, unsightly mills, with their countless rows of windows, their towering shafts, their jets of waste steam continually puffing in panting gushes from the brown grimy wall.[12]

At its industrial peak Bradford had over 200 chimneys serving its textile mills. *The Illustrated London News* printed an engraving of its skyline in 1882, dominated by these tall chimneys belching black smoke into the sky. It was at some point annotated with the title, 'the town is <u>not</u> supposed to be on fire'.

The mills not only changed the landscape dramatically, but also dominated the lives of families and whole communities. Mill owners built homes for their workers next to their factories and family and social life centred on these streets. Children played in sulphurous smoke and families lived with the constant backdrop of clattering looms that were operated day and night.[13] Effluent from the mills flowed directly into the streams, which were used for washing and drinking. Cholera and typhoid were common. A young German traveller called Georg Weerth, visiting Bradford for the first time in 1846, wrote about his impressions of it in an article for a German newspaper: 'In Bradford ... you think you have been lodged with the devil incarnate. If anyone wants to feel how a poor sinner is tormented in Purgatory, let him travel to Bradford.' As well as being one of the wealthiest towns in the country, Bradford soon developed a reputation as the dirtiest.

> In the course of last week I have visited some of the most filthy and wretched abodes that the mind of man can conceive, in which misery of the lowest description was personified. In a portion of this town, there are scores of wretched hovels, unfurnished and unventilated, damp, filthy in the extreme, and surrounded by stagnant pools, human excrement and every thing offensive and disgusting to 'sight and smell'. No sewers, no drainage, no ventilation. Nothing to be seen but squalid wretchedness on every side, and the features of the inmates show a perfect and unmistakable index of their condition: All this is to be seen in the centre of this wealthy emporium of the worsted trade.[14]

Joseph was the last of ten children born to Abraham and Sarah Jagger. Abraham was forty-four years old and his wife Sarah was nearly forty when he was born, and he was given his mother's maiden name, Hobson, as a middle name. This was a family tradition extending both before and beyond Joseph's birth.[15] Joseph and his sisters Elizabeth, Nancy, Hannah, Mary Ann and Martha and his brothers Thomas, John, William and my great-great-grandfather Richard did not have to grow up in the very worst conditions of Victorian Bradford. The family lived in Pepper Hill in Shelf, a small hamlet which sits between Cock Hill and Hill Top, approximately 6 miles from the city centre. It comprised a handful of stone cottages, houses and farms with fields all around and the men and women who lived there were nearly all weavers.[16]

The Jaggers had been established in Pepper Hill for at least a century before Joseph was born. Jeremiah Jagger, his great-grandfather, was born in 1730 and lived and died in Shelf; indeed, it's probable that he never left the county of Yorkshire during his entire seventy-two years of life. He was married and buried in the nearby church of St John the Baptist, which became the hub of important family events for the next two generations at least.[17] Jeremiah's son John was born at Ash Tree Farm near Pepper Hill and married Lydia Longbottom at St John's. Their six children, including Joseph's father Abraham, were all born in Pepper Hill and baptised at the church. The Jagger men of these three generations – Joseph's father, his grandfather and his great-grandfather – all worked as weavers.[18] In this pre-industrialised era, this almost certainly meant they worked from home as part of a cottage industry that was fragmented around the hills and villages of the area.

> At that time the processes of farming and of manufacturing whether of cloth or other fabrics went hand in hand … and occupied themselves and their families alternately with the mixed labour of tilling their limited acres and in combing, spinning, carding and weaving … wool was brought about once a month from Leeds and other places to … villages in Bradford … to be carded, combed and spun … In summer time the women took out their spinning wheels to the village green and up on the hillsides … When the women had got a pound

of wool from a neighbouring farmer it was spun … and carried
aback to 't'maister' who gave it out … to the hand-loom weaver
who in turn had to spin it on to bobbins before weaving ….
The weaver [worked by] throwing the shuttle with one hand,
catching it with the other, and throwing it back again.[19]

Joseph's mother Sarah had her hands very full raising her children
and running the home. It's not certain how many of the Jagger
children survived to adulthood. Infant mortality in Victorian
Bradford was devastatingly high and death records for working-class
families can be difficult to trace. The children of textile workers in the
mills were hardest hit. Only 30 per cent of them reached the age of
fifteen and in 1840, the average life expectancy in Bradford was just
over eighteen years, one of the lowest rates in the country.[20] Hannah,
Mary Ann, Elizabeth and Martha and Joseph's brothers William and
Richard all survived to adulthood but there is no mention of Nancy,
Thomas and John beyond their teens. So in all likelihood they either
left home to work or to marry, or they died young.

Joseph and his siblings, like most working-class children of the
time, would probably not have gone to school and many of them
may never have learnt to read or write. They all worked in the
textile trade at one time or another and for their generation this
would probably have meant moving to the mills as they began to
take over production. When Joseph was three years old the first
British Factory Act was passed, making it illegal to employ children
under the age of nine in mills and factories and requiring those of
legal age to be protected from unsafe working hours and practices.
It was the first of a series of laws that sought to protect the women
and children that formed the vast majority of the workforce.

In the stuffmills there are employed, at the very least, a
score of women, boys, and children, to one man. The adult
males employed at the machinery are either the few who are
overlookers, or the rather larger number who are forced to

compete with women and girls at the powerloom. The great bulk of the male worsted population work at the unwholesome, easily acquired, and miserably paid for – because easily learned – labour of wool combing. Thus the average of wages is kept lower than in the cotton and cloth, and about as low perhaps as in the silk, districts. The average wages of adult male workmen engaged in the stuff trade cannot be above 10s. a week, at the most liberal estimate. That of women ranges closely up to them – for a female weaver will earn as much, or more, than a male comber. And as for the children, the average of the wages which they receive is kept down by the great number of 'halftimers' – boys and girls under thirteen years of age – who are employed. Exclusive of halftime workers and young persons, the average weekly wages of male and female adults may be reckoned at from 8s. 6d. to 9s. 6d. – lower by about 2s. 6d. than the average wages in the cotton districts, reckoning in both cases on a time of fair prosperity, and a period of ten hours' daily toil.[21]

Working conditions had always been at the discretion of the owner, and continued to be so. Some were very enlightened and provided safe conditions, entertainment and leisure time; most did not.[22] The atmosphere in the majority of mills was dangerous and unhealthy. Water was sprayed to keep the wool moist whilst it was worked, and the air was filled with dust and loose fibres. The noise was continuous, and many workers went deaf later in life. Accidents were common and accepted as part of mill life. The most frequent cause was having to carry out repairs while the machine was still working because to turn one off would affect production levels. Frequently the belts of looms or weaving shuttles would fly off and knock workers unconscious. Serious and sometimes fatal injuries were common but there was no compensation.[23] There were no trade unions to defend workers either at first, and it was illegal to strike. The mechanisation of the textile industry reduced wages and diminished living standards, and between 1811 and 1813 groups of workers in the north of England began breaking up machines in protest. They became known as Luddites. In response, the government revoked the Acts that criminalised strikes, giving workers the right to withdraw their labour. Trade unions sprung up all over the country as a result of this unrest among workers, but it wasn't until 1871 that they were given legal status.

With no political voice there was little that working men and women like the Jaggers could do about these conditions, but this was also a time when political reform was being demanded. There was a revolution in Paris in 1832, and in Britain the populations of the new large industrial cities like Bradford were demanding representation in Parliament and the right to vote. This had always been the privilege of land and property owners, but things were changing. The Representation of the People Act (or the first Reform Act) passed in 1832 created the Parliamentary Borough of Bradford and gave the right to vote to some of its new middle classes, who were thriving with the industrialisation of the country. These new political rights were only extended to a minority, however. It would be decades before working-class men would win the right to vote and further decades before the franchise was extended to women.[24]

Growing up in Victorian Bradford played an important part in shaping the man that Joseph would become. The town's foundations were shifting, broken apart by the forces of industrialisation, and when the pieces settled, Bradford would be reformed into a very different state. Joseph grew up during this process of transformation. He witnessed men shake off their humble origins to make fortunes. He saw how industry and trade could provide a route to prosperity and power for men not born into the upper classes. Living in Bradford demonstrated clearly to him that the world was being remodelled by technology and that the ancient social hierarchies, which had held people in their place for so long, were being broken. For anyone with an entrepreneurial streak, this was a time of enormous opportunity.

2

MONTE CARLO

Whilst Bradford was growing and booming on the back of its natural resources and riding the opportunity presented by the Industrial Revolution, 1,800 kilometres away, Monaco was also transforming. The Grimaldi family, who had ruled the principality since 1297, were struggling to find a way of raising an income from their rocky land. Built on steep cliffs and outcrops along the Mediterranean coast, Monaco is blessed with a wonderful climate but few natural resources. Bordered on three sides by France, Monaco covers an area of only 2 square kilometres. It may be the world's second smallest country, but today the principality has more millionaires and billionaires per capita than any other country in the world.[1] Famed for its gambling and luxurious goods and services, it is one of the most expensive and glamorous destinations in Europe. By day and by night the small square outside the casino is host to a parade of designer-clad visitors and their supercars: Rolls-Royces from Russia, yellow Ferraris from Kuwait and Bentleys and Porsches from all over Europe. However, the transformation of this barren outcrop on the Mediterranean coast only came after many abortive attempts at creating an economy. This remote and relatively inaccessible agricultural region had no obvious way of making money. Lacemaking, alcohol distilling and perfume making having all failed (violets and other fragrant blooms were grown for the parfumier Rimmel), the principality struggled for income.[2] It was then that Princess Caroline, the wife of Prince Florestan I, noticed what was happening in Germany.

Under the pretext of taking the waters in the spa towns of Germany, a large number of people were engaging in gambling. The natural mineral waters to be found at Baden Baden in the south-west of Germany and Wiesbaden and Bad Homburg in the central German state of Hess had attracted those who sought cures for ailments such as skin disorders, gout and rheumatism, as well as those that came to enjoy the climate.[3] Queen Victoria and Kaiser Wilhelm I mixed with celebrities and the wealthy from all over the world, and Baden Baden in particular became the summer capital of Europe in the 1850s and 60s. These German spa towns developed into centres where luxurious and extremely successful casinos flourished. But the Grimaldis were to find out that the casino business was not as easy as the Germans made it seem.

Princess Caroline was to be the driving force behind the establishment of the first casino in Monaco. Her aim was to find a company that would finance and operate a gambling concession, building the hotels, baths, casino and restaurants that would generate money for her family and transform the Grimaldi finances. It would not be seemly for the royal family to run such a venture themselves. It proved difficult to find people prepared to take on the role but finally, after two years, on 26 April 1856, shortly before he died, Prince Florestan granted a thirty-year licence to Napoléon Langlois and Albert Aubert.[4] A Parisian businessman and journalist respectively, the pair were enthusiastic but lacking in experience. They were also lacking in funds. They did not have the reserves to offer anything but the lowest table limits, which was a disincentive to the big gamblers, and they were barely able to cover the costs of running the casino.[5]

They also did nothing to solve the access problem. Committed by their agreement with Prince Florestan to build a resort with a casino and baths and to improve transportation from Nice, they had yet to deliver on any of these promises by the time that they were forced to sell their concession in December 1857. This first casino had operated from a house opposite the royal palace, but the Villa Bellevue wasn't fit for purpose.[6] It was neither smart enough nor well financed enough to support the high-end play that was needed for success, and given the failure to address the transport situation, it was very difficult to attract visitors at all.[7] Between 15 and 20 March 1857 the casino welcomed only one gambler, and he won only 2 francs.[8]

In their short incumbency Langlois and Aubert had, however, made one shrewd move which would secure the future of the casino ever after, even if it wasn't recognised at the time. They bought land where they had hoped to build a purpose-built casino, although the money to do so never materialised. The land was across the harbour from the promontory where the royal palace stands, an area known as *Les Spélugues* or the caves. These caverns were eroded into the rocky outcrop that jutted out into the Mediterranean. It was a good place to find sea urchins and mussels, and little else.[9] But for this very reason the land was cheap. Langlois and Aubert saw the potential of the location, and the owner was keen to sell.[10] He had improved his barren land considerably by using convicts to dig and carry soil to cover the bare rocks and had managed to raise a reasonable harvest of figs, grapes and citrus fruit, but he was now ready to realise any income that he could through a sale.

The new casino operator, Pierre Auguste Daval, began construction of the new casino building in *Les Spélugues* and the foundation stone was laid on 13 May 1858. But faced with the same difficulties as his predecessor, he also failed to pay any money to the prince and the company plunged 2 million francs into debt.[11] He was forced to sell the concession only a year later to the Duc de Valmy, who employed François Lefèbvre to run the resort for him. Valmy failed not only to tackle the transport issue but was reluctant to invest in the site or build the new facilities that were required. The casino building remained unadorned, and he scrimped on the supply of newspapers to the reading room and underpaid the casino's staff.[12] After failing to meet the prince's deadline to complete the new casino, he resigned on 1 January 1863.

In only six years, Monaco's nascent gambling concession had seen three operators try and fail to make it a success. The new casino was incomplete (as was the adjoining *Hôtel de la Grand Place du Palais*). It stood alone on rocky land that remained very difficult to reach. Offers of free land were made to anyone who would build homes or presumably cafés or hotels on the site, but nobody came forward.[13] Land that is today among the most valuable in the world could not be given away. The new ruler of the principality, Prince Charles III, was left with a partly built resort and no hint of the seemingly endless supply of money that his German counterparts were enjoying. It was a Frenchman, François Blanc, a business genius, who would bring about the rapid and long-lasting success of the casino and in turn create Monte Carlo, the most glamorous and exclusive entertainment centre in the world.

François Blanc and his twin Louis were both proficient card players and had observed the enormous profits being made in the Paris casinos, not by the gamblers but by the owners. They resolved to set up their own. Understanding how much capital was required, they set out to raise it through a share fraud. Realising that prices on the Paris Stock Exchange could take as much as a day to reach Bordeaux, where they were living, they bribed government officials to communicate this information to them via the *télégraphe aérien* so that they would have exclusive early knowledge of the stock markets. The *télégraphe aérien* was a simple semaphore system operated from a series of towers that linked Paris to the main cities in France. Officials held up messages which their colleagues read through telescopes and communicated to the next tower.[14] This state-run system was supposed to be reserved for messages of national importance only.

The Blancs' insider dealing and stock speculation was a success, increasing their capital to 100,000 francs (the equivalent of £400,000 today). Betrayed by the death-bed confession of one of their collaborators, the brothers were actually tried and convicted for their crimes in 1837; however, they were not imprisoned and only had to pay the court costs before being set free.[15] Their defence had managed to demonstrate that, with no law in place against insider dealing, they had simply been as ingenious as other businessmen. The Rothschild banking family, for example, had allegedly used special agents with trained pigeons to communicate information.[16] The twins had sailed a little too close to the wind, but they had been able to keep hold of the capital raised by their scheme and now had enough to start their casino. But almost straight away their plans were jeopardised when France banned public gambling in 1838.

The gambling operations in the spa towns of Germany were thriving in the meantime, and the brothers spotted an opportunity in Bad Homburg, in Hess. The town had rich natural resources in the form of mineral water and the ruling *landgraf* (equivalent to a duke) needed money, so he accepted the Blanc brothers' rather modest bid to set up a gambling operation in the town in 1840.[17] Despite Louis' death in 1852 and their shared lack of experience, the brothers' gamble on Bad Homburg brought enormous dividends. It was a huge success. The *Kursaal*, their main casino building, opened in 1843 and the Blancs used their genius for bending the truth and for publicity to compete with the well-established, glamorous competition at Wiesbaden and Baden Baden. They employed a group of professors from the Sorbonne in Paris to say that Bad Homburg's waters were superior to the rest.[18]

Bad Homburg was frequented by the royalty of Europe, and was particularly popular with the Russians. François Blanc's success was brought to the attention of Prince Charles III of Monaco, who invited him to meet his agent on 31 March 1863 with the aim of persuading him to take over the concession for the casino in Monte Carlo. First impressions of Blanc were deceptive:

> A small, bespectacled man with a straggling moustache, nervous manner and heavy provincial French accent, he was obliged to stand throughout the negotiations because of a boil on his behind.[19]

He was a ferocious negotiator. When the deal did not seem favourable, Blanc used ruthless brinkmanship. He opened his wallet revealing a fortune in notes and declared that the prince could take the deal today or he would walk away.[20] The Grimaldis took it. In 1863, Blanc was awarded the concession to run the casino until April 1913 in return for a payment to the Grimaldis of a sum of 1.5 million francs.[21] A management company, the *Société des Bains de Mer et du Cercle des Étrangers* (the Society of Sea Bathers and Circle of Foreigners), had been established to manage the concession and Blanc was now at its helm. He and his family owned most of the shares. Blanc was in no doubt of just how lucrative the arrangement would be for him, and so added to the deal the astonishing sweetener of promising to pay for Monaco's army, roads, police, hospitals and schools. This arrangement ensured that no citizen of Monaco would ever pay tax again[22] – nor would they ever be permitted to enter the casino or to gamble there. As the title of Blanc's new company asserted, this was a place where only foreigners would lose their money.

Blanc masterminded a complete transformation. He inherited a partly built casino on an arid, rocky plateau and created in its place an exciting playground that would attract an international clientele. Only the name remained to undermine the potential success of the casino complex, and in 1866 the rather disreputable *Les Spélugues* was rebranded as *Le Quartier de Monte Carlo*, or Mount Charles, after its Grimaldi sponsor, Prince Charles III.[23] At the heart of the Monte Carlo resort was the *Place du Casino*, a wide circular space which Blanc carved out in front of the casino so that carriages could drive past or park and be displayed. The newly completed casino building which stood on the *place*, parallel to the Mediterranean coast, was smaller than the one that stands on the spot today. The first building occupied the footprint of the area that is now the Atrium and had only four rooms. Blanc masterminded two phases of significant expansion. The first began in 1878 under the creative eye of Charles Garnier, the architect of the Paris Opera House. He expanded the principal gaming room and redesigned its interior, renaming it the *Salle Mauresque*. Its name, 'the Moorish Room', came from the complete transformation of its décor in line with the fashion for the Orient which reached its height in the mid-nineteenth century:[24]

> Everything, in short, is so sumptuous, that the visitor is inclined to ask himself, in silent wonder, 'How is all this paid for?' Let him present his card at the entrance to the *Salle de Jeux*, and his curiosity will quickly be satisfied. ... decorated in the Persian style, and rivalling in splendour any of the royal palaces at Versailles, the Louvre, or Fontainebleau, with polished oak floor.[25]

The second phase added an Opera House (now called *La Salle Garnier*) to the building, which opened in 1879, giving the casino its distinctive white turrets. It became renowned for its daytime and evening concerts. Eating wasn't allowed inside the gaming rooms but the terrace provided a space to dine and to enjoy a drink.[26] Reading rooms were available to card holders, and a Billiard Room too.[27]

Below the casino, at the foot of the terraces, jutting out into the Mediterranean was a green semi-circular platform, netted at the far end. This was *Le Tir aux Pigeons*, and here from 1872 some of the best shots in Europe, as well as wealthy visitors, came to shoot live pigeons. Although many enjoyed watching the sport, others were disgusted by the blood sport and its intrusive noise:

All the morning, all the afternoon at intervals of, a minute or two, the sides of one of the five boxes fall, collapse, and disclose a tailless pigeon, which occasionally walks out, but as a rule flies a yard or two before an unseen figure at, the blind end-of-the-path fires. The single, or generally double, report is heard everywhere. You, cannot escape the noise … Everyone, man, woman, and child, watches the birds. Some fall dead on that one fresh green space. Some struggle to the wire. Some fall into the sea or on to the rocks. Some circle inland and fall, perhaps on the terrace among the fine ladies, perhaps in the streets or on the hills.[28]

In 1881, a new room for playing *trent-et-quarante* was added to the east of the main gaming room and became known as the Garnier Gambling Lounge (now *La Salle des Amériques*).

Blanc understood that the principal reason why the casino had been so close to financial collapse before he took it over was because it was difficult to get to. There was also the lack of accommodation and the few facilities available. To make his customers more comfortable and to provide places to stay, in 1864 he completed the partially built hotel on the west side of the *place* and renamed it the *Hôtel de Paris*. On the right side he built the *Café Divan* in 1868.[29] Now there was a luxurious hotel and a restaurant, which alleviated the need for gamblers to travel to and from Nice in a day, and would encourage them to spend their money in Monaco and not in France. However, for this to be a possibility Blanc had to tackle the arduous and difficult travel arrangements.

There was a road route into Monte Carlo from Nice but it was a dirty and dangerous overland journey of three to four hours via precarious mountain roads; it was expensive, too, with carriages costing 50 francs.[30] Passengers then had to endure a one-hour walk down the rocky cliffs.[31] More popular was the sea route, which only cost 4 francs for a return journey but was very unreliable. An ancient steamship, *The Palmaria*, could make the 15-mile journey in about two hours but the service was unpredictable and unpunctual. If the weather looked stormy the passage would be cancelled until the next day.[32] When it did run, passengers were delivered into Monaco's harbour by about five o'clock in the afternoon and transported to the casino.[33] Blanc knew just how crucial it was to make Monte Carlo easier to reach and so he hired a fleet of horse-drawn carriages to ferry visitors comfortably by road from Nice to Monaco and chartered a steamship that could carry 300 people to provide a reliable sea route.[34] Most importantly, he made sure that the railway was extended to Monaco. Blanc transferred land free of charge to the *Paris à Lyon et à la Méditerranée* rail company so that track could be laid, and supposedly donated money too.[35] In 1868, the Monte Carlo station opened just below the terraces and gardens that ran from the casino down to the sea so that travellers could disembark and enjoy a short walk straight up to the gaming halls.

The arrival of trains was a crucial development. Travel time between London and Monte Carlo was reduced from days to hours and opened up the resort to more than just the very rich with leisure time to fill and the money to enjoy it. Tourists came for the first time, people who could stay just for a week or two instead of renting a villa for the entire season. Visitors flooded in. It is no exaggeration to say that the arrival of trains created Monte Carlo. Some 70,000 people visited the casino in 1864, and by 1870 the number had risen to 120,000.[36] By 1879 the principality welcomed

315,000 visitors.[37] The nouveaux riche could now mingle with the royalty and aristocracy of Europe, and the *Hôtel de Paris* was in demand so far beyond its capacity that Blanc ordered its expansion.

However, the increase in the number of visitors arriving and their greater diversity, encouraged by railway access, did nothing to dilute the exclusive nature of the casino. Blanc instituted a system that required those wanting to gamble to fill out a registration card. This green *carte du jour* came with a small charge, but entry could be denied. It was dependent on the presentation of identification papers and on being smartly dressed. Passports had taken on the role of official British identity document in 1858 but were not required for international travel until the First World War.[38] Every applicant to enter the casino had to state their name and nationality and their last address.[39] After three or four days a white *carte du mois* or *carte blanche* could be applied for, which removed the necessity of the daily visit to the bureau.[40] Anyone with a criminal conviction was automatically refused entry, as were those who had previously tried to cheat, all domestic staff who did not have the permission of their employer and some wives whose husbands had arranged for them to be banned (this latter stipulation did not apply the other way around).[41] Because it could be refused, having a card came to be perceived as a symbol of status and, of course, of good character.[42]

The advent of trains also changed the mode of play in the casino. Blanc recognised that the arrival of the middle classes into his resort necessitated a sea change in terms of the experience that he offered. The style of play long enjoyed by the aristocratic patrons of the casinos was an adversarial one. These scions of the royal and noble houses of Europe enjoyed games where they duelled against each other, and they were not afraid to lose large sums of money. Games like *hoca* and *biribi* thrived at the courts of France and England. But the new patrons in Monte Carlo weren't interested in challenging each other, they were interested in defeating the casino and winning enormous sums. This new

breed of player wouldn't stake high bets but was prepared to play with small amounts for a long period. To meet the needs of this new mass market, Blanc concentrated on *roulette* and *trente-et-quarante*, the games that pitched the player against the bank. He then devised ways to encourage gamblers to stay on longer, introducing concerts and orchestras, fine food and other entertainments that provided a veneer of cultured sophistication. In this way he generated enormous profits whilst maintaining the exclusive reputation of Monte Carlo.[43]

With every facility in place to encourage visitors to spend and enjoy themselves, Blanc launched a publicity campaign to promote Monaco as an elegant resort where fortunes in gold could be made. He had spared no expense in creating an earthly paradise to greet those arriving in Monte Carlo and he needed to get this message out. This was the time when a mass print media was beginning. Newspapers were affordable and prolific, and Blanc paid regularly for expensive adverts in return for positive press coverage. In a single year he spent more than half a million francs on newspaper adverts, the equivalent of half his annual wage bill.[44] His campaign extended well beyond the usual press publicity, however. The very popular French newspaper *Figaro* was owned and edited by M. Villemessant, and Blanc arranged for him to be able to purchase building land in the *Condamine* (the area adjacent to Monte Carlo) at well below the market rate. There followed a series of articles extolling the wonders of Monte Carlo and the casino and of Blanc's genius, concluded by Villemessant stating that he would live there for the rest of his life if he could.[45]

Although both were open all year round, Blanc presented his German casino at Bad Homburg as the place to gamble in the summer and Monte Carlo as the place for entertainment during the warm and sunny Riviera winter. However, in 1872, Blanc's thirty-year ownership of his casino business in Bad Homburg came to an end when Germany banned public gaming. His sadness at handing over the keys of his beloved *Kursaal* must have been tempered by

the enormous success of his casino in Monte Carlo, and because the end of gambling in Germany created an unique opportunity for Monaco. With the closure of the German casinos, Monte Carlo was one of only two places left in Europe where roulette could be played legally in public. When the casino in Saxon-les-Bains in the Swiss Alps closed in 1877, it became the only one. To make absolutely certain that the Monte Carlo casino didn't suffer the same fate, Blanc used some of his enormous wealth to bankroll the French government and thereby win support in powerful places. In 1874 he had loaned 4.8 million francs to the minister of public works to fund the rebuilding of the Paris opera house. Its architect, Charles Garnier, was delighted in return to contribute his talents to the creation of the Monte Carlo resort. The French government also approved investment to further improve the rail connection between France and Monaco.[46]

In less than a decade, Blanc had transformed a Monegasque agricultural backwater into Monte Carlo, one of the most valuable pieces of real estate in the world, home to a casino and a business that until recently was still the primary source of income for both the Grimaldi family and the Monaco economy.[47] The Riviera was now the most popular winter destination in Europe.[48] It proved to be not only a lifelong safe haven for Blanc, but the basis of an enormous family fortune and the route to social success. Blanc's eldest daughter, Louise, married a Polish aristocrat, Prince Constantine Radziwill, and his youngest daughter, Marie, wed Prince Roland Bonaparte, the grand-nephew of Napoléon Bonaparte. When he died in July 1877, François Blanc left an estate worth 88 million francs (approximately £300 million today), perhaps proving the well-known maxim that the casino always wins in the end.[49] Blanc's wife ran the casino after his death, but it was his eldest son, Camille, who would eventually take over as managing director.[50] Camille had served a long apprenticeship under his father, watching him achieve dazzling success. He was ready to take his turn.

3

THE RISE OF
THE NON-CONFORMISTS

Joseph Hobson Jagger had also grown up with an example close
to home of just how socially mobile an able and ambitious man
could be. His father, Abraham Jagger, was no typical weaver. He
had ambition enough to move himself out of the industry that
his family had worked in for generations, prompted in part by
his religious convictions. Abraham was born at a time when a
huge wave of Evangelism had hit West Yorkshire, eroding the
centuries-old support for the Church of England and challenging
it with religious non-conformity. Bradford became the centre of
dissent and was, by 1851, the third most non-conformist urban
centre in England.[1] This ideological change was a direct result
of industrialisation, and its effect was felt strongly among men
like Abraham's father – the weavers and combers that were
out-workers for the textile trade. Some of these men developed
aspirations and saw opportunities which they believed were
frustrated by the landed elite and by the Anglican Church. Non-
conformity created a new Christian outlook that justified and

encouraged the pursuit of wealth and social and political change. Their ideal was to work hard, worship earnestly, grow rich and rise slowly but surely in society. Non-conformity also gave people some order as well as companionship and support in a world that must have seemed to be transforming in the most fundamental way. The chapels that were built in Bradford for the Methodists, Baptists, Congregationalists and numerous other non-conformist groups facilitated the growth of businesses and opportunities among like-minded people and provided a framework within which they could help each other.

Abraham and his siblings had been baptised as non-conformists in the last decades of the eighteenth century.[2] They are listed in the records as 'Independent', a denomination in Bradford that was Methodist in doctrine. Growing up in this dissenting religious environment must have influenced Abraham's view of the world and its possibilities. He learned to write his name and moved away from textiles and into trade.[3] Abraham became a grocer.[4] This brought with it the greatest change of all. Abraham qualified to vote in parliamentary elections, perhaps the first in his family to do so and certainly the only man in Pepper Hill to be enfranchised.[5] The new electorate created by the first Reform Act passed in 1832 included men who owned property worth over £10 (£852 today) as well as the 40-shilling freeholders who had previously been allowed to vote in county elections.[6] The property qualification had been broadened to include small landowners, tenant farmers and shopkeepers and anyone who paid a yearly rental of £10 or more. Men like Abraham Jagger. The Jaggers of Pepper Hill were not a wealthy family, but Abraham did support his family well through his trade as a grocer, saving enough to eventually buy a small property in the village.[7]

Abraham demonstrated to his ten children what hard work and ability could achieve. Some of his children learnt this lesson better than others. His son Richard, my great-great-grandfather, stayed close to home. In 1834, when in his early twenties,

Richard married seventeen-year-old Mary Oates, a girl from nearby Cock Hill.[8] After their marriage Richard and Mary moved there, establishing a home close to Mary's parents where they soon welcomed an enormous family.[9] Of their children, those to survive into adulthood were William, Joseph, Oates, Alfred, Linus and the only girl, my great-grandmother Lucy Jagger. Richard and his three eldest sons worked in the textile industry, as their ancestors had done.[10] Richard's brother William moved further afield. He followed his grocer father into a retail career rather than a textile one and became a confectioner.[11] He almost certainly met his Leeds-born wife when he was working in the city, but eventually William moved her and their children Martha, Solomon and Mary Ann back to his home town of Bradford.[12]

Options for women were of course much more limited. Abraham's twenty-year-old daughter Hannah had a baby when she was living with her parents and working as a weaver. She called her daughter Sarah, presumably after her mother.[13] Hannah was not married and here all trace of her ends. By the time of the next census in 1851 neither she nor Sarah were living in the family home in Pepper Hill. Perhaps she married a man who would take her and her illegitimate daughter; perhaps she and Sarah simply moved on and are lost among the many unrecorded working-class lives of the period.

Abraham's other daughters are easier to trace. Mary Ann married a farm labourer, Joseph Sowood. They had four daughters – Maranda, Abergail, Naomi and Sarah Hannah – and one son, Sidney. The family grew up in Shelf close to her parents and Sidney was working as a worsted spinner by the time he was eleven years old.[14] Martha married Joseph Oates, almost certainly related to Mary Oates, the woman who married her brother Richard.[15] A brother and sister from one family marrying a brother and sister from another was not unusual when children didn't move far from their parents and when whole communities were employed in the same factories and mills. While Pepper

Hill was populated with very many Jaggers, neighbouring Cock Hill was home to an extended Oates family. Martha and Joseph stayed in Pepper Hill, raising their children close to the Jagger family home.[16]

Joseph and Elizabeth, Abraham's two youngest surviving children, remained at home with him after their mother's death in 1846. Joseph was only sixteen when she died. Eventually Abraham's granddaughter, Martha's child Sarah Oates, moved into the house at 38 Pepper Hill to help the widower Abraham.[17] She was only a teenager, and younger than both her uncle Joseph and aunt Elizabeth, but they were both out at work and there was nobody to run the house. Abraham had premises in Bradford now, a true shopkeeper.[18] As the youngest of this large family, Joseph had plenty of opportunity to observe closely the lives of his siblings and to learn from his father's example.

At twenty years old Joseph was working as a warehouseman.[19] Although a relatively unskilled job, the warehouse was a place where a person with imagination could see the worldwide reach of the wool industry and begin to understand the processes that made it a success. Working in the warehouse meant welcoming in the raw materials – wool, cotton, silk, dyes – and sending out the finished cloth to towns and cities in England and to places all over the world. An observant man could begin to see where the demand lay and to understand the dozens of skilled and unskilled roles that were needed to meet it, from weavers and spinners to dyers and wool sorters to overlookers and fabric checkers.[20]

Over the next decade Joseph worked his way up, studying and developing his skills, including learning to read and write. By the age of twenty-one he was able to sign his name on his marriage certificate. For those like Joseph, whose class and finances precluded university, the acquisition of training and qualifications was difficult. Liberal reformers in Bradford, particularly non-conformist ones, set up Mechanics' Institutes where working men could have access to books, lectures and practical training on working with fibres and machines.²¹ Exams were offered to help men achieve promotions and take on more skilled jobs. The institutes were publicly funded, with many working men contributing to their cost, and they led the way in adult education for decades. The main Mechanics' Institute in Bradford opened in 1832 and is now part of Bradford University. Joseph acquired the skills in his twenties to become first a bookkeeper and then to work in partnership with others in the textile industry.²²

Joseph worked in a co-partnership with Charles Aykroyd at Lady Royd Size Works in Manningham, just to the north-east of Bradford's city centre. They operated under the name of Charles Aykroyd and Company and worked as warp sizers.²³ Warp threads are those that run vertically down the cloth, held taut by the frame of the loom. A new thread is passed in and out of the warp threads horizontally to create the fabric, these are the weft threads. If the warp is not really strong it can snap or fray during the weaving process, which slows or stops production, so warp sizers were employed using sizing machines to coat the warp threads in solutions that would increase their strength and flexibility. Sizing was an important part of making fibres manageable during all of the stages of textile production. It used a range of sizes made from fatty greases, with different recipes for different products.²⁴ Joseph and his partner Charles probably had an arrangement at Lady Royd Size Works allowing them to rent or store their equipment on the premises. Or it is possible they were employed as contractors. Joseph formed a new co-partnership sometime in the 1850s with Alexander Roberton, operating as Alexander Roberton and Company of Pitt Lane, Bradford, stuff finishers.²⁵ Finishing was the final process that took a woven cloth and improved its appearance or feel by combing, pressing or treating it, using finishing machines.

By the time he turned thirty Joseph was no longer part of a partnership but had set up on his own back at Lady Royd Size Works as a warp sizer.²⁶ A young man with his own business in the textile industry, Joseph had come a long way from his weaver ancestors. He had made monumental leaps forward in this career through hard work, study and most likely a huge degree of confidence and determination. However, Joseph was also probably helped enormously by the company that he kept, by the supportive nature of the non-conformist community, which provided opportunities for likeminded men who saw that there was virtue in hard work and that ambition should be rewarded.

4

AN UPWARDLY MOBILE COMMUNITY

On 15 August 1851 the twenty-year-old Joseph married Matilda Townend at the parish church in Shelf. The young couple had both grown up there and worked in the textile industry, so if they didn't work together they would have come across each other in the tight-knit local community. Joseph lived with his parents in Pepper Hill up until the wedding and Matilda with her family in Lower Witchfield, another village in Shelf, and not far away.[1] Her father Nathaniel, a cordwainer, or shoemaker,[2] and her mother Hannah had three daughters – Matilda, Margaret and Martha – and they all worked as worsted loom weavers. Matilda had given birth to her first child, Louisa, two and a half months before the wedding, and when she left home to start married life with Joseph and their baby daughter, her eldest sister Martha must have felt a tinge of envy. She was the unmarried mother of Jemima.[3] Not as fortunate as her sister, she was left to raise her child alone.

Joseph and Matilda were soon joined by three more children. Alfred, their eldest son, was born in 1854, followed by Mary two years later and finally Walter two years after that. By 1861, with their family complete, Joseph and Matilda had moved to 77 Girlington Road in the prosperous and desirable suburb of Manningham. Their presence there suggests not only that the young couple who met in the mills had done quite well for themselves during their first ten years of marriage, but that they were living in a community that could support Joseph's ambitions. It is likely that living among the aspirational, newly enriched men of Manningham, many of whom were also non-conformist, was of tremendous help to the young couple.

Manningham was one of the four townships that originally surrounded Bradford: Manningham, Bowling, Great Horton and Little Horton. As Bradford grew into an industrial giant in the second half of the nineteenth century, the outlying townships felt the impact; Manningham was transformed from a thinly populated countryside village into a residential and industrialised suburb. The factory where Joseph found work, the Lady Royd Size Works, suggests the area's rural past. This commonly used name in the area, 'Royd', means 'a clearing in the wood'. The change that came over Victorian Manningham was a result of its proximity to Bradford and what it promised to those who wanted to escape the pollution and noise of the city. Lying as it does on a gradual slope of land between the two arms of the Bradford Beck, which flows into the city, the new industrialists of Bradford soon saw what Manningham offered. They could move their families out of the city and into a cleaner and quieter rural location without living too far from the source of their wealth.

The first wave of new residents to the area was the new industrial aristocracy of Bradford. They had made their money in the mills and factories and now built classical and Gothic villas from local yellow stone, set in tree-lined streets near to the original heart of the village. These magnificent villas, some with porches and verandas, were set in spacious plots and built wherever possible to look down into the valley of the

Bradford Beck and the fields of leafy Manningham. At its peak, Manningham was regarded as the best place to live, a stylish community that indicated status and was seemingly part of a different world to the frantic, dirty, noisy, industrial centre of Bradford.[4]

But a second wave of change was to come, and the catalyst for this was the gradual creeping of industry from central Bradford into Manningham itself. By far the greatest impact was made by the building of a vast mill in 1838 by one of Bradford's greatest textile entrepreneurs, Ellis Cunliffe Lister. Manningham Mills (now known as Lister Mills) was built virtually on the doorstep of the Lister family home, Manningham Hall, as were the row upon row of houses built around it to accommodate its workforce. The establishment of a steam-powered factory with its belching chimneys and noise at the centre of a leafy and exclusive residential district marked a step change in the life of Manningham. The mill burnt down in 1871, and Samuel Lister replaced it with the largest silk-spinning and weaving mill in the United Kingdom. Its 78-metre-high chimney and colossal buildings dominated the area from all angles. An industrial corridor gradually built up along the Bradford Beck and on the valley floor which included worsted mills, cotton mills, wool combing works, the large dye works at Brown Royd and Thornton Road and the size works at Lady Royd where Joseph worked. By 1900 the fields and agricultural land of Manningham were covered with industry and the infrastructure that served it, including railway lines and residential areas for the people who worked there. As the very wealthy moved even further away, it became home to the prosperous and energetic middle classes, whose numbers boomed between 1860 and 1880.[5]

Girlington (together with Four Lane Ends, Whetley Hill, Lilycroft and Daisy Hill) was one of the five districts of Manningham and at this time was quite different in character from the others, which lay closer to Bradford. When Joseph and Matilda lived there it was still very rural, separated from Bradford and the rest of Manningham by fields.[6] The residential development of the area was, as with the rest of Manningham, encouraged by the arrival of industry and the need to house the workforce near to the mills and factories. However, in Girlington the unsanitary back-to-backs that had characterised Bradford housing were rejected in favour of a design which heralded a more enlightened and philanthropic view of how to house the working classes.

The old back-to-backs had developed as a way of maximising rental income on small plots of land. They usually comprised two rooms, one on the ground floor and one upstairs. Cooking was done in the downstairs room and the upstairs chamber was for sleeping as well as storage. Built as a double row of terraces, positioned back to back with no alleyway between them, these houses often shared three walls with neighbours. Windows and doors could only be introduced on one or perhaps two walls, resulting in badly lit, poorly ventilated homes and consequently very unhealthy living conditions. This style of building was banned in Bradford in 1860, but the move was so unpopular that the decision was reversed five years later, and after 1865 bye-laws ensured that all new back-to-backs were built with tunnels running between each pair of houses and with a privy in the yard.[7]

Joseph and Matilda lived in one of these tunnel back-to-backs built in Girlington in the 1860s. Their home, 77 Girlington Road, was built as part of a social experiment by some of the great Bradford philanthropists of the time. It was developed by the Bradford Freehold Land Society, which was formed in 1849 and was presided over by Titus Salt, a driving force in the improvement of the living and working conditions of the urban poor. In an impressive example of enlightened urban planning, Salt created around his own textile mill an entire village of houses, with a park, school, library, bath houses, hospital, concert hall, billiard room, science laboratory and outdoor sports facilities which became known as Saltaire. Under his leadership the Freehold Land Society used its members' contributions to buy up land and develop residential areas where the cost of purchasing the freehold could be significantly reduced. Between 1850 and 1852 the society bought a rectangular plot of land between Duckworth Lane and Thornton Road in Girlington and built houses in long, parallel streets following the slope of the valley wall: Washington Street, Kensington Street and Girlington Road. These new-style back-to-backs had small gardens or yards at the front so families could air their laundry, ventilate and light their houses and sit outside to take in the air. Many were also much roomier than the traditional model, some even built over three floors with heated bedrooms, coal cellars and sculleries.[8]

These new model houses didn't fill up with working-class families as expected, however, and the community developed slowly, with as many lower-middle-class as working-class migrants moving into the area.[9] Joseph and Matilda shared Girlington Road not only with others involved in the textile trade but also with dress and bonnet makers, a Post Office clerk, several teachers, a Baptist minister, a grocer, a professor of music and the incumbent vicar of the parish church of St Philip and his family.[10] Members of the Bradford textile elite continued to live in Manningham too, populating the classical villas that had been built in the area as early as the 1830s. The members of the relatively new and diverse community in Manningham must have relied on each other for support, entertainment and company. Joseph was establishing himself within it, and it seems likely that the relationships he made helped pave the way for him to establish himself in business and set his young and growing family on the path to a stable and possibly prosperous future.

There were a great many Aykroyds living in Manningham. Different branches of what may well have been the same family all worked in the textile business, usually as part of the finishing process and particularly as dyers. It is likely that the Charles Aykroyd, with whom Joseph formed a partnership, was part of this extended family. There was certainly a man of this name resident in Manningham in 1851, only a year younger than Joseph and working as a cotton dyer's clerk when he was nineteen. Charles was living at 74 Belgravia Place, and this road seems to have formed a family hub at the time. John Aykroyd, a dyer, and his family were living at No. 45, and William Aykroyd was at No. 80. William's elderly father (also Charles) was lodging with John Aykroyd, and so it seems clear that they were related.[11] These men were members of what was to become an enormously successful Bradford textile family. William Aykroyd was the man responsible for the fortune that they made. His company, William Aykroyd & Co., dyers, was founded in 1835 and he went on to partner with his sons as they came of age to become William Aykroyd & Sons. William's grandson, like many of the other hugely successful members of the Bradford textile elite, was made a baronet, and used some of the family fortune to purchase Grantley Hall. William was baptised as a non-conformist, as Joseph's father had been. If Joseph had found his way into the company of members of this up-and-coming family, then his future seemed very promising indeed.

5

GOING TO MONTE CARLO

Joseph was clearly a man on the way up. He was making a decent life for his family, but was not wealthy – so why, then, did he choose to take on the difficult and costly journey from England to Monte Carlo, the playground of the rich and famous? This has been one of the biggest mysteries surrounding this tale of bank-breaking. How could he afford to go? And why would he think to go there? This aspect of the tale has always been the most troubling. During the years that I have been researching his story, whenever I start to tell it, what everybody wants to know (apart from what happened to the money) is what Joseph was doing in Monte Carlo in the first place. I had never been able to answer this question satisfactorily and this, one of the gaping holes in my inherited narrative, was a factor in causing me to doubt that Joseph had broken the bank at all. However, I now believe I have discovered both his motivation for taking on this journey and how it was achieved.

There has been no consensus among those who have written accounts of Joseph's exploits in the past as to what might have motivated his journey. The newspaper articles in the Bradford archive that tell his story were written in the twentieth century and borrow details from each other, so it is difficult to tell which elements are based on fact and which are assumption and conjecture. The earliest version of events that I can find, which was written in 1901, doesn't discuss why Joseph went to Monte Carlo at all.[1]

The most frequently cited theory is that Joseph went on holiday and wandered into the casino out of curiosity. Anyone could enter the public gaming rooms free of charge if they applied for a card and were smartly dressed, and many tourists of the time did just this. I can imagine Joseph among the crowd, standing three or four rows deep around the table, behind the seated players, enjoying the atmosphere and, if he was lucky, watching a winning streak. Perhaps at such a time he was tempted to try his luck; roulette, after all, is a very straightforward game to play with no complicated rules to understand. Even for those who don't speak French, the language of the croupiers is no real barrier after a period of observing others play. I've done it myself. This seems plausible until the nature of Victorian tourism is considered.

Taking holidays abroad was a relatively new concept. Thomas Cook ran the world's first commercial tour in 1845, taking passengers from Leicester to Liverpool. During the three previous summers he had run train excursions to Temperance meetings in the local area, the first on 5 July 1842, which took 500 passengers a distance of 12 miles by train and back from Leicester to Loughborough for a shilling. The Liverpool trip was the first to be bookable and was accompanied by an excursion booklet, the first travel brochure. Thomas Cook didn't operate overseas until 1855, when a party was led through Belgium and Germany to Paris.[2] The French Riviera was a relatively new destination for anyone other than the very rich, and Thomas Cook didn't publish a guide to it until 1881.

Leisure travel overseas was only for those who had time on their hands and the resources to enjoy it. Monte Carlo in particular was the playground of the European elite, and in the nineteenth century its casino was the most glamorous destination of its day, enjoyed by the royalty and the social elite of every country. It became synonymous with grand dukes, tricksters, gambling systems and cocaine. Monegasques, the citizens of Monaco, were forbidden to gamble (as they are today), while outsiders were encouraged to do so. Visitors included King Edward VII and Queen Alexandra of England (when they were Prince and Princess of Wales), Emperor Francis Joseph of Austria, several Russian grand dukes and King Oscar of Sweden.[3] Professional gamblers, chancers and curious tourists flocked there: 'Everybody comes – anything can happen. Nothing is too strange to happen at Monte Carlo, and it is only ordinary things that never do.'[4]

The casino opened in the morning and play continued without intermission until midnight, even on a Sunday.[5] It was closed for one day a year only: the Prince of Monaco's birthday, 15 November.[6] Many gamblers remained at the tables for most of this time, as this account from the *Dundee Courier* of 12 April 1898 describes:

Duchesses, countesses, swindlers, shopkeepers, and soldiers mingle in the scramble for seats, and from that moment until midnight the play never ceases. After a short time, some of the crowd wander away to breakfast, served on the terrace beneath an awning which protects the customers from the blazing sun, and there are no better cafés than those at Monte Carlo ... Walks and drives, pigeon-shooting and flirting take up a few hours but as evening draws on the gambling rooms exert their fatal fascination. From now until dinner some of the heavier gambling takes place, and the great players are surrounded by a crowd of eager spectators ... Dinner follows at eight o'clock, and afterward ... more gambling, then supper, and to bed, at any hour of the morning.

It is possible that Joseph had an interest in gambling or that he was curious about the casino. Roulette had been banned from public play in England for generations before he was born. The English were still bound by a law passed in 1745, during the reign of George III, which decreed that anyone caught gambling in public on games of pure chance such as 'roly poly or roulette', faro and hazard could be prosecuted. George III's law was been relaxed a little in time to allow games of skill such as cribbage and dominoes to be played, but the playing of roulette in public still remained illegal in England.[7] As late as 1908 public gambling in London was still a risky business, as demonstrated in this report in the *New York Times* on 27 September that year regarding a game of roulette played with dummy money between two men who wanted to prove the validity of their theories about how the bank at Monte Carlo could be beaten:

> LONDON, Sept.26 – It appears that both Sir Hiram Maxim and the Earl of Rosslyn are liable to prosecution for playing the game of roulette in England ... Roulette is one of the few games expressly declared illegal by statute, for there can be no question as to its identity with the 'pernicious game called rolypoly or roulet', which is forbidden in an unrepealed act of Parliament of George III's time ... The tenant of the room in Piccadilly in which the contest is carried on is liable to a fine of £200, and each player ... £50 as an 'adventurer'.

By the time that Joseph went to Monaco, roulette had had a resurgence in England, but only among the upper classes who enjoyed it in their own homes or private clubs. In the early years of Queen Victoria's reign, gambling had become a national scandal. London's West End gentlemen's clubs saw vast sums of money changing hands between members and very many losing their fortunes. White's, which was established in the eighteenth century, is reputedly where in 1765 the fourth Earl of Sandwich asked for a piece of meat between two slices of bread to be brought to him so that he would not need to stop gambling in order to eat dinner.

In 1828 William Crockford, a cockney fishmonger, opened his eponymous gentlemen's club which was so lavish and so successful that he earned £1.2 million within a few years (approximately £108.4 million today). There were less reputable and grand clubs all over town, some of which didn't require membership, including dozens of illegal gaming houses called 'hells'. Here gentlemen rubbed shoulders with professional gamblers and crooks who made a living from cheating. Even Crockford's had a cockfighting pit in its basement and a secret escape passage that led on to Piccadilly which could be used in case of a raid.[8] Affronted Victorian politicians decided to act, and in a single night in 1844, police shut down clubs all over London.[9] The Gaming Act of 1845 tightened the regulation of professional gaming houses and many closed down. Gambling continued in private clubs but eventually the Crockford's club at St James's Street closed too.[10]

Perhaps Joseph had read about these clubs and about roulette or had been curious to see the game in action, but this seems unlikely. Other forms of gambling are much more likely to have drawn his interest before the rich man's game of roulette. Cockfighting, bear-bating and dog-baiting, although illegal from the mid-nineteenth century, were still popular and cheap forms of entertainment. Angus Reach's accounts of northern life in the *Morning Chronicle* attest to this: 'Another feature of the place was the quantity of dogs of all kinds which abounded – dog races and dog fights being both common among the lowest orders of the inhabitants.'[11] Horse racing would also have been very accessible to Joseph. Other more indigenous forms of gambling would also have been a daily part of life in Yorkshire at the time. Knurr was a traditional pub game in the Pennines area where a hard ceramic ball (the knurr) was launched from a sling or mechanised firing device and the object of the game was to hit the knurr with a stick as far as you could as it flew through the air towards you. The distance was measured and bets paid out accordingly. Joseph's brother Richard was known to play.[12] Would an interest in gambling be enough of a motivation to take an unusual, expensive and lengthy journey to the playground of the rich and famous? This seems unlikely given Joseph's Methodist background and financial circumstances, and there is no evidence that he was a betting man, even though his brother was.

To complicate matters further, Joseph worked in the textile industry. Despite being self-employed, this made it likely that he would have to fit in with an established pattern of holidays. In the early years of industrialisation, mill workers had time off on Sundays after church, on Christmas Day and on Good Friday. It took active campaigning by social reformers to convince politicians and employers that breaks from factories were essential, and this wasn't accepted until towards the end of the eighteenth century. The smoky, noisy and crowded conditions brought by the Industrial Revolution to cities like Bradford and the move towards creating better conditions for workers encouraged by the Factory Acts led to mills and factories closing for a week in the summer. This was the most economical way of running the business, effectively closing it for a week for maintenance but running at full strength for the rest of the year.

This period when all factories stopped and all employees took a holiday became known as wakes week, and each business set its own dates and sent its workers home. Wakes week was an unpaid holiday right up until the 1960s, and employees saved for it during the year by paying into a holiday club. Many families chose to spend their time off close to home, enjoying relatively cheap pursuits such as the pub, playing cards and listening to music. For those that could afford it, wakes week was a time to head to the clean air and healing waters of the seaside.[13] The northern towns that were situated beside the sea flourished at this time into tourist destinations. The Blackpool Tower was erected as part of this growth of seaside holiday resorts in 1894, the town itself being the main wakes week destination of the Lancashire mill towns.

Those from the West Riding, including those who lived and worked in Bradford, were more likely to head to Morecambe. Boarding houses and entertainments such as Punch and Judy shows and music halls were introduced to meet the needs of the city dwellers, who continued to head to the coast for their holidays well into the twentieth century. Joseph's circumstances were improving, and he and Matilda might have been able to enjoy a few days at the seaside, but he was not affluent and it seems inconceivable that he would think to spurn Morecambe in favour of Monte Carlo, then as now a destination for the extravagantly rich and famous. Besides which, it would have taken almost the whole week for him to travel there and back, leaving precious little time for gambling.

The family theory has always been that Joseph found himself in Monte Carlo while on a business trip and took the opportunity to visit the casino while he was there. Bradford was a world-class player in the textile industry, exporting its products all over the globe. Between 1860 and 1874 its textile industry was booming.[14] However, just as the Victorian northern towns had taken over from medieval East Anglia to dominate the wool trade, so a new commercial rival had emerged: France. During the early part of the 1870s, French manufacturers began to specialise in high-quality all-wool textiles, particularly those containing merino wool, which produced a very soft and luxurious cloth. Bradford's success had been based on specialising in the more cheaply produced mixed fabrics, and this was an advantage until traditional wool supplies waned. This coincided in the early 1870s with a sea change in the fickle world of fashion as customers were suddenly demanding clothes made from all-wool fabrics. It was a trend that was to last, and Bradford's looms couldn't easily or cheaply be adapted to deal with the shorter wool yarns that the French were using so effectively.

It is against this background of textile boom and bust and of French competition that those involved in the English industry might have considered a business trip to France. It would have been a good way of understanding the competition and learning more about the advances that were being made on the Continent. Members of the Bradford Chamber of Commerce did visit the Paris Exhibition in 1878 to assess what their French rivals were doing.[15] Is it possible that Joseph went on such a reconnaissance trip and decided to visit Monte Carlo to see the new resort at the same time? Again, it seems unlikely. He was not a member of the textile elite in Bradford who dominated the Chamber of Commerce, and he was not a mill owner. There is another explanation for why Joseph travelled to Monte Carlo, one that I discovered quite by chance but which I find completely compelling.

6

A DESPERATE ADVENTURE

Joseph's motivation for travelling to Monte Carlo was revealed in a piece of evidence that had gone unnoticed for years. Two years after our first meeting, I decided that I should speak to David and Joyce Jagger again, to let them know how my research was progressing and that I was still working on the book. We arranged to meet in York, in a café near the Shambles. It was a dark and gloomy February day but there was a fire lit and we settled down for a chat in the warm, oak-beamed interior. Peter, the last survivor of David's three older brothers, had recently died in New Zealand. Just as his brothers had done, Peter had spent many years trying to track down Joseph Jagger's story and continued to do so even after he emigrated. David had received a package of documents after Peter's death, the accumulated cuttings, letters and notes from his research. Many duplicated what existed in David's own collection, my father's papers or in the archives in Bradford with the exception of two that I had never seen before. The first was a poem said to have been written by Joseph Hobson Jagger to his nephew Sidney Sowood. I read it through, and it didn't make much sense. It was to take on a huge significance later, once I had followed up on the second document, which was a newspaper cutting.

Peter had clipped it from the property section of *The Mail on Sunday*, excluding the date from his cut but retaining the title: 'The man who broke the bank of Monte Carlo lived here.' It was an article placed as part of the marketing surrounding the sale of The Manor House in Cowick Lane, Exeter, a magnificent Grade II listed Georgian house. The agent's details claimed an extraordinary link between Devon and Monaco, stating that the manor was once owned by Joseph Jagger, the gambler who inspired the story of 'the man who broke the bank at Monte Carlo'. The article maintained that Joseph bought the house with his winnings in 1886. I had traced our family back eight generations, discovering every one of them to have been born and to have died in Bradford; it seemed strange to me that Joseph would have bought a property in Exeter. I couldn't ignore the cutting, though; he had travelled to Nice after all, and maybe this adventure had sparked a desire to see more, to start somewhere new or to break his links with the past.

None of the census records taken during Joseph's life list him as living in Devon, but they only provided a snapshot of where he was living at ten-year intervals, not what happened in between. The gaps between these records were very frustrating. The evidence would surely lie in the census results for The Manor House and in any deeds or directories for the area. I emailed a local historian in Exeter, Dick Passmore, and he and his colleagues in the local history society immediately began an investigation. This quickly revealed that no Jaggers are listed as having been resident in the parish and that for most of its history The Manor House was the property of the Earls of Devon. The mystery deepened when I consulted Historic England's *National Heritage List for England*, which identifies The Manor House as 'at one time known as Alphington House.

Said to have been the home of Mr Wells "who broke the bank at Monte Carlo".[1]

Charles Wells, the gambler and fraudster who broke the bank in 1891, and about whom the song was written, lived most of his life in France. He was arrested in 1892, sent back to England and sentenced at the Old Bailey in 1893 to eight years' imprisonment. Perhaps he'd bought the house with his winnings before he was locked up? His biography makes no mention of this, however.[2] The local historians then unearthed another piece of evidence that seemed to explain things: in 1893 the house was owned by Joseph Wells.[3] Ownership had clearly become confused over the years, and rumours had circulated locally about the Monte Carlo win as Joseph Wells became muddled with Charles Wells and Joseph Jagger. Whether Alphington House ever belonged to Charles Wells cannot be confirmed, but it seems probable that Joseph Jagger, Wells' fellow bank-breaker, never lived there.

This Exeter exploration was not, however, as dead an end as I first supposed. I'd relied on local historians to help me many times and this was another example of the willingness to help that exists within the online community of historians as well as the dogged determination to get to the bottom of a mystery. I'd shared my theory with Dick about the confusion of names and he emailed me to say that it had been a thoroughly enjoyable exercise for his fellow historians and that he was attaching some of the other things that they'd unearthed, although he assumed I'd probably seen them. Attached to the email were some documents, one of which I had not seen before. It took my breath away. Here, via a press cutting for a property for sale sent from New Zealand and an investigation into property ownership in Exeter, had come the answer to a question that I'd been asking since I started my research and which had dogged my ancestors for more than forty years: why did Joseph Jagger go to Monte Carlo?

The document that Dick had sent me was a notice printed in *The London Gazette* on 6 April 1860, which read,

INSOLVENT DEBTORS to be Heard in the Court House, at Lancaster Castle, in the County of Lancaster, on Friday, the Twentieth day of April 1860, at the hour of TEN in the Morning precisely ... JOSEPH HOBSON JAGGER (sued as Joseph Jagger and trading under the names of initials of J. H. Jagger) ..., out of business.[4]

By April 1860, then, Joseph had debts that he did not have the money to pay. Only a few years before, he had moved his family to an aspiring part of town and his future seemed stable and full of opportunity. Now he was facing financial ruin. He had lost his business and had been brought to court by his debtors. This was a very grave situation under Victorian law because insolvent debtors were held responsible for the money that they owed, and if they had no means of paying it they could be imprisoned until they did so, which could mean indefinite confinement.

Debtors' prisons were run privately for profit and were completely unregulated, a state of affairs which fostered numerous money-making schemes within them. In the notorious Marshalsea Prison in Southwark, London, there was a bar, shop and restaurant for those prisoners who could afford to use them. The majority of debtors, however, faced years of living at the mercy of their incarcerators, often finding that their financial situation worsened because of the extortion rackets operating inside the prison. It was routine for prisoners to be charged 'rent', to pay for their food and water, to furnish their own prison room and to pay for any legal help that they needed. They even had to pay for medical treatment. At its most brutal, this prison money-making system charged prisoners to have their chains removed. Some jailers applied several chains to each prisoner's arms and legs, removing them one by one only when money was handed over. There was no protection under the law for debtors, and even when they managed to pay back a little of what they owed this was not recognised. The debt could be inflated at the creditor's whim, and this, added to the cost of being in prison, resulted in situations where an ever-escalating debt was impossible to repay. When the Fleet Prison in London was closed in 1842, some prisoners were found to have been there for thirty years.[5]

This penal system encouraged communities of debtors to develop within the prisons. Whole families lived together there as few charitable organisations existed outside to support them. Babies were born in prison and children and spouses were allowed to leave on a daily basis to work to help their family raise any money that they could. Charles Dickens satirised this dreadful situation, most famously in *Little Dorrit*, which was published as a part work between 1855 and 1857. Dickens's father had been sent to Marshalsea in 1824 for owing a baker, James Kerr, a debt of £40 and 10 shillings (£3,271 in today's values). John Dickens was fortunate enough to be released after three months, but during that time Charles, who was only twelve years old, was forced to leave school and work for ten hours a day in a blacking factory. His mother and three youngest siblings moved into Marshalsea Prison with his father while Charles had to find lodgings and walk daily to work. Eventually he found a room close to the prison and was able to go there for breakfast and dinner with his family.

For those prisoners who had neither family nor friends to help them, and who had no way of earning any money for themselves, there was often only one fate: they died of starvation. A parliamentary committee reported in 1729 that at Marshalsea 300 inmates had starved to death within a three-month period, and that eight to ten prisoners were dying every twenty-four hours in the warmer weather:

When the miserable Wretch hath worn out the Charity of his Friends, and consumed the Money, which he hath raised upon his Cloaths, and Bedding, and hath eat his last Allowance of

Provisions, he usually in a few Days grows weak, for want of Food, with the symptoms of a hectick Fever; and when he is no longer able to stand, if he can raise 3*d* to pay the Fee of the common Nurse of the Prison, he obtains the Liberty of being carried into the Sick Ward, and lingers on for about a Month or two, by the assistance of the above-mentioned Prison Portion of Provision, and then dies.[6]

Lancaster Castle, where Joseph's case was heard, housed the largest debtors' prison outside London. This anonymous poem written in 1861, when Joseph was facing imprisonment there, illustrates its notoriety:

Most famed old castle of the North, time-honoured, old and grey,
Where John O' Gaunt for ever reigns a monarch of the day!
Where men of trade in thousands flock, when troubles are
    combined,
And who, like hunted hare or fox, a hiding place would find!
Where poor insolvent debtors seek a cure for all their woes;
And where both honest men and rogues do pay their friends
    and foes.[7]

Lancaster Castle's debtors' prison was, like Marshalsea, reasonably comfortable for those who could afford to pay for supplies. Food and drink was plentiful if prisoners had the money, and there was even a social club, but it was still a prison and it had strict rules. The dungeons were used to punish transgressors and debtors were incarcerated with criminals, even dangerous and insane ones, and so life was precarious. When Joseph's business failed, not only he but his wife Matilda must have felt terror at the prospect of the debtors' prison. They faced not only their own incarceration but that of their four children, the youngest of whom was only two years old.

7

MANCHESTER

How had Joseph come to this? Following the discovery of the insolvency notice, I researched further and found a report printed prior to his appearance at the court in Lancaster Castle.[1] This revealed that there had been a major change in the direction of Joseph's life and career. The business that he had just lost was based at 'Market Street, Manchester, in the County of Lancaster', a location that is confirmed in *Perry's Bankrupt and Insolvent Gazette* on 14 April 1860, in which he is described as a stuff finisher in Manchester. Joseph had left his finishing and sizing ventures in Bradford to cross the Pennines and ride the cotton boom in Manchester.[2] But, as will become clear, he picked the very worst time to do so.

Manchester was the centre of the cotton industry in England. It was at the very heart of the Industrial Revolution and saw the introduction of many innovations that caused it to thrive. England's first canal, the Bridgewater Canal, was built to take coal into Manchester's industrial centre in 1761, and it was succeeded in 1830 by the first successful railway to open in Britain, the Liverpool and Manchester Railway.[3]

Manchester developed the United Kingdom's first public horse-drawn bus service in 1824[4] and had one of the first telephone exchanges in Britain.[5] Raw cotton brought by sea from America was imported into Liverpool and shipped via the canal to Manchester, which was the commercial hub of the British cotton industry. Buyers came to purchase raw cotton for use by the textile mills of Manchester and more importantly the mills of the surrounding manufacturing towns of Lancashire. Once the cotton cloth was woven and finished it was sold in the Manchester Trade Hall and exported all over the world.

During the 1850s the cotton industry was experiencing unprecedented growth and it boomed between 1859 and 1860.[6] Joseph must have seen what was happening in Lancashire and, as an independent trader with experience in finishing and sizing, saw an opportunity to adapt the skills that he honed with wool to the cotton industry and ride its wave of success. Joseph and Matilda had moved to Girlington Road in Bradford sometime in the mid- to late 1850s, and as they were still there in 1860 it seems likely that Matilda and the children stayed in Bradford whilst Joseph lodged in Manchester, perhaps coming home when he could.[7] The Manchester enterprise must still have only been in its infancy when it fell into trouble, because there is no trace of Joseph Hobson Jagger or J. H. Jagger in the trade directories for Manchester in 1858 (or the preceding years); he must have headed to the city in 1859, at the very height of the cotton boom.

It would have been an exciting time for Joseph, with the prospect of success in a thriving industry that was new to him, in a great, unexplored city. He set up business in Market Street as a stuff finisher, at the hub of Manchester's cloth district. The Royal Exchange was on the corner of Market Street and Exchange Street, the latter being lined with great warehouses, which rose five or six storeys high. By day they belched smoke and at night they were brilliantly illuminated. Angus Reach's report on life in Manchester for the *Morning Chronicle* in 1849 recorded that there is a smoky brown sky over head – smoky brown streets all round long piles of warehouses, many of them with pillared and stately fronts – great grimy mills, the leviathans of ugly architecture, with their smoke-pouring shafts. There are streets of all kinds – some with glittering shops and vast hotels, others grim and little frequented – formed of rows and stacks of warehouses; many mean and distressingly monotonous vistas of uniform brick houses.

There are swarms of mechanics and artisans in their distinguishing fustian – of factory operatives, in general undersized, sallow-looking men – and of factory girls somewhat stunted and paled, but smart and active-looking with dingy dresses and dark shawls, speckled with flakes of cotton wool, wreathed round their heads.[8]

Manchester had grown through its co-operative approach to trade, which gave even small businesses a chance to develop through a 'room and power' system. Individuals like Joseph could rent a space with a power supply and house the hired equipment which they needed for their business. Raw cotton was very cheap to buy, and this business model allowed lone traders and small business owners to pay off the loan on their machinery with the surplus they made from the finished cloth before beginning to turn a profit. Finishing was a crucial part of the cotton manufacturing process, the stage that helped to make cotton fabric so very versatile. It included bleaching the yellowish raw cotton, raising fibres to create fluffy fabrics such as flannelette, rolling to make a smooth and sleek surface, printing, dying and even pre-shrinking to ensure minimal change to the fabric following laundering.[9]

Behind this façade of prosperity, however, problems were growing. Cloth was being produced at such a rate in the late 1850s that it far outstripped demand and merchants were hoarding it, speculating that they could force up the price.

The cotton industry had grown with such speed and to such an excessive degree that it was on the brink of recession.[10] Joseph entered the arena at this point, a small independent relying on a consistent supply of cloth to finish and sell to pay the rent on his room and repay the loan on his machinery. As the cotton industry faltered, Joseph and his fellow sole traders would have been among the first to feel the effects. Joseph's business probably fell into trouble very quickly and by April 1860 he couldn't go on, probably owing too much in rent and unpaid loans on his finishing machinery. Any chance of recovery was thwarted by the outbreak of the American Civil War and the order by the US President, Abraham Lincoln, to cut off all cotton exports in 1861. This blockade was intended to squeeze his enemies, cotton growing being the economic mainstay of the slave-owning southern states of America, but Lincoln's actions were to cripple Lancashire's cotton industry.

At first there was great ideological support for the President among the liberal, progressive population of Manchester. Despite the city's dependence on cotton, the fact that it was picked by slaves had long been a source of discomfort among a populace who in the main found slavery abhorrent. At a meeting in the Free Trade Hall on 31 December 1862, the chairman delivered an address from the working population of Manchester to Abraham Lincoln, expressing their support for the blockade on cotton:

> The vast progress which you have made in the short space of twenty months fills us with hope that every stain on your freedom will shortly be removed, and that the erasure of that foul blot on civilisation and Christianity – chattel slavery – during your presidency will cause the name of Abraham Lincoln to be honoured and revered by posterity. We are certain that such a glorious consummation will cement Great Britain and the United States in close and enduring regards.

On 19 January 1863, Abraham Lincoln thanked the cotton workers of Lancashire for their support, which he recognised came at a very great price to themselves:

> I know and deeply deplore the sufferings which the working people of Manchester and in all Europe are called to endure in this crisis. It has been often and studiously represented that the attempt to overthrow this Government which was built on the foundation of human rights, and to substitute for it one which should rest exclusively on the basis of slavery, was unlikely to obtain the favour of Europe. Through the action of disloyal citizens, the working people of Europe have been subjected to a severe trial for the purpose of forcing their sanction to that attempt. Under the circumstances I cannot but regard your decisive utterances on the question as an instance of sublime Christian heroism which has not been surpassed in any age or in any country. It is indeed an energetic and re-inspiring assurance of the inherent truth and of the ultimate and universal triumph of justice, humanity and freedom. I hail this interchange of sentiments therefore, as an augury that whatever else may happen, whatever misfortune may befall your country or my own, the peace and friendship which now exists between two nations will be as it shall be my desire to make them, perpetual.[11]

But support for a war on the other side of the ocean, even an idealistic one fighting for shared values, must have waned as it plunged Lancashire into three years of famine and depression. Workers who had been the most affluent in England became the most impoverished. Eighty per cent of the cotton imported into England came from America and now manufacturers in Lancashire could no longer make cloth. Supplies were held on to for as long as possible, and other sources such as Indian cotton were explored but they were often too brittle and unreliable, arriving full of stones and impurities so that far less finished cloth could be produced than from the excellent-quality American raw cotton. Workers' wages fell as production slowed and vast numbers were eventually laid off. In the winter of 1862/63, *The Illustrated London News* reported that

> nearly 7,000 of 11,484 operatives usually employed were out of work, and a large number of those employed were on short time. Of 39 cotton manufactories, 24 foundries and machine shops, and three bobbin turning shops in the town, only five were employed full time with all hands; 17 full time with a reduced number of hands; 34 on short time; and seven were stopped. A gigantic system of relief was organised in the town, and it is said that more than three-fourths of the population became dependent.[12]

Shopkeepers and small traders had nothing to sell and couldn't pay their rent. Neither could small mill owners who were heavily mortgaged with few finances to fall back on. Those businesses that survived did so by adapting, for instance changing their looms to take other forms of cotton or wool; by being frugal with limited supplies; or by diversifying, as, for example, factories in Stockport did by making hats. Unemployment among cotton workers was widespread. Many lived in terrible conditions while many more were evicted from their homes. Previously affluent families were plunged into the most terrible poverty.

> On entering their dwellings, you observe the little library of books gone, the Sunday coat and gown have followed, then the chest of drawers, the corner cupboard and mahogany clock, the wife's bonnet, the daughter's shoes, all but one pair, the little girl's latest frock, and the boys holiday hat; last of all, the chairs, the bedstead, and the bed...[13]

Many Lancashire workers went to Yorkshire in search of work, the irony being that Bradford's industry, the wool trade that Joseph gambled on leaving behind, boomed in the 1860s. Many more chose to take advantage of the offer of free passage by the governments of New Zealand and Australia and by the steamship companies, journeying to the other side of the world. In the town of Stalybridge in 1863 there were 750 empty houses and 1,000 residents had left. Money was sent from all over the world to the workers of Lancashire and local charities and relief organisations had to support whole communities. When raw cotton supplies from America resumed and the industry had begun to recover in 1864, thousands of vital workers had been lost. The heyday of the Lancashire cotton industry was well and truly over.[14]

Against this background, it's hard to think that Joseph had any chance of repaying his debts and recovering his family's security. The prospect of debtors' prison loomed large – but could it be avoided? For private individuals prison was inevitable, but for those engaged in trade or business there was another option, one created by the Insolvent Debtors Act 1842. Provision was made for the first time for a trader owing less than £300 (£26,000 in today's values) to obtain a protection order from the Court of Bankruptcy or a District Court of Bankruptcy, suspending all legal action against him on condition that he surrendered all his property to an official court assignee. Eventually this property would be distributed among his creditors in proportions relative to what he owed them.[15] A debtor whose business had failed could now declare bankruptcy and save himself from prison, but he'd have to give up everything he owned.[16]

This is the course that Joseph took. On 4 May 1860, the court in Lancaster appointed an assignee, Jeffrey Falkingham, to Joseph, who henceforth became Insolvent no. 90,965.[17] After this date, I can find no other official record of a case against him. Process notices in *The London Gazette* and *Perry's Bankrupt and Insolvent Gazette* cease.[18] Joseph managed to keep both himself and his family out of debtors' prison, but of course this came at a high cost in both financial and personal terms. With a failed business and the shame of becoming bankrupt to bear, the meaning of Joseph's poem to Sidney Sowood, which I had not first understood, now became very clear, and its significance obvious.

The poem is called 'On going to Monte Carlo'.

> Judge me by my style of action,
> Only have some mercy too,
> Such as sweetens rough distraction,
> Even this I ask from you
> Please to hear me when I plead
> Help me in this time of need.
>
> Honest men oft taste misfortune
> Others suffer for misdeeds
> But must your ear importune
> Saying while my conscience bleeds –
> Oh that life would backward turn!
> Never need my cheeks so burn.
> Join me in a conversation,
> Answer as your thoughts dictate,
> Graced by friendly consolation
> Good must come, although tis late;
> Eagerly my debts I'll pay –
> Rising in a brighter day.
>
> Dear Sir your kindness has been shown
> To me, but not to me alone
> For this I long to do my part,
> And thank you now with all my heart
> But here my pen more courage takes –
> I hope it mars not what it makes.

> I wish to ask one favour more,
> And hope you'll add it to the score
> Of all the kind deeds you have done
> To many a poor and needy one.
> I ask it with much pain and sorrow –
> Can you lend me five pounds tomorrow?[19]

Reading it again, but this time after discovering Joseph's insolvency, the poem is steeped in Joseph's shame and embarrassment. He clearly feels responsibility for the downturn in his fortunes, blaming himself for the decision to move to Manchester and wishing that he could turn the clock back. Joseph's agony at his situation can only have been enhanced by finding himself in the position of having to beg for money from a nephew to whom he'd so recently given a home. And not an insubstantial amount either, the equivalent of approximately £450 today. Sidney had lived for a time at Girlington Road with his uncle and aunt.

I doubt that Sidney was the only family member Joseph had to approach and appeal to; quite likely there were a procession of humiliating encounters including with his brother William and his sisters. His father was still alive but died in the December of that year, living perhaps just long enough to understand that his son had lost everything. Abraham may have been able to give his son a little, but he did not die a wealthy man. He left an estate valued at under £100, which equates to £8,620 today.[20] Joseph's determination to pay off his debts is clear as well, but this poem was written fifteen years after he was first taken to the Court for the Relief of Insolvent Debtors. Still reduced to borrowing money, Joseph and Matilda must have been struggling to keep the family safe for years.

By 1871, they had left their home in aspiring Girlington and moved back into the centre of Bradford, to 6 Greaves Street in Little Horton.[21] No longer the master of his own business,

Joseph was working as a 'piece taker in'. He might have been employed by a firm that undertook a part of the manufacturing process such as scouring, carding or finishing for a factory, possibly Brigella Mills, a worsted mill which lay at the heart of the Little Horton community and was run by the Briggs family.[22] More likely he was back to being an outworker, undertaking pieces of work at home and being paid a small amount for each, a remnant of the old cottage industry in Bradford.

Times were obviously hard, and the circumstances of Joseph and his family considerably reduced, but is this financial situation motive enough to travel to Monte Carlo? I think his poetic plea to Sidney suggests that it was. It represents more than just an uncle asking his nephew for a loan. Joseph Hobson Jagger was facing a situation so desperate that all he had achieved and the security of his family – indeed the very liberty of himself and his family – was in critical danger. The poem provides a glimpse of a larger fundraising campaign, a campaign by Joseph to fund a wildly imaginative plan that could clear his debts and allow him to rebuild his life. It is easy to imagine that he wrote in similar terms to other family members or friends.

International travel was not to be undertaken lightly by a man in Joseph's position. The price of a single ticket from London to Nice from Thomas Cook at the time was between £5 and £8 (approximately £450 to £730 for a single ticket in today's values), depending on the class of travel and chosen route.[23] Joseph was not in steady employment and was taking on piece work so would almost certainly not have been earning anything like the salary that a textile worker of the period could expect, which was approximately £85 a year.[24] Even if he had been able to earn this amount, the ticket alone would have cost him in the order of between one-eighth and one-fifth of his annual earnings.

Joseph's plan would also have required him to fund his food and accommodation for a period of time and to purchase or rent appropriate dress for the casino. There were boarding houses and pensions or villas in Monaco where all china and linen was included in the rent, and cheaper areas to find hotels such as the suburb of *La Condamine*, but even there a room cost about 3 francs a night. Breakfast, lunch and dinner (including wine) would have required Joseph to find an additional 6 or 7 francs a day.[25] At these prices, just to live in Monte Carlo might well have cost Joseph at least 10 francs a day, equating to approximately £3 a week at the time.[26] And this was before he even placed a bet at the casino, where the minimum stake was 5 francs for each spin of the wheel.[27] Knowing that he would have to remain in Monte Carlo for a number of weeks to put his plan into effect, Joseph would have needed to raise a considerable sum of money. A fundraising campaign on this scale must have been a daunting prospect for a man in Joseph's financial difficulties. He must have scrimped, borrowed and saved to get to Monte Carlo, and it must have taken him years.

Why Monte Carlo and why roulette? Both things were entirely foreign to him. Why not simply gamble on horse racing or hare coursing to raise the money he needed? The potential rewards of roulette were of course much greater; they could be life changing. As with lottery players today, it's easy to see how trying his hand in the casino at Monte Carlo could appear to Joseph to be a solution to his financial problems. But the plan involved so much more than just buying a ticket in a local shop and waiting for the weekend to see if the numbers matched. The costs and difficulties were immense, and Joseph must have known that the plan's chance of success was minimal. I believe the truth is that Joseph had tried all that he could to rebuild the family finances and at this point was facing a future so bleak that he believed his only means of escape was to take his chances on the roulette wheels of Monte Carlo. Even contemplating such a costly adventure seems extraordinary, except that Joseph had a source of help – surprisingly close to home.

8

THE RAILWAYMAN

Most working-class Victorian people lived and died within a few miles of where they were born. Joseph's family had lived for over a century in Bradford, marrying local men and women and raising their children close to home. The furthest Joseph had travelled was probably to Manchester, but now he was developing a plan that would require him to journey not only to the south coast of England but to cross the Channel and then travel the length of France. Joseph would have had to rely on modes of transport that were very, very new.

The railway system in Britain was in its infancy. The Leeds and Bradford Railway had opened as recently as 1846. There had been sixteen years of surveying and arguing about the best way to link the two cities, but finally trains had arrived.[1] Critical to the textile industry of the north and the major catalyst of the Industrial Revolution, the railways also provided a major new form of employment.[2] The job of the train driver was considered to be hugely exciting. At the very forefront of the new technology, these men, in charge of their own locomotives, were travelling as fast as it was possible to go at the time.[3] When trains first took to the tracks many people were terrified of their speed, believing that they would fall unconscious or that their eyes would be damaged. The driver's job was a very dangerous one in a very risky environment. Standing on open footplates, often with no cab or roof, drivers were exposed to the elements, the dirt and heat of their fires and the dangers of a transport system in its rudimentary infancy.

Vacuum brakes, which ensure that carriages when disconnected automatically come to a stop, were not compulsory until 1889. In the early days carriages had no brakes at all, and simply slammed into each other. Only a handbrake, which took quite some time to slow the engine, came between the driver and dangerous collisions. A crash at Bradford station on 27 February 1871 was caused by human error and an unreliable braking system, according to an accident report at the time. The train hurtled into the station, hit the buffers, left the tracks and hit the station wall, crushing to death a passenger who was standing there looking through a window:

> ... his tender brakes being hard on, thinking his speed was too high, [the driver] turned round to see if the guard was at his brake wheel, and perceived him sitting on his seat with his head down, appearing to be asleep; that he picked up a lump of coat and threw it at the end of the van, but that this did not rouse him...[4]

Pressure from the government had to be exerted before the railway companies would agree to introduce basic safety procedures. Block signalling, which ensures that two trains can't use the same stretch of track, wasn't mandatory until 1888. Before that companies used their own systems, and the lack of co-ordination, compounded by human error and confusion, meant that serious collisions and fatalities occurred regularly. The track into Bradford station was down an incline of 1 in 50, which required drivers to have excellent braking skills on the way in and the power to travel up the slope on the way out. A system was devised where heavy passenger trains with carriages could be pushed up the hill by lighter pilot engines. The rule on that area of track not to have two trains on the same stretch at the same time was regularly ignored to shunt trains up the incline, as this accident report of 1872 records:

> This collision was the result of an objectionable system of working. It is impossible but that accidents must again and again occur as long as it is permitted to continue. If I do not mistake, this is the fourth collision that has occurred on this railway owing to the same system of working during the last few months ...[5]

Horrible crashes were common. Charles Dickens was almost killed in 1865 on his way back from France with his mistress Ellen Ternan when the train in which they were travelling from Folkestone to London drove off a bridge. Engineering work in the area had been delayed and somebody forgot to tell the driver of the oncoming train. Ten people died and Dickens heroically went back to help the injured and to retrieve the manuscript of his novel *Our Mutual Friend*.[6] The crash was clearly a very traumatic event, as his letter written shortly after records:

> I should have written to you yesterday or the day before, if I had been quite up to writing. I am a little shaken, not by the beating and dragging of the carriage in which I was, but by the hard work afterwards in getting out the dying and dead, which was most horrible. I was in the only carriage that did not go over into the stream. It was caught upon the turn by some of the ruin of the bridge, and hung suspended and balanced in an apparently impossible manner ... Fortunately, I got out with great caution and stood upon

the step. Looking down, I saw the bridge gone and nothing below me but the line of the rail. Some people in the two other compartments were madly trying to plunge out of the window, and had no idea there was an open swampy field 15 feet down below them and nothing else![7]

In 1872, a pretty average year, 1,100 people were killed and 3,000 injured. Train drivers were penalised for running red lights or driving engines under the influence and rewarded for taking action that prevented accidents and saved the lives of passengers.[8]

Despite the dangers of its early years, no transport development since has had as great an impact on the imagination or on society as the arrival of trains. A settled world in which most people lived and died within a few miles of where they were born was transformed into a disturbing yet exciting world of infinite possibilities. Without the invention of trains and these first railway systems being laid through Britain and France, Joseph could not have travelled to Monte Carlo. Before them only the very rich, with plenty of time and plenty of money, could contemplate such a long journey. From 1868 trains were able to go straight into Monaco via Dijon, Lyon and Marseille.[9] At a stroke this extended service transformed a twelve-day journey into a thirty-hour one.[10] A traveller could board a train at London Bridge station first thing in the morning and be in Nice in time for supper the following day.

For the first time Monaco became a tourist destination, and Thomas Cook was prompted to publish a guide to the Riviera in 1881. *Cook's Handbook to the Health Resorts of the South of France and North Coast of the Mediterranean* focused on providing cost-effective travel for a clientele of more middle-class and professional travellers:

A cheap, comprehensive, and accurate Handbook to the numerous health resorts of the Riviera thus becomes a public necessity ... the rapid absorption of the first edition of this handbook has clearly justified its issue.[11]

Joseph's journey would have begun by boarding a train in Bradford bound for London, transferring on arrival to Charing Cross or Victoria to take a train to the coast. These boat trains took passengers straight to the dock where they boarded small steam ships to the Continent. There were five sea routes from London to Paris but the most popular were the shorter journeys from Dover to Calais or the cheaper and more scenic Newhaven–Dieppe route.[12] Once in France Joseph would have continued by train to Paris. He would have been delivered into the centre of one of the most modern, cultured and beautiful cities in the world. He would then have transferred to the Gare de Lyon from where, since the 1860s, the Paris–Lyon–Mediterranean Railway trains to the Riviera had departed between December and April, taking passengers through the heart of France to its southern coast.

This would have been a daunting journey for anyone, but for a man who had barely left Yorkshire before it must have felt almost impossible, and certainly not without risk to life and limb. It was possible to book the entire journey while still in England, but this sort of 'package' was relatively new. All the necessary information was published by Thomas Cook in its monthly newspaper, *Cook's Excursionist*, or its *Cook's Continental Time Tables*, and since 1875 Thomas Cook had offices in Manchester, Liverpool and Birmingham. They could provide combinations of tickets for passengers to travel 'by any route, any day, to all principal parts of the globe'.[13] Joseph could have booked a package, but this seems doubtful. I think that he had help from another, extremely coincidental and serendipitous source – assistance that helped with the details of the route and how to embark on it.

Oates Jagger was born in Cock Hill, Shelf, on 1 April 1839. His name came from the merging of his parents' names.

Richard Jagger was Joseph's older brother, and he married Mary Oates when they were both teenagers.[14] Oates' parents, like many of their contemporaries, couldn't write. On their marriage certificate from 1834, where his parents' signatures should be there are the two crosses which they have made instead, each labelled with their names.[15] Just like his father, grandfather and great-grandfather, Richard worked as a weaver[16] and then as a warp dresser, and his three oldest sons followed him into textiles in time; William as a mechanic apprentice, Joseph as a power loom weaver and Oates Jagger as a worsted spinner at the tender age of eleven.[17] It's possible that he began work at the age of eight or nine, as was quite usual at the time.

Mary died in her late thirties and Richard remarried soon after, choosing a local widow, Rachel Haigh (*née* Bairstow), as his second wife.[18] Rachel was obviously undaunted by adding seven stepchildren to her own brood of three because she and Richard went on to have nine children of their own. Perhaps it's not surprising that as soon as he was old enough to support himself Oates moved out and went to live with his uncle Joseph and Aunt Matilda at 77 Girlington Road. He was twenty-one, only nine years younger than his uncle.[19]

When Oates married he chose Sarah Ann Bairstow, possibly a relative of his stepmother. She already had a child, five-year-old Mary, born when she was twenty-two.[20] It's not certain if she was Oates' daughter, but the evidence suggests that she wasn't since the child kept the name Bairstow even after her mother married and on her own marriage certificate there is a blank where the name of her father should be.[21] Oates and Sarah married in June 1866, and a second daughter was born on Christmas Eve the following year.[22] Their happiness was short lived. The new baby was baptised Sarah Ann for the mother who died giving birth to her. Oates was only twenty-nine when he was left to raise their children alone. Falling between censuses as this date does means it's unclear where the young widower lived with his two small daughters, but it's possible that he moved back to Manningham, to the home of his uncle and aunt, letting Matilda help with the children while he went out to work.

Oates married again three years later, when he was thirty-one. This time he chose Jane Ellen Crowther, a spinster a couple of years younger than him.[23] They did not have children of their own but Jane Ellen helped to raise Sarah Ann, who was to suffer an early death like the mother after whom she was named. She died at the age of twenty-nine after her marriage; whether this death too was the result of childbirth cannot be confirmed, but it seems likely.

Oates Jagger's move away from his father's house before his first marriage and into the home of his uncle and aunt had been prompted by more than a desire to escape the crowded house in which his many siblings and half-siblings lived; he left because he no longer worked in the textile mills. Oates had joined a new and exciting industry. He had become a train driver. Railwaymen had to live close to stations, engine sheds or depots, and Joseph and Matilda's home in Girlington Road was within walking distance of Bradford's Forster Square station. There were engine sheds there, the most likely workplace for Oates, who was employed as an assistant engineman in 1861 when he was twenty-two.[24] Manningham, the area of Bradford where Joseph and Matilda lived, was one of the most important provincial railway centres on the whole of the Midland Railway system, and it was experiencing phenomenal growth.[25]

By the time that he was in his late twenties, Oates had worked his way up to become a train driver – quite an achievement for a boy who started work as a textile spinner.[26] A work progression from steam-powered mills to steam-powered locomotives seems logical, and there were plenty of opportunities for young men to make their way in this rapidly growing new industry. The role of engineman first class – train driver – was one of the most desirable jobs of the Victorian era. During the rise of the railways the train driver's job was as coveted as that of a professional footballer is today.

Men often took twenty to twenty-five years to work their way up from the job of a cleaner or labourer to being in charge of their own train. Many, of course, never made it.[27] For Oates to be a train driver by the time he was in his late twenties was quite an achievement.

Jane Ellen, Oates' second wife, must have been concerned about the safety of her husband but there is no doubt that he was ambitious and took full advantage of the opportunities offered. Shortly after the marriage he moved his new wife and his young daughters out of Bradford and into Bingley, a town just north of Manningham. Bingley's station had opened in 1847, and this prompted rapid growth and prosperity in the town. Oates and his family lived in New Road and many of their neighbours worked in the railway industry too. Next door was a railway carriage cleaner, and four houses away a railway guard.[28] Bingley was close enough to Bradford to allow men to work there too, perhaps lodging in the city during the week. Oates' neighbour may well have had to, as the carriages were stabled there.[29] By 1881 the family had moved again, even further from the city centre, this time to Keighley and a house on the Bradford Road, very close to the station.[30] The Midland Railway had an engine shed in the town that served the Worth Valley branch. Like many valleys in West Yorkshire, the Worth thrived as a centre of textile production. It had water and grassy slopes where sheep could graze, and over 100 worsted mills were built there. Coal was essential for the steam-powered machinery and had to be brought in while the textiles had to be transported out, and so the railway was a critical lifeline for the mill owners and their workers.[31]

It was while Oates was driving trains, and quite possibly while he was still living with his uncle, that Joseph formulated his plan to travel to Monte Carlo. Recognising the relationship that these two men had – two men so close in age, who had shared a home and the traumas of a wife's death and a bankruptcy – it's not too hard to imagine that Joseph would have shared his plan with his nephew. Putting Oates into events leading up to the Monte Carlo win introduces a new perspective. Joseph's audacious plan would not have been possible at a time without railways, and perhaps it would have been impossible without the help of a nephew who knew all about them, a man that Joseph trusted almost above all others. A man who, perhaps, could have helped to plan the route and gain access to the trains needed to deliver Joseph to Monte Carlo. Oates' employers, the Midland Railway, ran the line from Bradford to London, so perhaps he was able to purchase tickets for his uncle at a staff rate.[32] Maybe a colleague was persuaded to give him a lift, or perhaps Joseph offered to work his passage down to London. Men like Oates Jagger were the pioneers of a transport revolution that would change the face of the country and the lives of its people. This revolution, and his nephew's place at its forefront, helped Joseph to turn his incredible money-making scheme into a reality.

9

SIN, SCANDAL AND SUICIDE

What must Matilda's reaction have been when Joseph announced that he was planning to leave Bradford for Monte Carlo? It was notorious as a hotspot of sin and scandal; a place where huge amounts of money could be won, yes, but also where life savings – and lives – could be lost on the spin of a wheel. Fortunes, trust funds, children's legacies, money raised from the sale of a house could be, and often were, lost in days. The casino made a point of preventing from gambling anybody who was an official trustee or responsible for other people's money in any way, and clergymen, priests, officers and men in uniform were all forbidden too.

Blanc had made provision to assist in the most desperate cases and could loan a player their fare home on the understanding that if it wasn't paid back they would never be able to enter the casino again. In the early years, disgruntled and destitute gamblers were in the habit of running up hefty dinner bills at the *Hôtel de Paris* and then refusing to pay their bill before returning to Nice. This problematic situation was one of the reasons that Blanc introduced the *Viatique* (which translates as 'pocket money for the trip') to bail out those who had no money left.[1] It was claimed in 1895 that the *Inspecteur du Viatique* loaned £40,000 (approximately £4,250,000 now) to such destitute gamblers each year.[2]

For the most wretched, returning home was not an option; suicide seemed the only course of action. The newspapers were full of stories of tragic deaths. Young women were reported as throwing themselves from their rooms into the sea, players hanged themselves in their hotel rooms and men shot themselves in the casino, as this report in the *North Devon Journal* on 6 May 1875 records so graphically:

> One wretched victim blew out his brains at the table. 'He might have had the good taste to go and do it outside' was the remark of the other players as the mangled corpse was taken off, and the bloody pool was mopped up.

Sarah Bernhardt, one of the greatest French actresses of the era, gave the inaugural performance at the casino's new Opera House in 1879, dressed as a nymph. She attempted suicide after losing all that she had in just three hours of gambling. Returning to her room in the *Hôtel de Paris*, she took an overdose of sleeping tablets. Fortunately, her friend the Viscount de Rohan discovered what she'd done, rescued her and paid off the 100,000 franc debt.[3] The selling of poisons and firearms was banned in Monaco after François Blanc had to grab a gun from the hands of a man who was intent on killing himself in the casino gardens.[4] New visitors to Monte Carlo were advised to learn quickly to differentiate between the shots from the pigeon shooting terrace below and those of suicides.[5] One young woman visiting from England and enjoying the view from the terrace in front of the casino was apparently inconsolable on hearing a quick succession of gunshots. It had to be explained that what she heard was not brave men blowing their brains out after losing all they had, but the sound of pigeons being shot for sport.[6]

Speculation about the suicides in the casino had begun publicly when in 1875 the Bishop of Gibraltar condemned gamblers at Monte Carlo and their callous attitude to the desperate players who took their own lives in front of them.[7] The press picked up this clarion call, claiming that these cases were often suppressed so that the public didn't hear about them, and that officials were instructed to register these deaths as accidents rather than suicides.[8] Rumours abounded of chambers in the casino where dead bodies could be secreted before being whisked off by train and of discrete areas in Monaco's graveyard where they could be buried.[9] An article in *The Daily Chronicle* on 26 January 1897 claimed that the casino tried to cover up these incidents by not properly recording the deaths, stating that their accounts were a sham and rarely mentioned suicides even though during the season that year there had been sixty-five. A sixpenny edition of *The Secrets of Monte Carlo* claimed that the suicide rate in Monaco, 'with its four thousand inhabitants, has been more than one a day'.[10] A report in the *North Devon Journal* on 6 May 1875 shared the opinion that a great many suicides were being covered up,

> Of course a few lucky hits are made occasionally ... and these are sure to find their way into the papers. But the large winners are nearly sure to be large losers, for they are encouraged to play enormous stakes, with the all but certainty of losing at last. While these exceptional winnings are published far and wide, and serve as advertisements to attract other visitors, the tragedies ... are rarely made known.

These newspapers may well have been right. Blanc put aside an annual budget of £10,000 (approximately £1 million today) for what he euphemistically called 'publicity', as it included the practice of paying money to editors to keep the more scandalous stories about the casino out of the press.[11] Other accounts claim that the suicide problem was so great that it could not be hidden:

> If we residents of MC could only be spared the one blot upon the escutcheon – viz. the terrible and obvious necessity of daily witnessing the scores of corpses being withdrawn from the bushes in the exquisite gardens, with those specially made long rakes, also the queue of wagons in attendance simply longing for biz (these cannot well be concealed from the public gaze) … This notwithstanding, life at MC, in summer and winter alike, spells, in short, Paradise.[12]

Others defended Monte Carlo, claiming that stories of suicides were an exaggeration by those who wished to see the casino closed down – principally Christian groups. The journalist Adolphe Smith asserted that the suicide rumours were begun by the Bishop of Gibraltar after his request to open an Anglican church in Monaco was refused by Prince Charles III. Smith's analysis of the population of the principality, the statistics published, the probity of the local medical practitioners and his knowledge of the area led him to conclude that

> there is absolutely no secrecy; no corpse, whether a suicide or otherwise, can be buried without a medical certificate and a legal permission. Monaco, apart from its own love of law and justice, is too near to Paris, to Rome, to London, to Berlin, for it to be possible secretly to inter hundreds of people in the course of a season. It is an insult to the civilisation of Europe to imagine such a thing.[13]

Many went to great pains to point out that not every suicide in Monaco was directly attributable to the casino in any case. Some were the result of boredom experienced by people over fifty,[14] others because the victims were already desperate and unbalanced when they arrived and took their lives only when their gamble to win their money back at roulette had failed. Other suicides occurred amongst those that did not gamble:

> Then there is the gardener. He was terribly worried by his wife, who complained that she was never well enough dressed. If the casino did not attract so many beautifully dressed women to Monte Carlo, this gardener's wife might have been less anxious about her own appearance and would not have so worried her husband that he committed suicide by jumping off the rock at Monaco. Is this a suicide caused by the casino?[15]

These stories illustrate graphically just what a lurid and titillating reputation Monte Carlo had in the imaginations of the general public and what a frightening prospect it must have been for the far from worldly wise Joseph Hobson Jagger, contemplating this possible escape from his desperate financial straits. Blanc knew only too well what many people thought of his creation at Monte Carlo, and that's why his management company, the *Société des Bains de Mer*, or sea bathing company, was so named – to distance it and the Grimaldis from the real source of its income, the frowned-upon casino. *Bradshaw's Continental Railway Guide and General Handbook*, the bible of the Victorian traveller, described Monte Carlo and its casino very positively: 'Beside a fully supplied Reading Room, there is an elaborately decorated *Salle de Fetes* and widely known *Salles de Jeu* (Gaming Rooms). High-class music twice daily. Splendid view from the Terrace.'[16] Thomas Cook's first tourist guide to the principality, however, was scathing:

> It is not the province of the compiler of a handbook to moralise upon the subject of play, as practiced at Monaco. The whole question has been taken up by an influential Society, which is

endeavouring to induce the French Government to put an end to what is regarded as a plague spot infesting one of the most beautiful corners of Europe.[17]

This review was almost certainly influenced by the company's Baptist missionary founder. Thomas Cook took the Temperance pledge in 1833 and his organised excursions combined his two great passions: his heartfelt belief in the destructive influence of alcohol on the working classes and his faith in the power of the new railways to transform society and provide new opportunities. Joseph had been brought up a non-conformist among Baptists and Methodists in Bradford who frowned on both alcohol and gambling. If he used Cook's guide, as I think he must, then the shame he felt at his bankruptcy was surely compounded by being linked to the 'questionable visitors who now haunt the neighbourhood'.[18] Joseph would be throwing his lot in with this scandalous world, facing the moral judgement of his community and perhaps his own conscience. He would also be facing almost insurmountable odds. He must have feared for the consequences should his system fail. Was he really prepared to die in pursuit of his solution?

Did Matilda beg him not to go? Did she ask him to at least take somebody with him to support him? Or did she think it an opportunity for her entrepreneurial husband to rescue them from debt and financial disaster? Perhaps Joseph didn't tell her at all, or shared only a fragment of his plan, but if she knew then she almost certainly would have feared for him. Travelling to the south coast by the trains that had only recently arrived in Bradford, then crossing the sea in a steamship before entering a foreign country for the first time must have been a daunting prospect. She must have worried about her husband's safety and the money that they couldn't afford to lose on the roulette tables, but most of all she must have felt that she had little choice but to let him try.

10

SYSTEMS AND PLAYERS

The game of roulette as we know it today was devised in France. It is first recorded as being played publicly at the *Palais Royal* in Paris in the years following the French Revolution of 1789.[1] The palace was the home of the aristocratic Orléans family who had, before the Revolution, converted it for use by shops, cafés, social clubs and as apartments in order to make the property viable enough to hold on to. Eventually gambling rooms flourished there, attracting the elite of Paris, including Queen Marie Antoinette.[2] Despite the Duc d'Orléans losing his head on the guillotine and the palace being seized by the state, gamblers continued to flock there after the Revolution.[3] The execution of the royal family and much of the aristocracy does not seem to have affected the gambling economy in France, in fact it adapted and flourished. The new game appears to have been a hybrid version of a number of games that had been played in Europe for some time.

Hoca (or *Hocca*) was one of the games that the courtiers of Louis XIV of France enjoyed during the seventeenth century. Players bet on the turn of a card, or, in the Italian version, *biribi*, placed bets on a numbered grid. Gambling on games of chance like these became one of the main preoccupations of the court at Versailles and aristocrats were encouraged to wager enormous amounts. Some of the noble families of France lost their fortunes. The associated distress and bad behaviour caused by cheating, corruption and ill-afforded losses led Louis XIV to try to contain this obsession with gaming. In 1691 he imposed heavy fines and even imprisonment on those participating in gambling, but to little avail.[4]

Roly-poly had been played in England since the 1720s, and, like the French games, because of the enormous bets usually placed was very much the preserve of wealthy aristocrats. A letter sent to the Countess of Suffolk in 1731 recorded that Sarah, Duchess of Marlborough, had lost a great deal of money playing *roly-poly*.[5] The game centred on an un-numbered black-and-white spinning wheel containing a series of slots. A small ball was spun around and bets were made, but if the ball fell into any of the slots designated to the banker then all of the player's money was lost. *Even-Odd* or *E/O* was similar to *roly-poly* but used a wheel which was divided into twenty sections marked 'even' and twenty sections marked 'odd'.[6] Two of them contained holes, the equivalent of the *roly-poly* slots that gave the bank an immediate victory.[7] By 1800 *E/O* dominated the London clubs of St James's. Colonel Panton was one of the greatest players of his time and built a street, named after himself, near Leicester Square with his winnings.[8]

There are differing opinions as to when the name *roulette* was first used. It means 'little wheel' in French, which does seem to confirm its origins and give some credence to the theory that it was spread throughout Europe by the nobles who had escaped the French Revolution. The term seems to have been used at different times to describe games of chance played out on wheels. *Roly-poly* was certainly referred to as roulette on occasion (for example in the George III Act of 1845). However, there can be little doubt that the game that was first played at the *Palais Royal* in 1796 established the form of the game that is known as roulette today. It took the concept of numbers used in *hoca* and *biribi*, and added compartments numbered one to thirty-six, to a spinning wheel borrowed from the English games of *roly-poly* and *E/O*. The colours of the wheel were changed from black and white to alternating red and black. Two additional compartments, a red one numbered 0 and a black one numbered 00, were included, an updated version of the slots in the *roly-poly* and *E/O* wheels. These zeros were the bank's numbers, and gave the casino the financial advantage; if the ball fell on either, the best the gambler could hope for was to get his or her stake back.

François and Louis Blanc modified the thirty-eight-compartment wheel in their German casino by removing the 00 compartment, therefore improving the gamblers' chances of winning and then publicised it widely to attract players to their casinos.[9] This is the form of wheel that is used all over Europe today, while in America roulette is still played with a 00. The betting combinations of red/black, even/odd, single number and columns were all established by this French game launched in 1796.[10] Roulette, the game that had begun in France and was honed in Germany, was to reach its apogee in the casino at Monte Carlo.

Roulette is now, as it was at its genesis, a game of pure chance. Despite the evidence, many of the players drawn to the casinos of Europe during the Victorian craze for gambling still held on to the belief that a winning system could be found, that roulette wasn't just a game of chance, that they could beat the odds. Most professional gamblers entering the casino chose to play *trente-et-quarante*, a card game rather like poker, where the player had to keep track of the cards and with mathematical skill bide their time to make the right bet on the right hand. The odds of winning were higher than with roulette. But for everyone else, the roulette tables held the greatest attraction; a game that relied on the laws of probability must surely give a fair chance of a big win.

The method of play is unchanged. It begins when the *croupier* invites bets to be placed: '*Faites vos jeux, messieurs.*' He starts the wheel and throws the white ball in, sending it spinning around the bowl. As the wheel begins to slow he reminds the players that betting is ending – '*Les jeux sont faits*' – and then confirms that no more bets may be made as the wheel slows further and the ball jumps between the partitions: '*Rien ne va plus.*' When the wheel stops, the croupier calls out the number and colour on which the ball has fallen.

Gamblers choose the level of risk they want to take. The most likely way of winning is to lay money simply on red or on black and win double what has been staked. If players want a little more excitement they can place their bet in the centre of a group of numbers, reducing their chance of winning but increasing their payout if one of their numbers comes up. If they bet on a group of four numbers, for example, they will win nine times what they bet if any of the four come up; or they can bet on one of the three blocks of twelve numbers (1–12, 2–24, 25–36) and win 2/1.

As well as betting on individual numbers or groups of numbers, players can also bet on the evens chances: red/black; high/low; odd/even. Individual number betting is the riskiest of all but is the route to enormous wins and enormous losses. It requires nerve. While the laws of probability dictate that the real chance of winning is 1 in 37 (or 1 in 38 if you're playing with a 00), the actual odds paid out by the bank ignore the zeros and are only 35 to 1. This small margin, which means that the casino wins almost everything staked if the ball lands in the 0 (or 00), is, remarkably, all the advantage that the casino has over the player. And, even more remarkably, it is enough to ensure that in the long run the house always wins and the player generally loses, as this report from the *Manchester Courier & Lancashire General Advertiser* on 8 January 1881 explains.

On the whole, viewed merely as betting, it is a bad way of risking money ... If you and I play roulette ... we stand to lose or win on an average at an equality with one another. We back our luck at no special disadvantage. But if we play with a bank which gives itself one extra chance out of every 37, we are backing our luck against unequal odds. In the long run the bank must win from us.

People had beaten the odds before, of course, and their success was widely publicised. The casinos in the early years were terrified of a gambler appearing who had developed an infallible way of beating the roulette tables. Professional surveillance officers scanned the room and observed play, looking for any signs of cheating or early indications of a winning streak. Systems of play abounded, and books and magazines outlined a myriad of different methods, all of which promised certain success in Monte Carlo. Some were complex, and some were surprisingly simple.

In the main, systems of play centred on a method of placing bets. Usually these methods were based on a clear mathematical progression and an understanding that the laws of probability give gamblers an equal chance of a win with every spin of the wheel. In other words, each spin of the wheel is completely independent of those spins that have gone before and those that will follow, and so every outcome has an equal chance every time. Most systems also stated that gamblers should increase their bets with every loss, in order to try to recoup each loss as quickly as possible.

The d'Alembert System (or the '*montant et descendant*') was based on this belief that the laws of probability, or in this case the 'Law of Equilibrium', applied to roulette. D'Alembert was convinced that in any game of pure chance, whether it was cards, dice or roulette, the odds would eventually equalise. If you toss a coin 10 times you might expect more heads than tails (or vice versa); toss it 100 times and you'd expect the number of heads and tails to be equal; toss it 1,000 times closer still to equilibrium; and so on. The betting system that he devised was that a player should add one unit to his stake every time he lost and deduct one every time he won, so that when the equilibrium occurred he would be the winner. So, for example, if he lost five times in a row he will have lost 1 + 2 + 3 + 4 + 5 = 15, and if he then won on the sixth spin and the next four, he would have won 6 + 5 + 4 + 3 + 2 = 20, so a net win of 5 units.

The Labouchere system, or 'Labby', also required the gambler to put more of their money on the table each time they lost and to reduce their stake every time they won, in an attempt to use every win to wipe out the previous losses. Those who played the system kept track of their calculations, how much to bet and when. The principle was to always stake the sum total of the top and bottom figures on the score sheet. So, if they began by writing down '1, 2, 3' then they'd bet 4 (1 + 3). If they lost then they'd write 4 at the bottom of the list which now read '1, 2, 3, 4' and add it to the number at the top so in this case the next play stake would be 5 (1 + 4). If they won then they'd cross out the 1 and 4 and have a score card that now read '2, 3', and so their next bet would be 5 (2 + 3) and so on. If they crossed out all of the numbers, they began again with 1, 2, 3. The Martingale System, the Fitzroy System and the Wrangler System all operated on a mathematical progression of one form or another, with bets increasing with losses.

Unfortunately, play didn't always follow the expected progression. D'Alembert was, of course, absolutely right that given sufficient time the laws of probability will ensure that a player, where the game gives everyone an equal chance of success, will eventually win. The problem in the context of roulette is exactly how much time can be considered sufficient time. If time is infinite then the odds will eventually be equal, but over a shorter period, for example the course of a single day, red could win far more often than black, for example, producing a long run of losses. If weeks or even months are necessary for the laws of probability to equalise the odds then a player would need a vast amount of funds to carry on playing at that rate against a bank with much larger resources, particularly if they're losing more than winning, and their stake is gradually increasing with every spin of the wheel. Add to this the mathematical advantage that the bank has, the vagaries of the croupiers' involvement (their signature spin and throw of the ball), the emotional fallibility of a player caused by stress, lack of concentration or alcohol and the chances of winning are minimal. The odds are always with the bank, regardless of the system that a player uses to try to defeat it. All system players know this. The only way to win and keep a fortune is to play until you hit a lucky streak, maximise the money you win while your luck lasts and then walk away as soon as you start to lose. It's all about timing, and has nothing to do with any system.

This is the approach that Charles Deville Wells, the bank-breaker and subject of the famous song, appears to have taken during his two visits to the casino in 1891. He first arrived in Monte Carlo in the summer with stake money of £400, or £4,000 in today's money, and left after a five-day stay with winnings of approximately £40,000, equivalent to £4 million today. He broke the bank several times, playing roulette for eleven hours a day and claiming to have an infallible system.[11] This phenomenal winning streak came to the attention of other gamblers and the press in England, and 'Monte Carlo Wells' became a household name. When he returned to the casino in November 1891 he was recognised at once and became the subject of immediate press attention. He broke the bank again several times and journalists were able to interview him on the spot. *The Times* observed, in an article published on 9 November 1891, that his success stemmed from not being afraid to play for long periods of time while risking big sums of money:

After watching the game of this gentleman for some hours, it does not seem to me that he has made any very novel discovery in the science of playing roulette ... The secret of his success rather seems to be in the courageous way in which he attacks the tables and his cool-headed manner ... few have the courage to risk repeatedly for 11 hours a day close upon a thousand pounds at almost every coup.

Of course, it helped that the vast amount that Wells staked on each turn of the wheel belonged to someone else. He had a long history of persuading investors to back inventions that never materialised. His bets at Monte Carlo came from a pot of money that his backers believed had been invested in inventions that he had patented and were now in development. Arthur Bower, another Englishman who broke the bank, had a very similar *modus operandi*. A former bankrupt with convictions for fraud, who had also patented inventions, Bower should not have been able to gain access to Blanc's casino. But using the name Captain Arthur de Courcy-Bower he broke the bank five times and won the maximum pay-out eighteen times in a row during his visit to Monte Carlo in 1911.[12]

There were some exceptions to the rule that gamblers should always raise their bet after a loss. These reverse systems didn't require more and more of the gambler's money to be put on the table as he or she lost but rather the reverse. Players following the *tiers et tout* system, for example, split their capital into three and bet only one-third. If they lost they then had to bet the remaining two-thirds, effectively doubling their bet in an attempt to recover their loss. If they won, they would bet a third again. This system was perhaps feared more than any other by the casinos because of its greatest proponent, a Spaniard called Thomas Garcia. Garcia, a travelling salesman and gambler with a history of marking cards and using loaded dice, is said to have invented the *tiers et tout* system, and he put it to devastating use in the casino in Bad Homburg in 1860, nearly bankrupting Blanc. Over the course of two visits that year, and despite some losses, he left Germany in September with nearly 800,000 francs of the casino's reserve. Blanc had no option but to reduce the dividends paid to shareholders, causing some disgruntlement among them and among staff, some of whom began to question his management.[13] Garcia became a minor celebrity while he played, as did many successful gamblers, enjoying great attention while he was on a winning streak.

> They say that when the croupiers see him place his money on the table, they immediately prepare to pay him, without waiting to see if he has actually won, and that they have offered him a handsome sum down to desist from playing while he remains here. Crowds of people stand outside the *Kursaal* doors every morning, awaiting his arrival, when he comes following him into the room, and staking as he stakes. When he ceases playing they accompany him to the door, and shower on him congratulations and thanks for the good fortune he has brought them.[14]

Garcia returned the following year and lost heavily, revealing that his system was not unbeatable. He did not visit Bad Homburg again but instead descended on Monte Carlo in 1863, just a few weeks after the new building at *Les Spélugues* had opened, and won 45,000 francs playing mainly *trente-et-quarante*. His fame and success struck fear into the casino operators, who did not know when he might return with more funds to play again. Garcia proved to be the final straw for the struggling concession owners, and it was soon after this that François Blanc took over the casino.[15]

Most of these systems placed bets on even chances, usually red or black, and most encouraged players to pause in their betting after a certain number of losses. In the early 1890s, a partnership between Lord Rosslyn and Sam Lewis broke the bank in this way by betting repeatedly on black. For seventeen spins of the wheel, the ball fell onto black and hundreds of people watched as the two men broke the bank. But on the eighteenth spin, the ball fell on to red and their winning streak was over. Sir Hiram Maxim said that it was the longest run that he had ever witnessed at Monte Carlo.[16] It was generally true that gamblers who played any of these systems beyond their means would lose, especially where there was progression betting, which caused stakes to get incredibly high after a string of losses. Many gamblers chose to play as teams or with money raised by syndicates (or with other people's money, like Charles Wells) to minimise the problem of the enormous capital required, but this did nothing to improve their chances of winning. Others simply played along as they saw others win, copying their betting patterns.

The logic of the mathematical progression was eschewed by some in favour of more creative means of play, for example the *Décavé's* (or stony broke) system.[17] All that was necessary for this system was a good dress-suit and a confident and respectable appearance. The gambler then strolled around the room looking for someone who had a lot of bets scattered around the roulette table, a player who perhaps wasn't keeping track of what was where. What happened next was clearly illegal but was practised with some success. The gambler moved to the table where the target was playing and relocated one of his or her many pieces without anyone noticing. Any wins could be claimed, and if caught the gambler just had to apologise for not remembering where he'd put his own pieces and hope that his charm and smart suit would be convincing. The advice was to *hire* a suit, in case of any unpleasantness where the suit could come in for some rather rough treatment. Working with an accomplice was also recommended, and although it would necessitate the sharing of any profits it would be very helpful in the event of emergency: 'If you happen to know a fellow swindler as aristocratic in appearance as yourself, one who wears a monocle, for choice, the game will be easier.'[18] This ploy could be repeated on several tables in an evening.

This sort of manoeuvring was only possible because the casino allowed almost any form of currency to be used on its tables; gold, silver and paper money from many countries were thrown down on to the baize. French francs and Italian lire were the most common, but American dollars were often used. Gamblers could also use mother-of-pearl or ivory plaques for particularly large bets. Sometimes it was difficult to tell whose stake was whose. Croupiers were rigorously trained to ensure that they could keep track. It wasn't until the 1880s that chips began to be used regularly, but these first examples were relatively uniform, bearing no design and in a limited range of colours, so confusion was still likely. This uncertainty over whose bet was whose was only really resolved in the 1890s when the casino began to issue players with their own set of chips with a colour and design that could be clearly distinguished from those of other players.[19]

Many players relied on talismans and dreams, and even touching the humps of hunchbacks. Some always sat when they gambled, and some always stood. There was at one point a craze for lucky china and golden pigs, which were placed by the player to bring luck.[20] One English lord attended church on Sunday morning and then wandered into the casino, where he couldn't get that morning's hymn out of his head. He placed bets at several tables, choosing the number of the hymn, in this case thirty-two. He enjoyed quite a lot of success and so the following Sunday many of the congregation followed his system until eventually the horrified vicar was forced to decree that no hymn with a number under thirty-seven could be sung at the Monte Carlo church.[21]

Almost all of these well-known systems were based on controlling the amount of money bet, not on picking particular numbers on the basis that they had a better chance of coming up. It was taken as read that every number had an equal chance of catching the ball after the wheel had been vigorously spun by the croupier. Most systems, were based on the hope that, over time, the evens chances that they were gambling on would come up more frequently than those that they were not gambling on and that this would happen on the spins when they happened to have the most chips on the table. In 1908, Sir Hiram Maxim (he who had been liable for prosecution for playing roulette in public) was goaded into playing to prove his steadfast belief that a winning system was impossible. His challenger, Lord Rosslyn, believed that anyone with the money and the courage could beat the banker's odds. Despite having lost heavily in Monte Carlo by playing continuously on red and increasing his bet with each win, he still believed that he could break the bank in this way. After two weeks of play, Lord Rosslyn, in debt and admitting defeat, acknowledged that Maxim was victorious.

Blanc himself knew that given enough time the bank would always win: 'He who breaks the bank today will assuredly return to be broken by the bank tomorrow.'[22] For the vast majority who played at Monte Carlo, losses were more common than gains. Even the big winners usually went on to lose all they had gained. Very few walked away following their winning streak, instead continuing until their luck changed, with devastating consequences. In 1893 Arthur Cockburn broke the bank three times playing *trente-et-quarante*, winning £8,000 (over £800,000 now), but kept on playing till it was all gone. Days later another player called Peel won 50,000 francs but lost it all the next day.[23]

It is among the famous bank-breakers of Monte Carlo, professional gamblers or fraudsters in the main, that Joseph Hobson Jagger's name has often been quoted. Despite the near-impossibility of truly confounding the casino, he has been cited as one of those to have beaten the odds. How could this working-class Bradford man, who had never left England and almost certainly never seen a roulette wheel, have achieved the near-impossible when so many more experienced people had failed?

Even more surprising is that the two brief mentions of his story in previous accounts of exploits at the Monte Carlo casino have singled him out for a unique accolade. They attest that Joseph didn't play one of the forty or so known systems; instead he used a method that nobody had used before, and in doing so, proved to be the 'one man who actually did win a fortune by means of a system. What is more, it was an infallible one.'[24] Perhaps even more importantly to his descendants, he is credited as being 'the only man ... ever heard of who completely defeated the Bank at Monte Carlo by fair means, and won and kept a large sum of money'.[25]

11

THE KEY

This suggestion that Joseph was the only man to have beaten the odds at Monte Carlo by fair means and to have kept his fortune is at once tantalising and frustrating. Despite this brief mention, previous accounts and the family stories that have been passed down, if he had truly developed an unbeatable system for winning at roulette, surely there would be more evidence? Certainly there was none to find in the newspapers or in his rather modest will. Blanc had confidently offered a prize of 1 million francs (£40,000 then and approximately £4 million now) to anyone who could demonstrate a guaranteed way of beating the bank. Joseph didn't claim this enormous sum; indeed it has never been claimed. My research had given me an insight into just how extraordinary a journey to Monte Carlo would have been for a man like Joseph to make, but it had also thrown up a compelling motive for it. After all, what greater impulse could there be for a risky adventure than to save your family from ruin? And yet where was the proof that Joseph had actually put this plan into effect – or ever left home?

A recent biographer of Charles Wells, perplexed by the same lack of facts, had even concluded, 'The story has been told and retold many times: however, I doubt whether it is strictly true ... "Jaggers" may be an imaginary character.'[1] I had to return to the hunt for evidence.

At the beginning of my search, the story of Joseph's life promised to be a vivid tapestry. But I soon found it to be full of holes, with so much of its detail lost and numerous threads come loose. Some of these threads I had picked up early in my research, but I didn't know enough then to realise how they should be woven back in. Such was the case now. I went back to my files to look again at the documents, letters and notes that I'd compiled over the years. It had become my routine method to return to them regularly to check details and sources, but this time the search felt futile. The search for proof of Joseph's win in Monte Carlo had narrowed to a final trawl through my research, but the trail already felt cold.

I began with the letters and notes that I'd been given at the very start of my search. I reread the correspondence between my dad and Derek Jagger which talked of arranging a meeting that never took place. The letters showed that they'd tried off and on to meet up over the course of thirty years. In a letter that my dad wrote in reply to Derek at the end of 1991, or perhaps early 1992, he'd mentioned the annual family trip to Bradford that had taken place every year throughout my childhood and suggested that they meet up during that summer's trip. They had both been dead for over a decade when I revisited this letter again, and so I'd never be sure why they had not been able to meet each other. This seemed such a shame as my dad's letter anticipated just how much family information they had to share. It was then that I noticed a detail that I had missed:

By the way, you refer in your letter to a key but I am not clear what you mean by this.

I could find no trace of the letter that Derek must have written mentioning a key and which prompted this query, nor could I find any follow-up letter responding to it. I'm certain that my dad never found out what Derek meant before he died in 1999. He had certainly never mentioned it to me or written about it in the account that he left behind, as he surely would have done. What could the key be?

Derek's brother David Jagger solved the mystery. He placed in my hands a mahogany-coloured leather box with a slightly worn brass plaque attached to its lid. Still very clearly legible were the words engraved on it.

Presented to
J.H. Jagger Esq.
By his friends and admirers
On the occasion of his great and unprecedented
success in the ROULETTE
Which he achieved over the BANK at MONTE-CARLO;

I lifted the lid and there, held in place by a pristine pink satin lining, was a key. But it wasn't a conventional key. Made of stainless steel and constructed around a thermometer, it was an unusual item and clearly a commemorative gift, commissioned by Joseph's friends and admirers. Maybe it was intended to hang on the wall as a decorative piece, an amusing reminder among friends of a quite remarkable achievement by one of their group. Touching it was thrilling. This key had been held in Joseph Hobson Jagger's hands and kept pristinely in its original case ever since. The connection to him was palpable. So too was the connection to all of the family members who lived between his time and mine. It had been hard to feel a personal connection to Joseph, to remember that he and I are related, that his story is my story too, but I felt it while holding the key. It had been treasured, handed down through the family and kept safe, a reminder of a quite remarkable achievement and the only known artefact relating to the Monte Carlo story. Finally, here was the key, the proof that I'd been looking for. Joseph had broken the bank at Monte Carlo.

The account that follows is, I believe, the most accurate that there has been of how events unfolded after Joseph entered the doors of the casino. I have reviewed evidence in the public domain and compared it against the findings of many years of research, which has included access for the first time to the private archives of three branches of the Jagger family. I have found the truth behind the story of a poor working-class Yorkshireman who went to Monte Carlo and won a fortune. It's a story that has never been fully told. What is more, it's the story of perhaps the only man to have ever found a truly infallible means of beating the casino at roulette. Joseph's method was unique, one that didn't rely on the laws of probability, that didn't require vast reserves of money and time in order to win and which overcame the mathematical advantage of the 'o'. His system rendered all of the bank's advantages null and void. It's a story that makes a case for a reconsideration of Joseph Hobson Jagger, a man whose very existence was doubted by some, but who should perhaps be regarded now as the greatest of all these famous bank-breakers.

PART 2

'THE MAN WHO BROKE THE BANK AT MONTE CARLO'

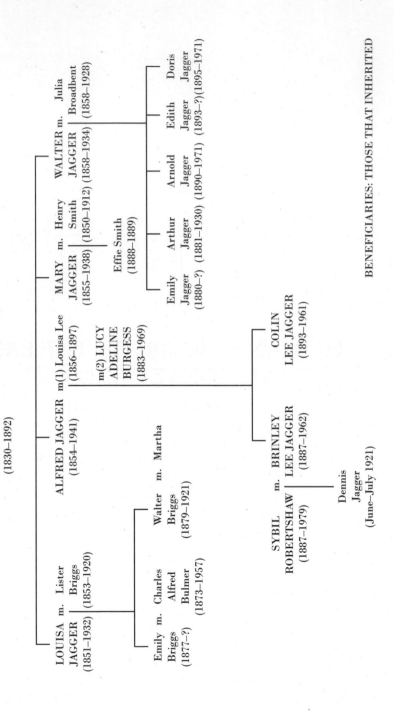

JOSEPH HOBSON JAGGER (1830–1892) m. MATILDA TOWNEND (1830–1902)

LOUISA JAGGER (1851–1932) m. Lister Briggs (1853–1920)

ALFRED JAGGER (1854–1941) m(1) Louisa Lee (1856–1897) m(2) LUCY ADELINE BURGESS (1883–1969)

MARY JAGGER (1855–1938) m. Henry Smith (1850–1912)

WALTER JAGGER (1858–1934) m. Julia Broadbent (1858–1928)

Emily Briggs (1877–?) m. Charles Alfred Bulmer (1873–1957)

Walter Briggs (1879–1921) m. Martha

SYBIL ROBERTSHAW (1887–1979) m. BRINLEY LEE JAGGER (1887–1962)

COLIN LEE JAGGER (1893–1961)

Dennis Jagger (June–July 1921)

Effie Smith (1888–1889)

Emily Jagger (1880–?)

Arthur Jagger (1881–1930)

Arnold Jagger (1890–1971)

Edith Jagger (1893–?)

Doris Jagger (1895–1971)

BENEFICIARIES: THOSE THAT INHERITED

12

BREAKING THE BANK

Arriving at the station in Monte Carlo by the edge of the sea, Joseph's first glimpse of the casino was a turreted white facade looking out over the Mediterranean from a hollow in the hills above. Flaming and shining in the hot sun, it was almost certainly the most exotic building Joseph had ever seen. Between him and it wove the lushly tropical gardens and terraces that stretched up to the casino from the sea. It seemed that winter never came to this place where even in November the air swooned with the scent of flowers, sunlight danced on the waves and palm tree fronds swayed gently in the breeze.

Walking up the hill through the casino terraces, they saw the exotic blooms of the oleander, hibiscus, verbena and bougainvillea that had been planted with cacti among the native pines, olives, date palms and citrus trees. The shade of the casino gardens was welcome as the men strolled, taking in every new smell, shape and colour. Their arrival in the Cote D'Azur was an assault on the senses, intoxicating and thrilling and so very, very alien. The terraces were full of people, strolling or sitting admiring the view. The lilt of myriad languages filled the air as elegant women walked under parasols, escorted by smartly dressed men. Feeling conspicuous in his old-fashioned suit, Joseph saw dresses that he'd only seen before in the Bradford newspapers and elaborate hats that came straight from Paris.

Arriving at the topmost terrace, the men paused for a moment and gazed at the magnificent view of the blue bay below and the boats moored on it. Music drifted out of the casino and mingled with the chatter of the people dining at the terrace tables and with the footsteps of the waiters hurrying to and fro with trays of drinks. They walked around the casino building, through the gardens to the main entrance on the *Place du Casino*. The square in front of the casino was bustling with activity. People were there to see and be seen. A distinguished man in uniform was arriving outside the *Hôtel de Paris* with a retinue of servants, and staff were flocking to assist with luggage and to welcome him. At the *Café Divan* opposite, all eyes were on the scene, wondering who he was. As they ate their sorbets, women gossiped about whether he could be royalty.

The men turned away and walked towards the casino entrance. A flight of stone steps led up to it, and at the top the 'dress police' flanked the doorway. Unsmiling in their blue and red uniforms, bedecked with gold braid, they scrutinised everyone who approached. Ahead of Joseph an elderly man in a shabby coat was beckoned to one side, while an unaccompanied woman in a rather revealing dress was quietly led away. The men passed inspection and entered the cool interior. It took a little while for Joseph's eyes to adjust to the darkness of the entrance hall. Paved with marble and with its ceiling held aloft with great pillars, it felt familiar. The columns and brass lights reminded him of the buildings that a booming Bradford had thrown up, symbols of its rapid success like the Wool Exchange.

His rented suit of clothes had felt stiff and added to his discomfort before, but now, feeling a little more at home, he took off his hat and sought out the office where he could request entry to the casino. The bureau was just inside the entrance, to the left, and here a small queue had formed in anticipation of the opening of the gaming rooms. Admission was impossible without a green *carte du jour*.[1] Joseph knew that François Blanc had, from the very start, insisted on all visitors being decently attired, which meant for men a frock coat and high hat.[2] These rules were Blanc's way of trying to curb the number of pickpockets and petty thieves who frequented the gaming rooms. Joseph took a firm hold of his *carte du jour*, grateful that his hired clothes had passed muster, and with the rest of the men walked quickly on, further into the casino.

An atrium called the *Promenoir* opened up before them, a vast, pillared hall with many doors. It was, as usual, full of people chatting, smoking, hoping to be admired or listening to the very fine orchestra that played in the afternoons and evenings. Three doors led into the *Salles de Jeux*, or gaming rooms: the left was for players with a daily entrance card, the right for those with a monthly card, and the centre door was reserved as an exit.[3] They showed their cards and were waved through. The principal gaming room, the *Salle Mauresque*, was as beautiful and luxurious as anything money could buy. It was smaller than Joseph expected but more exotic than anything he had seen before. Its name, 'the Moorish Room', came from its very fashionable transformation into an exotic, Eastern-inspired salon only three or four years before.[4] A series of elaborate arches ran around its edge, decorated with red, gold and silver tiles bearing decorative motifs of plants and Eastern-inspired patterns and shapes. The mosaicked walls twinkled in the light thrown into the room from the ornate brass filigreed lamps that hung down from the ceiling, casting silver and scarlet blazes on to the polished wooden floor. Joseph felt like he was a character in *Arabian Nights*, a stranger in a strange place. He swallowed hard, gathered his nerve and began to walk around.

There were leather couches and chairs placed around the room's edge and in the middle a circular leather couch with plants at its centre which rose high above those who sat there, adding to the intoxicating atmosphere of the room. Joseph took a seat. With a creeping nervous nausea, he realised that from any of these seating positions it was possible to observe everything that was happening. He could sit at the side of the room and be aware of play on every gaming table. Any excitement, any unusual activity, any unexpected action attracted attention and could be quickly focused on.

Joseph felt more nervous than at any point in his adventure so far. His plan depended on being able to play roulette while being as unobserved as possible. He began to doubt that this would be as easy as he had hoped. The room was so much smaller than he had expected. Joseph had hoped to merge into the throng, to find anonymity at one of the many roulette tables among the crowd, but he saw to his horror that the *Salle Mauresque* had only four. One table stood in each bay of the room; three were reserved for roulette and the fourth for *trente-et-quarante*.[5] The roulette wheels were placed on top of long green baize-covered tables that were nipped in at the waist like cellos at the point where the wheel sat. The betting grids were drawn on the green baize that spread out from each side of the wheel and covered the length of the long tables.

Suddenly there was a commotion. A solemn procession of casino staff entered the *Salle Mauresque* carrying heavy chests. Reaching the tables, they opened them and revealed the coins within, enormous quantities of gold and silver to fund the many hours of gaming that would follow, enough to pay off every win and certainly a quantity to be added to by every loss. With the money box on each table fully stocked, the casino was ready.[6] Play could, at last, begin. The gambling elite of Europe crowded with the chancers and tourists to gather around the tables. Many had to jostle to find a place to stand and watch while the players took their places at the long tables, sitting on the upholstered wooden chairs that were positioned along both sides. Small rakes were available to help players reach the furthest parts of the grid to lay their bets. Losing bets would be quickly gathered and winnings handed out by the croupiers who sat in the leather-backed chairs adjacent to the wheel and at both ends of the table. From these positions they could also keep an eye out for any suspicious play. Behind the croupiers sitting nearest to the wheel, a raised chair was occupied by the table supervisor, the *chef de partie*, allowing him to observe all play on the table. Soon the click of the wheels and calls of the croupiers fractured the hubbub of the room. '*Faites vos jeux, messieurs*!' Bets were placed and watched with feverish anticipation as the balls spun and croupiers raked in piles of coin.

Joseph's attention was drawn to a table where a finely dressed Italian was seated. The Italian was playing well. A pile of coins sat at his elbow, and he was surrounded by young women who were flirting and trying to catch his attention. He was smiling, enjoying his game. Joseph walked across and stood behind his chair, observing the play, watching the wheel spin and the ball fall. The Italian was betting repeatedly on black and it took only three spins and three unlucky reds to destroy his winning streak. The girls floated away, the feathers on their hats bouncing with the momentum that moved them on to find the next winning player. Meanwhile, the Italian was reduced to trying to borrow money from the players around him. Cursing, he leapt up from the table and slipped out, either to lick his wounds or to telegram home for extra funds.

Joseph watched similar scenes at most of the tables. There were French women who played cautiously, making small bets and winning modest amounts, there was a Russian grand duke who threw a pile of gold on to number twelve in an act of bravado and just managed to keep his smile fixed as the croupier swept it away, and there were others who played with rabbits' feet on the table to bring them luck. If Joseph had ever doubted the risk he was about to take, the evidence was all around him. The chance of a big win was small. Much more likely was the loss of everything he had begged and borrowed. The scenes of winning and losing played out as the evening drew in, and only the cast of characters changed.

Joseph watched every wheel in the room, observing the pattern of play but all the time looking closely for something more specific. Now, so far from the home where he had conceived an idea of how to beat the odds at roulette, Joseph waited patiently for any indication that his theory might actually work in reality.

Months before, sitting beside the fire at home as night fell, he had been struck by an idea. Perhaps it was a dream, perhaps a random but brilliant mental leap, but the image of a casino had come into Joseph's mind. He saw a roulette wheel spinning, its numbers turning in a red-and-black blur until the white ball settled and the wheel came to a standstill. At that moment it was clear to him that roulette was not a game of pure chance. Joseph had spent his working life depending on machinery and spindles that rotated wheels. He'd learned to be vigilant in his own business, he couldn't afford for production to be slowed down or the quality of cloth to be affected by a mechanical malfunction. Stopping or slowing equipment was rarely an option, and so he had learned how to adjust his machinery without having to wait for a millwright or technical engineer, and often without turning the machine off. Joseph had even had to be prepared to pick up severed fingers and keep production going while he did so.

This practical experience and expertise, gained through the necessity of running a business, drove Joseph's idea forward and fleshed it out into a coherent plan. But the initial spark had come from another source. The newspapers were always full of stories about Monte Carlo, but on this occasion there had been a drawing of a roulette wheel. Joseph had never seen one before and his engineering mind was intrigued as he examined the illustration. The enormous riches won in the casino were the direct result of this wheel's function in throwing a ball on to a number. He knew that, despite the incredible technological progress that had transformed his world, nobody could guarantee that a wheel would spin perfectly evenly with a perfect balance. If wheels in northern England could spin and not remain perfectly level, then why should it be any different for the spinning roulette wheels of Monte Carlo? Surely the wooden bowl, turned by a spindle, would have a tilt – an almost imperceptible one, but enough to throw the ball on to the same set of numbers more frequently than would be expected through pure chance? If this was true, then an observer could record the play on each of the wheels and wait for a pattern of numbers to emerge.

Now he was in the casino watching, waiting and recording the order of play. It was a meticulous and time-consuming task, and Joseph had always known that he couldn't do it alone; he couldn't afford to. He'd borrowed the money to travel to Monte Carlo, with sufficient funds remaining to rent an acceptable suit of clothes, but staying there was fiendishly expensive. The hotels around the casino were well beyond his means, so he had found simple lodgings in Nice and paid each day to travel into Monte Carlo. His expenses were mounting quickly. He needed to eat, needed to clean his clothes, and eventually he'd have to start placing bets. Sharing the workload was a necessity. Joseph had known this from the start, and that's why he had not come to Monte Carlo alone.

While planning his daring adventure and borrowing the money to fund it, Joseph had shared his plan with men whom he trusted absolutely. His success depended on their willingness to keep the plan secret and not to use it for their own profit. Now these colleagues were in the casino with him. They stood at the same table as Joseph, watching the play closely without acknowledging that they knew each other at all. The size of the room, the vigilance of the gaming officials at the tables and the presence of the security team, attuned to and seeking out any irregularities in play, all counted against them. As numbers won they had to be recorded and a sequence searched for, but writing down anything at the table would have drawn attention to them instantly. If any player had a system then they had to rely on their memories; any evidence of writing down play or concealing the means of doing so could have led to instant ejection.

Joseph and his colleagues had to remember every winning number and how often each won, and then calculate in their minds if the number of wins exceeded the expectations of probability. Before they had left England, they had practised. Never having seen a roulette wheel until they arrived in the casino, they used images from the newspaper and trained themselves to remember sequences. Now, in Monte Carlo, in the feverish atmosphere of the gaming room, they concentrated on the roulette wheel and its numbers, avoiding the distractions around them. For an entire month they did this, keeping Joseph's secret day after day.

Late one evening, Joseph was resting in his lodgings, enjoying bread and cheese after many hours at the casino. Even here in Nice the smell of jasmine and orange filled the air, reminding him constantly of how far he was from home. Despite his fatigue, he was too exhilarated to sleep yet as tomorrow morning he would begin to play roulette. He glanced again at the data that they had recorded at the end of that day's play, reassuring himself that there really was a pattern. They had needed to be so discreet inside the casino. Each night they relaxed together at the Nice lodgings, away from the prying eyes of the casino, to discuss the events of the day and exchange information. On this evening it had become clear that a sequence had emerged. Nearly every table in the casino had a bias, but on one particular wheel it was more pronounced. Here was the evidence of a mechanical flaw in the casino operation that Joseph had been looking for, a technical and entirely legal loophole that he had travelled so far to exploit.

Shortly after the casino opened, Joseph walked in, his fingers resting reassuringly on the small number of coins in his coat pocket. He had to wait for a space at the right table, but as people left to take lunch on the terrace a seat became free and he took his place. Cautiously at first, he began to play. Quietly and steadily, his money grew. As he played he concentrated on the game alone, ignoring the lures of women, alcohol and conversation that so often distracted the attention of players. Joseph battled with himself to remain calm, not to draw attention, to suppress the growing tide of excitement within him. It was the most thrilling experience of his life. Making sure occasionally to bet on random numbers to distract attention from his sequence, Joseph's remarkable run of luck continued into the afternoon and evening. He returned to Nice with more coins in his pocket than he'd left with that morning and the confidence to repeat his mode of play the next day. This was Joseph's routine for the days that followed.

Despite his discretion, Joseph could not hope to hide a winning streak from the casino's surveillance staff, who were paid to spot big successes and uncover any cheating or suspicious play. They grew ever more anxious as Joseph continued to win and casino staff were ordered to target the bearded Englishman and put an end to his successful run. They scrutinised his actions, stood at the table writing down his bets to seek out a system, looking for any evidence that he might be cheating, but they couldn't understand the pattern of his game. He didn't seem to be using one of the recognised playing systems; instead he seemed to be betting randomly on the wheel, and always on numbers, never colours. Joseph knew that he was attracting attention. All eyes were on him. He had to remain calm in the spotlight, confident and focused on his game. The casino did all it could to distract him. Women approached him to make conversation, someone nudged his elbow when he was placing a bet and drinks were spilt, but Joseph played on. He took no notice of the people jostling around his chair, the other gamblers pressing around him, their hands eagerly placing coins where he placed his.

As his pile of gold grew, the croupier's voice inciting gamblers to lay their bets was all that could be heard. Play had long since ceased at the other tables, everyone now intent on watching Joseph's game. The crowd was silent as the last bets were laid. '*Les jeux sont fait.*' The croupier spun the wheel and the clattering of the ball was the only sound in the room. The wheel slowed: '*Rien ne va plus.*' The croupier gave a nervous cough, and then it was over. '*Vingt-huit!*' was the shout from the crowd. '*Bravo monsieur, bravo!*' The croupier slid Joseph's winnings towards him and signalled to his colleagues. A bell rang out and a cloth was brought to the table, its colour matching the black uniforms of the croupiers. It was draped over the roulette wheel, a table now in mourning for its loss. The bank had been broken.

The casino erupted with cheers and congratulations. Everyone was trying to reach Joseph to bask in his good fortune. Struggling to comprehend that he was now a very rich man, Joseph was swept along by the excitement and only the vast pile of gold in front of him confirmed the truth. He stood up, shook hands with the croupier and left the building. His colleagues had slipped out as the tumult began and were waiting for him on the terraces. The men embraced each other silently, with a mixture of elation and relief.

Despite the ceremony laid on at the casino to mark the breaking of the bank and the respectful treatment of the winner, this was not a moment to celebrate. The casino's greatest fear, the dread that had been harboured since François Blanc opened the doors of the first Monte Carlo casino, was now concentrated, with the utmost intensity, on the bearded Englishman who would surely return. A stranger to them, Joseph Jagger was nevertheless the focus of all their attention now. Was it possible that he had an infallible system? What was to stop him now from winning ever bigger sums for many days to come?

The next morning, buoyed still by the success of his theory and excited about the prospect of winning again, Joseph returned to play. He took his seat at the same table. He was recognised at once, of course, and the space around him soon became crowded with onlookers, as well as security staff who circled the table, keeping a wary eye. Joseph placed a bet and settled down to the business of winning. But luck was not with him. As Joseph's bet disappeared under the croupier's rake he saw in horror that his sequence had failed. Again and again the ball seemed to fall randomly, his numbers no longer yielding wins. The crowd melted away in search of the next flurry of excitement and a big win.

Joseph felt a creeping nausea. The shocking prospect of losing his recently acquired fortune was compounded by the fear that his theory was wrong. Had he been a fool to think that a man who had barely ever left Yorkshire, whose experience was limited to the textile industry of northern England, could outwit the most successful casino in the world and the expertise of the Blancs, which had been build up over decades in Germany and here in Monte Carlo? Newspaper reports were full of accounts of huge wins; he'd read them himself. But there were more often tales of devastating losses. Big wins became news and made players famous or infamous depending on the circumstances, but the odds were always against the gambler from the start. Joseph only had to look about him at the sumptuous surroundings, the profits of the casino and its main investors and the personal wealth of the Blancs and the Grimaldis to realise that.

The likelihood was that those glorious winning days had merely been a fluke. No longer in control of the roulette wheel, Joseph's dream of paying off his debts and keeping his family from the workhouse was fading fast. Seeing the ashen faces of his colleagues and realising that something was very wrong, he rose from the table and hurried from the casino, taking with him what was left of his winnings.

The management congratulated its team and celebrated their coup. They had worked out the reason for the Englishman's winning streak and put a stop to it. Their expertise was greater than any gambler's; it had to be. So confident were they that they knew every one of the forty or so systems being played in casinos around the world that they had looked elsewhere for an explanation of Joseph's success. One of the croupiers had suggested that maybe there was something at fault with the wheel. This seemed plausible enough to investigate, and so overnight they were all swapped around. Without understanding fully how Joseph was exploiting the mechanics of the wheel, the casino had taken the one action that would defeat him. With the wheels relocated, Joseph could no longer be sure which was which. His advantage of knowing their unique bias was lost and his number sequence was rendered useless. Joseph's system was no longer infallible.

Blanc's relief was short lived. Joseph was not the sort of man to be so easily deterred, and he continued to enter the casino every day, not playing but walking around the room. His colleagues were there too; more anonymous than their frontman and unknown to the casino, they could observe play freely. The casino authorities watched Joseph carefully, but while he was not playing they had nothing to fear – and besides, they felt certain they had ended his winning streak. One evening, to their surprise, after a short hesitation the Englishman approached a roulette table and placed a gold coin on a number in front of him.

It had taken all of Joseph's courage to return. If he was wrong, he faced the prospect of losing all that remained of his winnings. Anxiety turned to relief as, slowly but surely, he began to win again, once more in control of the wheel and working with its tilt. The casino authorities were astounded and confounded. Joseph and his partners had been watching very carefully, at last understanding that the casino must have swapped the wheels. With the detailed eye of an engineer, Joseph had identified each one by the slightest of imperfections or tiniest of scratches and had paired each with a set of numbers. He was now playing at a different table, but with his winning wheel. Joseph's money began to accrue once again, steadily and consistently, and other gamblers began to follow him, betting where he bet, winning where he won. Financial ruin for the casino was a very real and terrifying prospect.

In desperation, suspecting still that there must be a mechanical fault but not understanding what it was or how to prevent Joseph taking advantage of it, the casino managers looked to Paris for help. A representative was sent by train to meet with the head of the company that manufactured the roulette wheels. This skilled manufacturer soon understood what was happening. He knew as well as Joseph did that it was impossible to make a wheel that would spin absolutely true and concluded that this was the Englishman's winning method. Despite tremendous pressure from Monte Carlo, where Joseph was continuing to win and the casino was facing a ticking time bomb of financial ruin, the manufacturer held his nerve. If a tilt could not be prevented then the solution must lie in reducing the gambler's ability to exploit it, and so he focused on the numbered partitions, realising that if they could be moved then the advantage of a tilt would never fall on the same number two days running. Orders were given to the manufacturer to create a new design with moveable partitions that could be swapped from wheel to wheel every day. These new wheels, intended to defeat the Englishman once and for all, were promptly installed in the casino at Monte Carlo.

Joseph's first encounter with the new roulette wheels was decisive. Seated once more at the table with his lucky wheel, he lost rapidly. Something was not right. The ball was not being thrown on to the numbers where he knew it should land. Joseph understood that big winners always returned, playing on longer than they should and more often than not losing it all. He needed to win, but he knew when to stop. Realising that he had met his match, that he no longer had an infallible system, Joseph collected his winnings and walked out into the warm, sunny air of Monte Carlo. Shaking with exhilaration and relief, he breathed in the exotically scented air. His partners followed him out on to the terraces, clapping him on the back and shaking his hand. Joseph calmed himself and allowed the enormity of what he'd achieved settle in his mind. He had travelled far from home and faced the shame of begging and borrowing from his friends, but he had been right. He had defeated the casino for long enough to ensure that his family's financial difficulties were consigned to the past. Joseph strode away from the casino with the modern equivalent of nearly £7.5 million in his pocket.

13

A PROLONGED ADVENTURE

The foundations of this story of how Joseph Hobson Jagger broke the bank at Monte Carlo were laid down in previous accounts. I have been able to extract the consistent elements and dismiss those that seem spurious. I have chosen to include facts that seem plausible, and I have tried to fill in some of the gaps with my own research. This has enabled me to speculate on how Joseph travelled to Monte Carlo, how he lived while he was there and where he stayed. Reading contemporary newspaper accounts of Monte Carlo and what happened to other winners and losers has helped me to recreate the atmosphere in the casino when Joseph won his millions, including the dramatic draping of the table in black cloth when the bank was broken, a ceremony that François Blanc had copied from the Wiesbaden casino and used as a publicity stunt.[1] Insights into what was involved in the recruitment of his team, how it felt to be in the middle of a successful run and the extent to which a casino might go to stop it all come from an account written by a successful gambler in the 1970s.[2] The result is the fullest account so far of what happened when Joseph visited Monte Carlo, and one which I believe is nearest to the truth.

The earliest account, *Monte Carlo Anecdotes and Systems of Play*, was written in 1901 by The Honourable Victor Bethell. An aristocrat and younger brother of Lord Westbury, Bethell was a prominent figure among the gambling elite of the Riviera. He was assistant manager at Smith's Bank and then looked after the financial interests of wealthy English visitors through his senior role at the Monte Carlo branch of the French bank *Comptoir National d'Escompte*. Popular and courteous, Bethell handled the delicate issue of losses and loans with great discretion, understanding when to allow a cheque to be cashed for those who needed ready funds. His impeccable credentials helped him deal with his elite clients, as this account published in 1927 in the *Illustrated Sporting and Dramatic News* reveals:

> Having lost a great deal of money at the tables, I wended my way to Smith's Bank one morning in order to cash a cheque ... Victor Bethell glanced at my visiting card and remarked, 'I think I must have been at Eton with your elder brother?'[3]

For over thirty years, Bethell's influence extended beyond the bank into the heart of the Monte Carlo gambling establishment. He and his wife were popular figures on the Riviera, appearing alongside their aristocratic friends in the regular gossip columns of the *Sporting Times* and *The Bystander*. Bethell was also honorary treasurer for the Queen Victoria Memorial Hospital in Nice.[4] He was acknowledged as an authority on bridge and wrote a guide to the game in 1908. Victor Bethell's book on the casino, its systems and winners, is the work of a man who was immersed in the world of Monte Carlo for many decades, a member of its elite and privy to the day-to-day mechanics of funding gamblers' plays and losses. He was also a player and a gambler, a man who understood roulette and his account was written closest to the time when Joseph broke the bank.

Bethell confirms the family story that Joseph's strategy was based on an understanding that delicate machinery can never work in perfect condition and so wheels must have a bias. In devising this theory, and by putting it into devastating action, Bethell grants Joseph a unique accolade:

> ... the only man I ever heard of who completely defeated the Bank at Monte Carlo by fair means, and won and kept a large sum of money.[5]

Bethell also claims that Joseph employed a team of six clerks to work with him to record the results of the play on each table.[6] It is from his account too that the information about the casino's remedial action comes. He states that they changed the roulette wheels from table to table every night and that Joseph eventually realised this and was able to recognise each from a slight scratch or speck on the paint. Bethell's account also provides the detail of how the casino consulted with the head of the roulette wheel manufacturing firm in Paris[7] and how new wheels with movable partitions were constructed.[8] He also suggests that other gamblers played along with Joseph, thus increasing the threat that he represented to the casino: 'It was a constant drain on their resources, and as others were beginning to follow him wherever he staked his money, it meant ultimate ruin unless they could put a stop to it.'[9] This scenario is supported by the chaotic events which were to occur later, following Charles Wells' winning streak. The *chef de partie* at the time recounted that other players flocked around his table, several ranks deep, all trying to copy Wells' numbers. The casino was forced to limit the number of people permitted to play, which almost caused a riot as angry people accused the *chef de partie* of trying to prevent them from winning too.[10] The same frenzy accompanied Garcia's winning streak at Bad Homburg:

> A crowd of eager hands are immediately outstretched from all parts of the table, heaping up silver and gold and notes on the spaces on which he has staked his money, till there scarcely seems room for another coin, while the other spaces on the table only contain a few florins staked by sceptics who refuse to believe in his luck.[11]

In 1937, Joseph's win was documented for a second time. *Monte Carlo Casino* was written by General Pierre Polovtsoff, a Russian gentleman and former military attaché to the Russian Embassy in London who had become president of the International Sporting Club, the inner circle of the Monte Carlo elite. He mixed with aristocracy and royalty, attending balls and dinners, and was a well-known personality in the principality for many decades; in 1956, he hosted a pre-wedding gala for Prince Rainier and Grace Kelly at the International Sporting Club.[12] Polovtsoff was a casino insider and so a credible source for wins and systems and historic anecdotes. He wrote an article in *The Illustrated London News* on 22 May 1937 to support the publication of his book, which sums up the story as he understood it. Although it does not mention Joseph by name, it draws very much on Bethell's account and so there can be little doubt that he is its subject:

> Once upon a time an engineer won, and went away with, £70,000. He had realised that it was impossible to construct a perfect machine: 'there were bound to be slight inaccuracies in the bearings which, in the case of a roulette wheel, would cause certain numbers to appear more frequently than others'. For weeks he employed clerks to take down the numbers as they came up on all the tables. 'The statistics bore out his theory, and he found that one particular wheel gave certain numbers with

considerable frequency. In this way he found no difficulty in winning 360,000 in four days.' The Administration, realising what had happened, changed the wheels from table to table. On the fifth day the engineer, playing against what he thought was the same wheel, lost £40,000. He saw light. 'He had noticed that on the wheel on which he had been playing there was a tiny scratch, and this enabled him to identify it.' Next the Administration replaced the old roulette wheels by new ones with interchangeable parts, and not only were the wheels themselves changed from table to table every day, but the component parts were shuffled too, so that each table started the day's play with what was basically a new wheel ... The practice of changing the wheel in this way has, of course, been continued ever since.[13]

Most importantly, Polovtsoff distinguishes Joseph from other winners: 'I have only heard of one man who actually did win a fortune by means of a system. What is more, it was an infallible one.'[14]

Finally, *The Big Gamble: The Story of Monte Carlo* was written by Charles Graves in 1951. Graves was a journalist and writer, and the brother of the author Robert Graves. He worked on the *Sunday Express* and *Daily Mail* among other newspapers and published forty-six books, including five on the subject of life in the Riviera and Monte Carlo in particular. With a journalist's eye for fascinating characters, extraordinary events and gossip, *The Big Gamble* focusses on the history of the casino and offers a behind-the-scenes view of its operation. Graves's telling of Joseph's story is clearly based on Bethell's, with some minor variations, and he also added some embellishments of his own. Graves states that Joseph occasionally played numbers that he knew wouldn't win in order to conceal those that he knew would.[15] Although not recorded anywhere else, I've used this piece of information in my version of the story as I think a strategic thinker like Joseph might play exactly like this.

Perhaps most importantly it is Graves's account that introduces for the first time the series of numbers that Joseph identified on the wheel with the bias and thus used to win his fortune.[16] My dad's own telling of the story in 1960 in Bradford's *Telegraph and Argus* drew heavily on *The Big Gamble*, and subsequent newspaper articles drew very heavily on my dad's. Consequently, the numbers 7, 8, 9, 17, 18, 19, 22, 28 and 29 appear in his and most subsequent newspaper accounts as Joseph's winning numbers. It's not clear how Graves knew this. Perhaps they appeared in an account that I have not yet found, but this seems unlikely. For these to be Joseph's winning numbers they would need to be grouped together on a standard roulette wheel so that an almost imperceptible tilt in the wheel would regularly throw the ball into them when it spun. The numbers 28, 7, 29, 18, 22 and 9 are grouped together but 19, 17 and 8 are spaced out around the roulette wheel. It is possible that 19, 17 and 8 were the numbers Joseph played to throw the authorities off his scent as he knew they wouldn't win, but this is pure speculation. Graves may well have made up the numbers to give his account more plausibility.

Graves also added some new detail around Joseph's contest with the casino authorities which I suspect he thought would improve the story. He writes that Joseph had been winning at table one and that the casino moved that roulette wheel to table six. Joseph was able to spot it because it bore a tiny scratch, which some believed Joseph had made himself in order to recognise it.[17] I haven't used these details in my account because it is very hard to believe that Joseph could have scratched the wheel himself (or had it scratched by a partner). I have played roulette in the room where Joseph won and its size would make it very difficult to be inconspicuous, particularly in the attempt of an illegal act like vandalising a roulette wheel. It's possible to sit at one edge of the room and see clearly to the other side. The tables are monitored closely from all angles and it is known from reports about Charles Wells' win that security guards followed anyone they suspected of foul play or indeed anyone who was doing too well. Surely Joseph would have been under close scrutiny from the moment that he first started winning on a large scale. Nevertheless, these details do appear regularly in later accounts. It's likely that the table numbers, which aren't mentioned in the previous accounts, are an embellishment too. Joseph could not possibly have moved to table six – there were only four in the *Salle Mauresque* at that time.[18]

Graves also differs from Bethell in his account of how the casino finally thwarted Joseph with their redesign of the wheels. He states that a representative was sent to Paris by train (a piece of information that I have used as it is probable) to bring back to Monte Carlo any available spare parts so that the casino could modify its wheels by moving their sections around.[19] Bethell's account seems more credible here with its explanation of how moveable partitions could overcome a natural tilt and how such a specialist piece of machinery would surely have to be constructed by a skilled manufacturer, which would have taken some time when the casino needed a quick solution. It is unclear what sort of 'rejigging' the casino would have been able to effect themselves with a set of spare parts or indeed what that means. Graves seems to have glossed over the process, but perhaps he didn't have an engineering mind.

Winning in the way that Joseph did must have required a great deal of preparation and then a period of time spent observing play in the casino. In their telling of Joseph's story, the previous accounts vary on the duration of his stay in Monte Carlo. The timescale of events seems to accelerate with each new telling. Bethell writes that Joseph and the clerks watched the tables for a month to spot the tilts and the numbers to bet on before starting to play.[20] Forty years later, Graves says that it took only a week to identify a pattern.[21]

Bethell gives no timescale to the events that followed once Joseph began to play, but Graves does. He states that he played for a week before the authorities realised that they had to move the wheels. Joseph's realisation of what they had done was then startlingly quick; Graves claims only ten minutes. The casino's counter-reaction happened equally swiftly, with their dispatch of a representative to the wheel manufacturers in Paris that same night, so that forty-eight hours later all the wheels in the casino had been rejigged. By the time my dad was writing in 1960, the entire course of events had happened in eight days and there is no longer any mention of the newly engineered wheels from Paris.[22] This is an interesting example of how stories can change in the telling and how important it is to go back to the earliest sources. I find it hard to believe that the process of identifying the numbers and the thinking required by both Joseph and the casino to get the upper hand could have taken place over the course of only eight days, and so my account has the narrative playing out over many weeks, if not months.

None of the earlier accounts say anything about the year in which Joseph broke the bank. All of the twentieth-century newspaper articles say that he won in 1875; this begins with my dad's, which specifically claims that Joseph's first bet was placed on 7 July that year. I don't know how my father was able to be so specific (and so confident) about that date, but my research suggests that he was almost certainly mistaken. Monte Carlo was a not a place for summer leisure; its season was December to April. It was open every day of the year except for the Prince of Monaco's birthday on 15 November, so a July date is *possible*, but it is unlikely that Joseph visited in 1875. My suspicions were first aroused when I read Joseph's letter to his nephew Sidney Sowood asking to borrow money for his journey to Monte Carlo. The letter is dated 5 November 1875, too late to be of any use if he'd travelled in the summer of that year. Bethell's account gives a possible clue as to when these events actually occurred when he says that the win happened over twenty years ago. Given that he was writing in 1901, this points to a date in the 1880s rather than 1875.

In the census of 1881 Joseph is not listed as being in the house in Greaves Street where he and Matilda lived. The census was taken on the night of 3/4 April, and of course this could mean that he was staying the night elsewhere as the census simply records who is where at that moment, but Joseph does not appear on any other United Kingdom census record that I can find for that night. Anyone working or living overseas would not have been listed. Then in October of that year Joseph wrote his will, and it is the will of a man of property and assets.[23] This suggests to me that he was abroad in April 1881 and was home again by the autumn to make a will to protect his newly gained wealth. The census for this year reveals another important fact. It does not describe Matilda's relationship to the head of the family – Joseph – as 'wife', as would be expected. She herself is listed as 'Head'. Does this suggest that Joseph's absence from home was a more permanent state of affairs? Why would Matilda style herself or be described by the census taker as the head of the family unless she was in sole charge of the property and the family for a considerable period? Then I remembered the first time that I saw the commemorative key given to Joseph by his friends and my surprise when I read the full inscription on its box:

Presented to
J.H. Jagger Esq
By his friends and admirers
On the occasion of his great and unprecedented
success in the ROULETTE
Which he achieved over the BANK at MONTE-CARLO;
Extending over a period of FOUR YEARS.
Having thus accomplished what the whole world, had
failed to do for more than a century
Monte-Carlo 1st May 1884

The key was given to Joseph by people who knew him, perhaps even people who witnessed his win, and the inscription provides strong evidence for revising the timescale of Joseph's adventure in Monte Carlo. It seems clear to me that he did not defeat the casino during one week in the summer of 1875 but first went to Monte Carlo in 1880 or 1881 and that the events that I have described may have happened over many months or even many years.

The real significance of this timescale is that it throws a different light on Joseph and Matilda and their family life. Following bankruptcy, they struggled for twenty years to make ends meet while their children grew into adulthood. When they lost everything their eldest child, Louisa, was only eight years old and Walter, the youngest, was two. All of the children had to go to work as teenagers. Mary was working as a weaver at fifteen and Walter as a mill hand at thirteen, hardly the life that they had expected when they moved to Girlington Road and Joseph set up business in Manchester. Into this stressful mix was thrown Joseph's plan to travel to Monte Carlo. Rather than being apart for a few weeks of one summer, it is possible that the couple spent a considerable period apart in the early 1880s, perhaps with Joseph living away for several years or travelling back and forth between Bradford and Monte Carlo regularly.

The photo that I inherited supports this theory. It is a *carte de visite*, the new form of calling card patented in France in 1854, which was the first form of mass-produced photograph. They were enormously popular as collectibles during the Victorian period. The picture of Joseph has rounded corners, is not full length and is mounted in an oval vignette. All of these features suggest that it dates to the later years of *carte de visite* production, most likely between 1877 and 1885, when the oval vignette was most prevalent.[24] Bienmüller's studio, where Joseph's photo had been taken, was based at 7 rue Gioffredo, Nice, in 1875 – the year when Joseph was supposed to have broken the bank – but Joseph's portrait was taken in his studio at 49 rue Gioffredo. Frustratingly, information about when the photographer might have moved to that location is obscured by the incomplete records in the archives for that period.[25] However, I think there is sufficient evidence to throw doubt on this photograph having been taken in 1875. Dating the portrait in this way does more than merely suggest the date when Joseph travelled to Monte Carlo; it implies that if he took the time to sit for a portrait in Nice and to have visiting cards made then this was more than a fleeting visit to Monaco. What began as a desperate adventure could have ended up a dramatic change of lifestyle. Joseph may have restored his family's fortunes, but at what cost to his relationship with Matilda and his children?

14

THE RETURN

Stepping off the train at the station in Bradford must have been the moment when Joseph realised just how much his life had altered. The size of his win in Monte Carlo has left previous accounts divided, and yet it is the one thing that people most want to know. Victor Bethell records that Joseph took home about £80,000, while Polovtsoff and Graves estimate the level of his win to be between £60,000 and £80,000.

Here a newly discovered source has helped me considerably. During the course of my research, while exploring family archives, I came across a handwritten set of notes that were produced by the same Pam Hill who had been in contact with Derek Jagger in the 1990s. The notes record that Joseph had initially won £120,000 but then lost £40,000 of it, presumably during the course of his battles with the casino and the modification of its roulette wheels. Joseph finally left Monte Carlo with winnings of £80,000. At this point I was unsure who Pam Hill was, but I was to discover later that she was a very credible source indeed. Her quote of a £80,000 win also corroborates Bethell's account, and this seems compelling. All of the evidence suggests that

Joseph Hobson Jagger took home to Bradford approximately £7.4 million in today's money.

Joseph returned to Little Horton and to 6 Greaves Street, the house to which he had brought his family after his business failed, where he had struggled to make ends meet working hand to mouth as a piece worker, the house where he had been forced to confront a bleak future of ever deepening debts and possibly prison. How must he have felt upon opening the door? Did the familiar feelings of despair descend on him when he entered the house that represented all that he had lost? How long was it before he could brush these thoughts aside, knowing that his financial struggles were over and that he had returned from Monte Carlo a very rich man?

Matilda must have known, of course. Joseph surely would have telegraphed her from Monte Carlo, reassuring her that his great gamble had paid off. But it's by no means certain what her reaction would have been. When Joseph embarked on his journey to Monte Carlo, Matilda was left to cope alone with their business gone and labouring under the burden of keeping the family together. The older children had already left home. Whilst they might have been able to help their mother financially, she probably had no choice but to find work. She may have taken on piece work as Joseph had done after his bankruptcy, or perhaps she was forced into the humiliating position of having to take in washing from her neighbours in Little Horton. It must have been a stressful and unhappy time for her, imagining what might be happening in Monte Carlo while trying to make ends meet at home. It's quite possible that long periods of time passed with no news at all. Matilda could have been left wondering when Joseph would be coming home and likely feared that his venture had been unsuccessful. She had first-hand experience of his initiatives not always being a success – his relocation to Manchester, for example, which had marked the start of all their financial troubles.

Considerable strain is always put on family life when parents live in different countries for long periods, and there could have been a cooling of the relationships between Joseph, his wife and children. On 21 November 1883, Joseph and Matilda's youngest daughter, Mary, married in Bradford in a ceremony that was witnessed by her older brother Alfred.[1] Alfred signed the marriage certificate as the male representative of her family, so clearly Joseph did not attend the wedding. Was he in Monte Carlo? If so, why didn't he come back? What could be important enough to keep a man from the wedding of his daughter? Perhaps it was too expensive for Joseph to travel home, or perhaps the wedding needed to be organised in a hurry. Mary's wedding day could have fallen in the middle of a sustained campaign of noting numbers, at which point Joseph couldn't interrupt his system without losing the momentum. Or maybe the excitement of life far away in Monte Carlo, the Riviera social life, was simply too good to miss. Joseph may have felt that this planned and prolonged campaign in the casino was necessary to accumulate his winnings, but he may also have returned time after time just for the thrill of it. If Joseph was away for the full four-year period, only returning occasionally, this might well have further strained his relationship with his family.

Matilda may have resented the situation, feeling that she'd only condoned Joseph's big gamble due to their desperate situation, agreeing to support a solution to their problems that perhaps she didn't approve of and which caused her great stress. She might even have found it hard when he returned home and she had to learn to share a house again. Matilda might have been justified in feeling that the gamble was never-ending if she had to sit by and wait as Joseph tested his luck repeatedly at roulette in a faraway country. Each time he would have risked all they had, spending on travel and accommodation and staying away for lengthy periods of time, leaving her to struggle on. Or maybe Matilda greeted Joseph's return with joy and gratitude, thankful that her entrepreneurial husband had found such a creative and astonishingly successful solution to their problems.

Under such extraordinary circumstances, Matilda may have felt all of these emotions. But there is one thing of which we can be sure: Joseph did rescue his family from disaster. He and Matilda had met as young, poor workers in the mills of Bradford and now they were multi-millionaires. That their lives had changed was clear. With the prospect of seeing her children grow up inside a debtors' prison firmly consigned to a difficult past, Matilda must have felt unimaginable relief. How she must have prayed then that the change would be a positive and long-lasting one for the family, that Joseph was not prone as most gamblers are to the thrill of the big win. What if he just couldn't resist going back to play again, lured by the excitement and intoxicating thrill of the game? What if Joseph got a taste for gambling success and went back again to Monte Carlo, victim to the addiction upon which the casino thrived?

Charles Wells had returned to Monte Carlo in January 1892, and this time his system had failed him, as it always eventually did. He suffered heavy losses, and the timing could not have been worse. Wells had spent his Monte Carlo winnings on a yacht which he renamed the *Palais Royal*. Whether or not this nod to the casino in Paris where modern roulette was founded was deliberate, it was a very appropriate name. The yacht was listed the following year as the seventh-biggest privately owned yacht in the world. Only Queen Victoria, the Tsar of Russia and the Khedive of Egypt had bigger yachts.[2]

Wells had been enjoying a very public and very lavish lifestyle, but the cost of his refurbishing, crewing and operating his yacht was rising. To replenish his bank account, he returned to the fraudulent ways that had proved so lucrative in the past. He persuaded two of his regular funders that the *Palais Royal* was powered by a new fuel-saving device that he could only test while the boat was actually sailing. Cheques were sent, but Wells' frauds became even more reckless as his desperation rose and his schemes were uncovered. He fled on the *Palais Royal*, but in 1893 was arrested and extradited to England to stand trial at the Old Bailey on charges of obtaining money by false pretences. This evidence from a police inspector at the trial, reported in the *Reynolds's Newspaper*, outlines as series of bogus patents:

> I searched the records at the Patent Office ... for patents applied for and a patent completed by Wells. It appears that between 1885 and 1892 he filed 192 specifications of inventions in respect of which he applied for provisional protection, but that he only completed the formalities necessary ... in twenty-seven instances. Of the 192 applications ... I can only find one case in which Wells completed a patent and disposed of it. This was in 1887 ... A musical skipping rope, which he sold for £50. In the other cases in which complete specifications were lodged at the Patent Office, it appears that this was done under pressure from persons from whom Wells had obtained money to take out a patent. Beyond the ... skipping rope, I cannot ascertain that Wells has patented or disposed of a single invention...[3]

Wells was found guilty and served eight years of hard labour in prison. Now, with a criminal record, he could never return to the casino in Monte Carlo. On his release, he continued with his fraudulent behaviour, enacting one confidence trick after another as well as setting up companies, attracting investors and embezzling funds. Two short periods in jail followed, but Wells and his mistress Jeannette accumulated investments and kept one step ahead of the law until in 1911 their final fraud trapped them. Wells and Jeannette were arrested on board their yacht in Falmouth and extradited to France, where Wells was sentenced to five years in prison. He was now in his seventies. On his release, he was given a small annuity to live on while his creditors were paid off until his death in 1922 in London aged eighty-one.

Thomas Garcia also lost his fortune. His fall was not as public as that of Charles Wells, and so some uncertainty surrounds his fate. Blanc had been vigilant, expecting the Spaniard to return, but he need not have worried because when Garcia did come back to Monte Carlo he was a broken man. He had been frequenting the private gambling 'hells' of Paris and had been found guilty of cheating.[4] He served five years in prison, and because of this sentence Blanc was able to refuse Garcia entry to his casino. According to Charles Graves, Garcia died shortly afterwards in poverty.[5] However, Adolphe Smith, who had a source among the casino croupiers, claims that the Spaniard retired from the world to become a Trappist monk.

Among the tales in the press of winners and losers that so titillated the public, there were cautionary tales aplenty. How Matilda must have hoped that Joseph would not leave again and, like the other men who had broken the bank at Monte Carlo, lose everything he had won – or, worse, end his days burdened with the shame of a prison sentence as a convicted fraudster. Matilda did not want to return to the life that she had so recently left behind.

15

BUILDING A FUTURE

A man in Joseph's position, a new millionaire with wealth at his disposal, might be expected to change his life conspicuously on his return, like a lottery winner today spending winnings on a new house, a car or the holiday of a lifetime. Charles Wells bought a yacht that was so enormous only members of the royal families of Europe could rival it with their own. Kenneth Mackenzie Clark (the Scottish industrialist father of art historian Kenneth Clark), who enjoyed regular luck at Monte Carlo, used his roulette winnings to buy a Riviera golf course at Sospel. He built a hotel in its grounds.[1]

The story passed down within the family is that on his return Joseph spent some of his millions on a mansion in Pepper Hill where he had grown up. He was unhappy living there, however, and eventually moved his family back to Greaves Street. I was even shown a picture of the house, but there is in fact no evidence that Joseph bought a mansion at all. The truth is that Joseph did something quite different with his winnings on his return to Bradford, and in doing so he chose a much more measured and discrete path. In 1881 he bought No. 6 Greaves Street, the humble house that he had rented for years, and also the two neighbouring properties, Nos 8 and 10. These three properties are described as cottages or dwelling houses with yards at the back and gardens at the front, together with outbuildings.[2]

From this point until his death Joseph invested in other properties close to home. He bought mostly small houses in the streets of Little Horton and others slightly further afield, but all were in Bradford. These weren't isolated investments, though; Joseph purchased rows of houses. In 1886 and 1888 he bought houses in Ida Street and Spicer Street, possibly as many as eleven.[3] Close by, he bought a further eight houses in Montague Street, between 1886 and 1890.[4] In Clayton, a part of Bradford near to Little Horton, Joseph bought a plot of land from Ellis Robinson. It lay between Beaconsfield Road and Pasture Lane, and the purchase included nine houses that had been built on Pasture Lane.[5] In total Joseph seems to have bought at least thirty houses. Becoming a property owner enfranchised Joseph. For the first time in his life, aged fifty-six, he could vote.[6] The Second Reform Act, passed in 1867, granted the vote to all householders in the boroughs as well as lodgers who paid rent of £10 a year or more, doubling the electorate from 1 million to 2 million men. Joseph may well have voted in the General Election of 1886, when Gladstone was elected Prime Minister for a third term.

Joseph's only public concession to his new wealth was to eventually upgrade the family home, but even that was a modest move. He chose to stay in the same street and move to one of the larger properties. By 1883 Joseph had acquired the freehold of 25 Greaves Street, and he and Matilda lived there for the remainder of his life.[7] Built from warm local stone with decorative stone jambs around the door and curved stone heads to the three large front windows, No. 25 was a substantial property compared to the back-to-back houses in the area. Set back from the road with its own small front garden, it was one of a row of terraced houses where working-class residents lived alongside those who had entered the middle classes. Men and women living off their own means, professionals such as teachers and clerks and the owner of Brigella Mills (who lived at No. 42) were neighbours with worsted spinners, combers, weavers, overlookers and warehousemen.⁸ Joseph's other properties were only a short walk from home, and when he chose to rent them out it would have been possible for him to be an active and present landlord.

By renting his properties out, Joseph invested and managed his roulette winnings in a prudent way, demonstrating a key trait of his character. He had no desire to spend his money conspicuously on material goods. He could have moved his wife and children to a palatial home outside Bradford as the family story has it, but he didn't. Instead he invested wisely, ensuring their financial security. Joseph was a risk-taker and capable of incredible daring, as his Monte Carlo adventure clearly illustrates, but he was a calculated risk-taker. To have contemplated such a complicated and expensive journey was indicative of Joseph's desperation, but even more so of his non-conformist, entrepreneurial spirit, which was shaped by his upbringing in the booming industrial powerhouse that was Victorian Bradford.

Joseph's resolve that men must shape their own futures was honed by growing up in a city that demonstrated that anything was possible. He was not the type to bemoan his fate and to wait for things to get better; he believed in taking action to help himself. His was not an impulsive, reckless move. Joseph had carefully considered what he was going to do when he got to the casino and had weighed up the risks. He had an idea of exactly how he could break the bank at Monte Carlo before he left Bradford. He didn't enter the casino and play with the desperate hope that he'd make some much-needed money quickly, instead he worked out a method by which he was almost certain that he could win. When he returned home, Joseph didn't live a millionaire's lifestyle. His motivation was, and had been from the start, to save his family from debtors' prison and financial disaster. Joseph wanted to make sure that his hard-won money would not only save Matilda and the children from their immediate hardship and precarious finances, but that it would last. Perhaps too he wanted to stay in the community of Little Horton, which had been his and Matilda's home for over a decade, where they had friends and where their grown-up children still lived.

Although appearing to simply return to his old existence and disappear back into anonymity, Joseph's life was tangibly transformed by Monte Carlo. He no longer had to work (and neither did Matilda). He was a homeowner, a local landlord and now, with a vote, he had a political voice in the community in which he'd chosen to remain. But it was perhaps the lives of his children that were to be changed the most. Whether their relationship with their father had become strained during his time in Monte Carlo or not we cannot know, but on his return Joseph set about making sure that their futures were secure, building up an inheritance which would support his children for years to come.

Louisa, the Jaggers' eldest child, had been eight years old when her father was made bankrupt. Most of her life had been endured under the strain of making ends meet in the shadow of debtors' prison or the workhouse. Louisa, like many children of her generation, went to work in the mill as a child, following her mother Matilda to work long hours in the cacophony of the textile weaving sheds. She had married Lister Briggs, a cotton warp twister, when she was twenty-three and on her father's return from Monte Carlo she was still working in the mills.[9] Lister's job as a twister involved taking the spun woollen threads and twisting them together with cotton to make them stronger. The combined threads then became the warp, the vertical threads that are held taught by the loom, and Lister's job supplying the weaving looms with threads may well explain how the couple first met. Although male textile workers usually earned higher wages than their female counterparts, twisting was a fairly unskilled job after it became mechanised so it was often done by young men who were just starting out on their careers. Or by women. The couple would have been working long hours in the mill to support their children Emily and Walter.

The family were living at 32 Montague Street in Little Horton, not far from her parents, and when Joseph returned he bought the house.[10] Being able to live rent free and without fear of eviction in her father's property transformed the family's life. Louisa was able to stop work to raise Emily and Walter, who would not have to work in the mills as children as their parents and grandparents had.[11] Although there is no record of it, it's probable that Joseph also gave his daughter financial gifts to increase her comfort further. Eventually Louisa and Lister moved into 8 Greaves Street, another of Joseph's properties, but this time just across the road from him and Matilda.[12]

Walter, born in 1858, was Joseph and Matilda's youngest child. Just before his father had gone away he had married Julia Broadbent, a spinner, possibly from the same factory. They were both twenty-one years old.[13] He had started work as a teenager but already in his twenties had perhaps the most challenging job in any textile mill.[14] Walter was an overlooker, firstly of stuff weaving and then in the worsted-weaving process.[15] The role of overlooker was important, requiring one to act as a go-between who had to balance the needs of the workers with those of management. It required training and expertise. Walter would have been responsible for the smooth running of his part of the factory, ensuring that production flowed efficiently from spinning to weaving to finishing without any hold ups or stoppages. To ensure the optimum output at the factory the overlooker was responsible for discipline and health and safety and could fine and fire workers as necessary. Walter would have had to pass exams in order to understand the range of equipment, the technology of fibres (and how they would behave under the different processes) and mathematics so that he could boost productivity and reduce waste. He would have taken evening classes up to three times a week at the Bradford Technical College in his own time and at his own expense. Other training happened on the job, but workers were very protective and often training would be denied to those who weren't members of the Bradford Power Looms Overlookers Society.[16]

Joseph's win in Monte Carlo during the early years of Walter and Julia's marriage eased their financial circumstances. Julia gave up work and stayed at home to raise their growing family, which finally comprised five children: Emily, Arthur, Arnold, Edith and Doris. This home was provided by Joseph. After his parents moved to 25 Greaves Street, Walter and his family took up residence at No. 6, the house where he had grown up. He stayed there for at least twenty years, next door to his sister Louisa and across the road from his father and mother.[17] Providing a secure home for life for his children did more than transform their finances; it also allowed the family to live close together, supporting each other and sharing in the lives of the next generation as it grew.

While Joseph was away in Monte Carlo, his youngest daughter Mary lived at home at 6 Greaves Street, keeping her mother company and working as a worsted weaver like the other women of the family. Her income must have helped Matilda with the family finances.[18] When the twenty-seven-year-old Mary decided to marry in 1883, she chose Henry Smith. She was the only one of Joseph's children to marry after he became a rich man, so was Henry Smith different to the spouses chosen by her siblings, all of whom worked in the mills too? Did her father's wealth give Mary a broader opportunity to meet people and therefore a wider choice in the marital field? If it did then Mary certainly didn't take advantage of it, choosing as she did a widowed stuff salesman five years her senior who lived nearby in Little Horton.[19] Actually, it was probably Mary who was the good catch, already in such a good financial position at her marriage due to her father's win that she no longer had to work.[20] By 1891 Mary and Henry were living at 78 Donishthorpe Street, not a property owned by their parents but just a short walk across the fields from the rest of the family in Little Horton.[21]

Alfred, Joseph and Matilda's eldest son, born in 1854, had also begun his working life in his teens, as a factory assistant.[22] Unlike his siblings, who all married other textile workers, when he was twenty-five Alfred chose to marry Louisa Lee, an educated girl two years younger than him, who had been a teacher. They set up home in Boynton Street. By the time he was in his thirties Alfred had become a successful merchant selling colonial and English wool, and he and Louisa were living in Little Horton Lane with their two young sons, Brinley and Colin, and a servant, sixteen-year-old Mabeth Martha Littlewood.[23] Alfred was clearly prosperous enough not to need one of his father's houses to live in; he could afford one of his own.

The last years of Joseph's life were free of financial worry and he lived surrounded by family. He must have paid off all of his debts after Monte Carlo, for how else would he have been allowed to buy property? A respectable man, financially comfortable and a local landlord, Joseph had left the bankruptcy far behind him. He did not make his fortune in Bradford, like his first partners the Aykroyds and the other textile magnates that rose to riches on the back of the wool trade. Joseph did something much more interesting. He turned his ingenuity to roulette wheels rather than mill wheels, and for a time eclipsed them all.

Joseph's purchase of properties in Little Horton enabled his children to live within a few streets of him and Matilda, raising their families in close proximity to each other rather like in Joseph's own childhood in Pepper Hill. Even Alfred, who could afford his own house, did not venture too far from the family's Little Horton focus. Perhaps this helped to forge strong bonds between the three generations of Joseph's family, overcoming any distance that might have been created by his time in Monte Carlo. I'd like to think so. But Joseph's wealth could not protect them from the other ups and downs of life, and the family was not without its tragedies. Mary gave birth to a child, a daughter called Effie, in the summer of 1888. After five years of marriage her arrival must have brought great joy both to her and to Henry, and also to her parents. But in May the following year Effie died, aged only ten months.[24] Matilda and Joseph must have been grief-stricken for their grandchild and for their youngest daughter, who would never enjoy a family of her own. Mary and Henry were to have no other children, and in the years to come were to experience even more sadness.

16

A QUIET ACHIEVEMENT

Joseph Hobson Jagger died in the spring of 1892. His death was recorded in a simple obituary in the *Bradford Observer* on 26 April 1892: 'JAGGER – April 25th, at 25 Greaves Street, Little Horton, Joseph Hobson Jagger, aged 61 years.' He was buried three days later in Shelf very near to where he was born, in the graveyard at Bethel Chapel. His baby granddaughter Effie is buried with him. In the article about Joseph's life that my father wrote in *The Telegraph & Argus* he stated that

> his great wealth did not, alas, bring him happiness. He made the mistake of retiring to a life of luxury. This proved to be, literally, a fatal mistake for, hardly surprisingly, idleness did not suit one of his intellectual ability and he became subject to long bouts of acute depression and lethargy.[1]

Whether this was my father's sentiment or the family view handed down to my father isn't certain. It seems a very Victorian interpretation of life; that wealth encourages the destructive sin of sloth. Perhaps a man as energetic and entrepreneurial as Joseph did find it difficult without the challenge of work, and perhaps he missed the excitement of Monte Carlo, but I can find no evidence of a luxurious life after the win. There was no impressive house or conspicuous wealth, rather a continuation of the home life as it had been before, albeit with the stress of financial problems removed.

At home in Greaves Street there were no resident maids or cooks, although Matilda may have had daily help.[2] Joseph continued to describe himself as a manufacturer, appearing as such in his early property transactions and in his will of 1881 and consequently on the probate register in Wakefield. Later property transactions describe him as a 'gentleman', as does the census of 1891, but these legal documents probably reflect his status as someone living on his own means and not his perception of himself. Luxury is of course relative, and so perhaps life at 25 Greaves Street was so palpably different to what had gone before that it could be described in this way. Perhaps this story was told with a tinge of jealousy, and with a determination that it is not possible to be both rich and happy. If there is no evidence for a 'state of unhappy luxury', then what did kill Joseph? His death certificate records that he died of diabetes. A common symptom of Type 2 diabetes is extreme tiredness, and it's possible that Joseph's reported lethargy was not due to his being tired of life and bored by his wealthy lifestyle, but a consequence of the disease that would eventually kill him.

Despite his enormous success, Joseph Hobson Jagger's story has survived as only a footnote in histories of Monte Carlo. He is mentioned in passing, usually with brevity and without any of the detail that might be expected following such a win. Nor did he make a splash in the newspapers at the time. His win wasn't covered in the local, national or international press. *The Times* did stand aloof from advertising the casino (disapproving of gambling presumably, still an illegal public activity in England at this time and certainly a disreputable one), but what of the other newspapers who regularly titillated their readers with exciting and scandalous stories from the casino as well as accounts of the big winners and losers?[3] In particular *The Sporting Times*, also known as *The Pink 'Un*, and *The Bystander*, which later merged with *Tatler*, both published regular columns on activities in Monte Carlo which were full of casino stories, gossip and society tittle tattle and yet Joseph's name does not appear once in their editions. In contrast, the press helped to make Charles Wells a major celebrity in England, tracking his every move at home and abroad, even interviewing him in the casino. His fall from grace into prison in 1893 was covered in minute detail. After his win Wells' image was published worldwide, and yet there is no authenticated image of Joseph in the public domain. This absence of press coverage is one of the reasons why Joseph's win has been doubted, and why it has been mooted that he didn't exist at all, that Charles Graves made him up to add colour to his own account of big wins in Monte Carlo.[4]

François Blanc was a PR genius and deliberately publicised big winners to attract players to his casino. He had a huge budget for publicity and used it with great success after a big win, enticing readers with the prospect of winning a fortune and seeing the number of visitors to his casino rocket as a result. He even publicised Garcia, his Bad Homburg nemesis, turning the near-disaster of his enormous win into a commercial advantage by spinning stories of the Spaniard's black beard, gold rings and diamond cross and of the beautiful woman who hung on his arm.[5] Joseph broke the bank ten years before Wells, and, most unusually, did it legally and kept hold of the fortune that he won. So why no mention of Joseph's ingenious method and enormous win in the press? It would have made a terrific story.

The answer most likely lies in Joseph's ingenuity. The way that he breached the defences of the casino made him different, exploiting as he did the very mechanics of the roulette infrastructure in the casino rather than using a system that would eventually be thwarted by the laws of probability. This made him dangerous. Surely if a man like this, who had never travelled abroad and never seen a roulette wheel, could identify a flaw then what was to stop somebody with much more experience discovering yet more technical advantages? On this occasion the casino simply did not want the story of the win to get out. Publicising daring gamblers with unusual systems was one thing, but revealing that his roulette wheels had a mechanical flaw that could so easily be exploited? Well, maybe that was a story to keep out of the papers.

Blanc's publicity strategy must surely have worked both ways. He used it to draw attention to his casino when it suited him but he also buried inconvenient truths, and Joseph's win was certainly one of those. Perhaps this explains why there appears to be no record of Joseph's win in the Monte Carlo archives either. My dad wrote to the casino and was told that all papers relating to the period were destroyed during the First World War. I tried again, writing to libraries and archives in Monaco and France, and even tried approaching the Grimaldis directly when a friend's cousin married into the family. So far, these avenues have all proved to be dead ends. No record of Joseph's achievement or celebration of his win seems to exist in the principality.

The casino's desire to cover up Joseph's success was abetted by Joseph himself. He could of course have told or even sold his story to the press, dined out on it, sought fame from his win. The huge public reaction to Charles Wells' win a decade later demonstrated just how popular a Monte Carlo winner could be. The public were responding to 'one of us', an ordinary man, beating 'them' by getting the better of the casino. Joseph was the real deal, matching this image of a champion of the people much more than the well-heeled Charles Wells ever could. His was a genuine rags-to-riches story: a boy who worked in the mills then worked hard to make a life for his family but lost it all and used his intelligence and logic to beat the casino and become a millionaire. Imagine what a splash that would have made in the newspapers! However, I can find no evidence of Joseph publicising this. Not only did he remain under the radar of the local and national press but he did not cite his victory over the roulette tables as his greatest achievement. He is not heralded as 'the man who broke the bank at Monte Carlo' on his gravestone, or in his obituary, both obvious places for a showier man to brag of his extraordinary feat. He did not present the key publicly as the accolade that it surely was, and he did not make any public endowments or make any overt philanthropic acts that I can discover. Any financial gifts were made in a private and unrecorded way.

A strong desire to live a modest and quiet life could explain Joseph's actions. He took his gamble to save his family, not to become rich. Whether or not he came and went to Monte Carlo over a period of years it seems certain that a glamorous life in the spotlight had never been a motivation, and so on his return he chose simply to resume his old life with his old friends. The Jagger family had strong roots in Little Horton and perhaps they wanted to stay there even though they could have moved anywhere they chose. Perhaps they valued their community more than they would an affluent middle-class area where they simply would not fit in. Joseph's desire for privacy, to slip back into normal life after his great adventure, would go a long way to explain the lack of publicity surrounding events in Monte Carlo and his new-found wealth.

I believe there was another force at work too, a powerful emotion that encouraged Joseph to turn away from his Monte Carlo life and live as he had before, and that is shame. The Jaggers lived within a Methodist community which frowned upon gambling, and roulette was still illegal in England. There is a story told within the family that the Bishop of Bradford publicly condemned Joseph, and although I can't find any evidence for this it doesn't sound unlikely. A groundswell of criticism had risen as

Christian groups in particular condemned the debauchery and sin evident in Monte Carlo. High-profile representatives of both the Anglican Church and the Baptists spoke out against Monte Carlo and called for the closing down of its casino, which they regarded as immoral and a magnet for all that was most reprehensible in the world.[6] When Queen Victoria passed through the area during a visit to the Riviera in 1882, she spurned both the bouquet of flowers that was presented to her as well as the hospitality offered by Charles III.[7] This devastating and very public rejection must have sealed the reputation of Monte Carlo and its casino in the minds of all those Christians who considered gambling to be an ungodly practice.

This does beg the question of how difficult it must have been for Joseph to return home with money that would have been seen by some of his neighbours and friends as having been gained through illicit and sordid means in one of the most morally corrupt places in the world. Members of his own family may well have felt the same, including his wife and children. Joseph was certainly ashamed of his bankruptcy, as his poem to Sidney Sowood clearly demonstrates, and he may have felt the same about the desperate measures that he'd resorted to.

> Honest men oft taste misfortune
> Others suffer for misdeeds
> But must your ear importune
> Saying while my conscience bleeds –
> Oh that life would backward turn!
> Never need my cheeks so burn.

Financial failure at this time was a very public matter with a very public punishment which affected the whole family and, at its most extreme, could result in a lifelong loss of liberty. Joseph had to live under this stigma for twenty years before he went to Monte Carlo, struggling to keep his family afloat in a very tight-knit community where everybody knew everybody's business. If Joseph wanted to forget this episode in his life and also didn't want to brag of his gambling success and new-found wealth to his former debtors, then living a modest life, away from any public comment, was a sensible course of action.

In February 1892, just two months before Joseph died, the song 'The Man Who Broke the Bank at Monte Carlo' was performed in public for the first time and became the musical hit of a generation. Everybody knew it, everywhere around the world. I wonder how Joseph felt about this song that made a hero and a household name of a man who achieved what he had already done over a decade earlier? I would like to think that he didn't mind, that he might even have found it amusing to hear another man's exploits at the casino immortalised in a music hall song. Joseph had chosen to keep his achievement close to his chest, never seeking the celebrity that Charles Wells craved all his life (and which was to cause Wells' eventual destruction). It may also have been a salutary reminder of the most crucial aspect of Joseph's success: that he had kept his winnings when so many others had failed to do so. I'd like to think that he died a contented man, surrounded by his family, safe in the knowledge that he had beaten the odds, kept his money and secured their financial futures.

PART 3

'AND I'VE NOW SUCH LOTS OF MONEY, I'M A GENT'

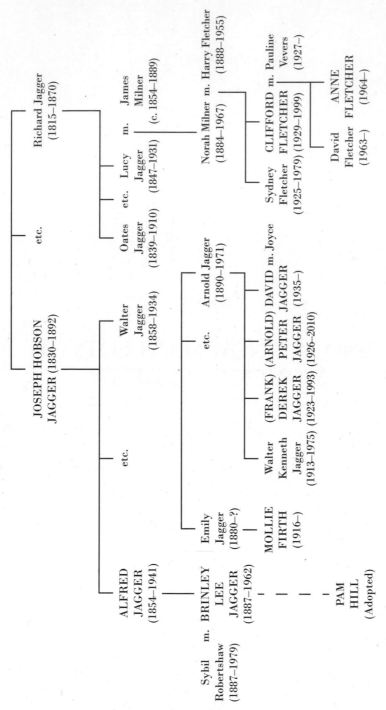

DESCENDANTS: THOSE THAT KEPT THE STORY ALIVE

17

LOST MILLIONS

During the years in which I have been researching Joseph's story, there has been one question more tantalising than the rest: what happened to the money? It is one of the first things that people want to know when I tell the story. But in the articles that have been written about his win, and in the brief mention of his success in books about the casino, nobody has been able to say. Some have even stated that it is a mystery what happened to Joseph's millions because he did not leave a will. This is not true. Joseph left very clear instructions in his Last Will and Testament, written on 7 October 1881, and his wishes were put into effect after his death.[1] His will bears all the hallmarks of a newly enriched man, instructing his trustees to put all of the properties in which he had so carefully invested his Monte Carlo winnings during his lifetime into a trust fund which would support his family, 'sell my real estate and to collect get in and convert into money my residuary personal estate and as to the moneys to arise from the sale ... pay my funeral and testamentary expenses and debts and to invest the residue ...'

A shrewd businessman, Joseph gave his trustees the freedom to make decisions about the fund and its investments, stating that they need not sell if the time was inopportune:

> My trustees may postpone the sale and conversion of my real and residuary personal estate or any part thereof for so long as they shall think fit ... my trustees may let any [properties] ... for the time being remaining unsold either from year to year or for any terms of years at such rents and subject to such conditions as they shall think fit and generally may manage the same in such manner as they shall think fit.

Continuing his own shrewd approach to investment, Joseph also authorised

> all monies liable to be invested under my will may be invested in or upon any of the public stocks or funds or government securities of the United Kingdom or in mortgage of freehold copyhold or leasehold estates securities of any Railway or other Company in Great Britain ... or of any Municipal Body or Corporation or Local board of Health in England or Wales.

Joseph also did something very important for his daughters. When he wrote his will in 1881, any assets that he gave his daughters would not have been protected by law if they were married as marriage nullified a woman's legal status. A wife was considered to be one person with her husband, or rather she was considered to be an extension of her husband. Any property or assets that she had owned previously went automatically to him, and she could not write a will or dispose of assets without her husband's permission. A wife had no authority over her children and she could not vote. Her husband was legally permitted to make all of these decisions on her behalf. Although the Married Women's Property Act of 1870 modified the situation by allowing wives to keep any money that they earned during their marriage, it wasn't until the Act was extended in 1882 that married women could retain control of any property that they had owned before their marriage.

Joseph wrote his will the year before this change of law occurred. Louisa was married and Mary was likely to wed, and so to prevent his daughters having to give everything that he bequeathed to them up to their husbands, Joseph did all that he could to protect them himself. In his will he asserted that 'all monies or effects payable or transferable to any and every female under this my will shall be paid and transferred to her for her separate use free from marital control'.[2] This clause gave Louisa financial independence from Lister and ensured that Mary could marry and not surrender her inheritance to her husband. At a point before married women were granted property rights that were equal to those of men, Joseph made sure that his daughters' inheritance would be secure. Joseph's daughters were both married women when he died, and this clause would prove to be a very prescient protection of Mary.

As would be expected now, Joseph's widow Matilda was the major beneficiary, receiving half of the income from the trust fund. However, a wife couldn't automatically inherit her husband's estate as she would today. Despite the changes to property law, it wasn't until a further Married Women's Property Act was passed the year after Joseph's death, in 1893, that wives would be recognised as being co-owners of property acquired during a marriage and therefore be able to retain it after their spouse's death. In law, all that the couple owned belonged to Joseph, and it was he who would decide what would happen to it after his death and even after Matilda's if she remained his widow. Joseph gave all of the contents of their Greaves Street home, called 'paraphernalia' in law, to his wife:

I bequeath to my dear wife Matilda the use and enjoyment during her life of all the household furniture, plate, linen, china, books, prints, pictures and other effects of the like nature ... and after her decease I bequeath the same articles to my daughter Mary Jagger ... in case she shall be un-married.

In the spring of 1892, after forty-one years of marriage, Matilda had to adjust to living without her husband. She was sixty-one years old. Unlike many other women of her generation, however, she did not have to rely on her children to house and support her because Joseph had left her well provided for. Matilda's half-share of the trust fund was intended to support her for the rest of her life, and she continued to live in the home that she had shared with Joseph, the house where he had died, 25 Greaves Street. Matilda had been used to her husband's absence and to struggling on without him, perhaps for protracted periods of time, and so her adjustment to living alone may not have been too difficult. She was able to remain in the home that she had run for over twenty years in a neighbourhood where she had friends and established pastimes and routines. In these last years of her life she also had her family close by.[3] Without money worries and with no one to please but herself, these could have been halcyon days for Matilda. However, four years after Joseph's death she chose to marry again.

Matilda became Mrs Samuel Raistrick on 8 February 1896 during a civil ceremony solemnised at Huddersfield Register Office. She was sixty-five and he was sixty-seven. Samuel Raistrick was a coal merchant from Huddersfield.[4] He came from a West Yorkshire textile family like Matilda's and had begun his working life as a weaver just as she had. Like her he had also lost a spouse. Grace, the mother of his four children, had died in the same year as Joseph. Their first child, Georgina, died in infancy but their three remaining children, Orville, Herbert and Amy, thrived and were raised in Huddersfield. Samuel's coal merchant's business must have made him a good enough living because he was able to send his children to school rather than the mill.

Orville became a teacher and Herbert a Post Office clerk, both professions requiring a good level of education. Samuel and Grace Raistrick were certainly able to give their children a better start in life than Joseph and Matilda Jagger had been able to give theirs.

The newly-weds began married life at 29 Calton Street in Huddersfield, the home that Samuel had shared with Grace, and this marks what I think was Matilda's final break with Greaves Street. It must have been quite a wrench for her, leaving behind the street where she had raised her children and the house where her husband had died. She chose to leave Bradford and remove herself from daily contact with her sons and daughters and grandchildren, starting life again in another woman's home in a town that she did not know. Matilda must have been motivated by a very strong need or by powerful emotions to contemplate such a change. Love, loneliness or new opportunities may have moved her towards this new marriage to a man who could offer companionship and a few exciting and stimulating years at the end of her life. Whatever drove her choice, it wasn't financial. In becoming Samuel's wife, Matilda relinquished her share of the Monte Carlo winnings. Joseph's will had decreed that her half-share of the trust fund depended on 'if she shall so long continue to be my widow'.[5] If Matilda remarried, she would forfeit it all.

Three days before the wedding on 5 February 1896, Matilda, her children and Joseph's trustees gathered to witness a document which reconfigured Matilda's finances for the rest of her life and removed from her the legacy of her husband's Monte Carlo win.[6] Her imminent marriage necessitated a new division of the trust revenue as Joseph's will explicitly stated, 'On the death or marriage again of my wife whichever shall first happen my trustees shall stand possessed of the said trust fund ... [that is Matilda's half of the trust].' Her new husband would now take on the responsibility of supporting her financially. Matilda and her children agreed that the trustees would take back the shares that they all held and redistribute them so that they would be held only by Alfred, Louisa, Walter and Mary. Despite this arrangement being exactly what Joseph had outlined in his will, his children and his trustees agreed that Matilda should still be supported financially by her family to some degree. Clearly they didn't want her to be totally reliant on her new husband, and so decided to pay her 'during her life the annuity or sum of One hundred and four pounds by equal weekly payments of Two pounds each'.[7] This provision is equal to approximately £11,000 a year today. The document outlining the agreement was signed by Matilda's eldest son, Alfred.

Matilda's personal and financial gamble did not reap the rewards that she must have hoped for. Samuel died only ten months after the wedding in December 1896, leaving her a widow for a second time. Samuel's will, written the month before he died, requested that on his death both his coal merchant business and his house in Huddersfield should be sold and the proceeds split equally between his two sons Orville and Herbert. After doing so his sons were to pay

> unto my dear wife Matilda Raistrick ... the sum of sixty five pounds [value of almost £7,000 today] and it is my desire that the aforesaid Matilda Raistrick take away the whole of the household effects that she brought to my house after our marriage. I also direct my executor to pay to my daughter Amy Elizabeth Raistrick the sum of sixty pounds and all the household furniture and the household effects that I die possessed of ...[8]

Matilda had left her home in Bradford and now lost her new house in Huddersfield too. She had her household possessions, the 'paraphernalia' that she had accumulated and treasured through two marriages, but no home of her own to put them into. Matilda had an income, a good one from both husbands, so she could have bought a property of her own but she chose not to. An old woman by the standards of the time, Matilda returned home to Little Horton to the emotional refuge and comfort that her children could offer. She moved in to the home of her daughter Louisa in Manchester Road where she spent her final years surrounded by children and grandchildren.[9] Matilda died there on 16 October 1902 aged seventy-two of a 'malignant disease of the stomach, presumably cancer'. Her daughters were by her side.[10]

I have searched for Matilda's will without any success, and there are only two possible explanations for its absence. If a will is not registered it could be because there is conflict surrounding it. It's easy to imagine that the will of the widow of 'the man who broke the bank at Monte Carlo' might well be the subject of family disagreement. None of Matilda's or Samuel's children attended their wedding, or at least it seems that way as the two witness signatures on the marriage certificate belong to none of them.[11]

Why would Matilda's children leave this most important event to be witnessed by others? It is possible that her daughters Mary and Louisa were there if women could not by law act as witnesses to legal documents, but the absence of both Alfred and Walter along with Samuel's sons Orville and Herbert does raise questions. Did Matilda and Samuel's children oppose the marriage? The Jaggers were clearly protective of their mother, ensuring that she would always have an income from her own family and independent of her new husband. Perhaps they did not approve of her choice of spouse, or perhaps of any remarriage at all. When she died they ignored it, choosing to bury their mother with their father, referring to her on the grave stone as Joseph's wife, a sign perhaps of just how much they disregarded the short second marriage of her twilight years. If Samuel's children were unhappy with the marriage too and what it meant for their legacy, then there could have been arguments at her death about her estate and their share in it.

An account in the *Bradford Almanack* (date unknown) states that there was a family rift after Joseph died, caused by confusion over his financial legacy: 'After his death there was a family dispute over the inheritance as Jagger did not leave a will.'[12] There is absolutely no truth in this. Joseph left a will with very clear instructions that were carefully followed. Is it possible that these stories relate to Matilda instead, the subject of the story being confused in its telling over time as so often happens? I think not, because there is evidence that her financial affairs were settled and not left to endless wrangling within Chancery. A later document relating to the administration of the family trust clearly states that Matilda Raistrick's 'funeral and testamentary expenses and debts ... have long since been paid and satisfied'.[13]

I think that the truth is more straightforward. At her death, Matilda had no house to dispose of and the annuities that she received from her children and from her second husband both ceased. Matilda Jagger, the wife of the 'man who broke the bank at Monte Carlo', the woman who stood shoulder to shoulder with him through bankruptcy and his desperate adventure in the casino and who welcomed him back as a multimillionaire, died with so few assets that a will was not required. This is the only other possible reason for a will not to be registered, but it does not mean that Matilda died in poverty. She was born at a time when married women had no right to property of their own beyond the household furnishings that they accumulated. However, unmarried women enjoyed much more freedom. They could own property, pay tax and vote in the local parish, none of which a married woman was allowed to do. The law changed twenty years before Matilda died, and married women were given complete ownership of their property, but Matilda, by then in her fifties, had no assets of her own and seemingly no desire to purchase a property. She was totally reliant financially on both of her husbands, but they provided very well for her, as did her children, and in her final days she was cared for by her daughters. Having been brought up with the expectation that she would never own a house or have access to her own money, this situation would have been the norm for Matilda and there is no reason to think that she died anything other than a very contented woman.

Joseph had directed the other half of the trust fund to be shared equally between his four children: 'As to the other half of the income ... divide the same ... between and among my ... children ... Louisa Briggs, Alfred Jagger, Mary Jagger and Walter Jagger'.[14] After Matilda's remarriage, the Jagger children added their mother's share of the trust fund to their own. The indenture produced to formalise this arrangement confirms that all of the property purchased by Joseph (at least thirty-two houses) was still in the possession of the family and that the children could continue to live off the rental income and other investments that it comprised.

From this point in 1896, Joseph's children became the sole beneficiaries of their father's Monte Carlo winnings, doubling the income that they had previously received from the trust that had been established to manage it. However, this income was not what might have been expected. Joseph was no longer a millionaire at the end of his life. The estate that he left behind had a net worth of just £1,710, the equivalent of £170,000 today, a considerable diminution of the sum that he had won. A £7.5 million fortune appears to have been eroded by an astonishing 97.5 per cent in a little over ten years. But how?

18

A GENEROUS GIFT

The contents of Joseph's will at first seem hard to explain. The absence of substantial wealth is evident within succeeding generations, some of whom saw no evidence of his enormous roulette win in their lives, making it hard to believe that their ancestor had really broken the bank at Monte Carlo at all. How was it possible for him to have been a multimillionaire when no significant money seemed to remain in the family? Death duty, the forerunner of inheritance tax, had been payable on estates since 1796 and would account for some of the loss.[1] The property portfolio contained within the estate no doubt fluctuated in value too, and may have been valued at a lower rate at the time of Joseph's death. However, I was told a story which might offer another explanation.

Mollie Firth is Joseph's great-granddaughter. Born in 1916, she is the oldest surviving member of the family. I was introduced to her by her nephew Chris Holdsworth after he read a short article about Joseph that I had written and tracked me down to find out more. Another branch of the family that I had not been aware of, they are the descendants of Joseph's younger son Walter. Mollie made a career at the BBC, splitting her time between London and her family home in Bradford, a quite extraordinary life for a woman of her generation. I drove to meet her in Yorkshire just before her 100th birthday and found a fascinating, funny and young-at-heart woman. One of her recollections was vital to my understanding of what might have happened to Joseph's wealth. Her older relatives had told her that Joseph had lost money to a conman in what they described as 'a typical investment scam'. Mollie knows no more than this, but I find it entirely credible that Joseph could have lost some of his fortune in this way.[2]

The burgeoning culture of investment in Victorian times saw more and more people putting money into business, stocks and shares, and this was fraught with danger. A significant number of flotations by companies on the stock exchange during the nineteenth century were in fact fraudulent, designed to take money from investors in return for non-existent shares.[3] In addition to stock crashes and frauds, investors also had to contend with the lack of auditing that was common within companies and which made their accounts untrustworthy. Large-scale banking and investment scandals brought ruin to many. In 1866, the banking house of Overend and Gurney went into liquidation after overextending itself with railway investments and share sales. Some 200 companies collapsed in its wake.

Swindles by individuals were also rife. Charles Wells, for example, is known to have advertised for investors who sent him money for non-existent inventions. In 1822, a British Navy veteran, Gregor MacGregor, arrived in London announcing that he had been made leader of a nation in Central America called Poyais. Investors rushed to give him money, excited by the prospect of a chance to settle in the new nation, but of course it didn't exist. When ships arrived there, they found only jungle.[4] In the 1850s the MP and director of the Tipperary Bank, John Sadleir, embezzled thousands of pounds of his customers' money to fund his own investments in mining and railway stocks, and then produced fake transaction records and balance sheets to cover his tracks. When his fraud was discovered in 1856 he killed himself with poison, but many individuals and companies were left destitute. So well known was the cast that Charles Dickens based his *Little Dorrit* character Mr Merdle on Sadleir when he wrote it the following year.[5]

Despite Joseph's discretion and the lack of publicity surrounding his win, his success must have been known locally and he might have made a lucrative target for someone who could present themselves as a financial expert. He was a man who looked for sound investments and had made many through the purchase of property, but perhaps on this occasion he was misled. Or perhaps he was simply unlucky, placing his trust in a bank or in a company that seemed to be a sound investment. Ironic, perhaps, that the only man known to have broken the bank at Monte Carlo by legal means and to have kept all of his money was divested of some of his winnings on his return by a confidence trickster. Nor would this be the last time that what remained of the Jagger fortune would fall prey to the actions of an unscrupulous individual.

Although this fraud, depending on its size, might be enough to account for the reduction in Joseph's wealth in the last years of his life, I believe a more important factor may be what happened to it in the years immediately after he won. In addition to his property purchases, it is likely that Joseph gifted sums of money during his life. Perhaps this is what he had always intended to do, to give financial help and security to those closest to him rather than enrich himself. Helping out friends and family is a natural instinct and he may have been very generous indeed. My great grandmother Lucy Jagger, his niece, said that she received £5 from him (worth a not inconsiderable £500 today).[6] The family believes that Joseph also gave sums of money on his return to those of his siblings that are known to have survived; William, Mary Ann and Martha. Perhaps the most intriguing story, however, is that

Joseph Hobson Jagger gave both of Alfred's sons £10,000 each.[7] This is a staggering sum. It equates to nearly £1 million each in today's terms (£925,000) and represents approximately a quarter of the sum that Joseph won in the casino. Why would Brinley and Colin have been the recipients of such a generous handout when neither the other grandchildren nor Joseph's own sons and daughters received such huge financial gifts? This question would eventually lead not only to an explanation of what happened to the money but also to an unexpected twist in the tale of how Joseph beat the casino.

Looking into the lives of Alfred's two sons and piecing together the details in an attempt to understand Joseph's gesture unearthed an event that immediately resonated with me. In early 1918, Brinley had married Sybil Robertshaw.[8] I'd heard that name before. When I had first been shown the commemorative key that Joseph Hobson Jagger's friends and admirers had given him after his Monte Carlo win, I was told by David Jagger that it had arrived into his branch of the family via a mysterious 'aunt Sybil'. She had given it to his father Arnold. David remembers visiting her as a child in her very grand and impressive house near Saltaire, just outside Bradford; she had a butler. He had never discovered who Sybil was or why she had the key and didn't know what the link was between her and Joseph. Surely Sybil Robertshaw, Brinley's wife, must be the mysterious 'aunt Sybil'? She was the right generation for David Jagger to call her an aunt, and she was clearly wealthy, as I imagined Brinley and his wife must be.

If I was to find out why Brinley and Colin were given so much money by their grandfather, I wondered if there might be surviving relatives in his branch of the family who would know. Could there be family stories that had never been shared just as there were in mine and in David Jagger's? Sybil outlived Brinley and they had no children and so my search began with her and her siblings.

Sybil Marion Robertshaw had three sisters: Gladys, Mary (also known as Isabel) and Mabel. They were daughters of a master butcher who later transferred into worsted manufacture.[9] Job Robertshaw and his wife Mary clearly made a good living because they lived in some style in Legrams Lane in Bradford with servants to assist them. Mabel and Mary married while Gladys did not, and it was Mabel who was to provide the link to surviving relatives that I was looking for. Sybil's will divided her estate into equal quarters and one of those shares was left to 'her friend' Pam Hill.[10] This must surely be the same Pam Hill who had exchanged letters with Derek Jagger in the early 1990s. I had found copies of her research notes among Derek and David's archive, but without knowing who she was I had been uncertain as to how much credence to give them. A second quarter of Sybil's estate went to her sister Gladys, and the remaining two went to David Wright and Gillian Stretton, described as her nephew and niece. In fact, David is Sybil's great-nephew, descended from her sister Mabel, who married a wool merchant called Edward Athelstan Holdroyd Wright. Gillian is his half-sister.

Sybil left Gillian her jewellery and personal effects, and so I assumed they must have had a close relationship. Knowing that her married name was Stretton, and making an assumption about her age and that she might still live in Bradford, I searched the electoral rolls, finding that there was indeed a person of this name, of the right age and listed in the city. Hoping that I was right, I wrote a letter explaining who I was, and my efforts were rewarded by a phone call only days later in which Gillian began to recount her memories of her great-aunt Sybil and great-uncle Brinley. She suggested that I speak to David Wright to find out more. David and I met at his lovely old rectory in Stonton Wyville, and it was here over a cup of tea that I was able to ask him about his branch of the family, what Sybil had been like and for his recollections of their family life. He could not help with my question about why Brinley and Colin had been given such a large share of the roulette winnings by their grandfather – he'd not been aware of that at all – but he could tell me about Pam Hill and who she was.

During the Second World War, Brinley and Sybil had been asked to take in two evacuees because they lived alone, with just their servants, in a very large house. Brinley had, however, agreed to take only one child. Pam arrived from London, and she never went home. The family story is that at the end of the war her family could not be traced. Perhaps they'd died in the Blitz, or perhaps they did not want her back, but whatever the reason she remained with Brinley and Sybil, whom she called Nunkey and Bid. Pam was very much a surrogate child, helping to heal the loss of their son Dennis William Lee Jagger, who had died of diphtheria at the age of six weeks in 1921.[11] Brinley and Sybil had no more children. A bright girl, Pam did well at school and became a teacher, only marrying and leaving the Jagger home in her mid-forties.[12]

Fascinated by the Monte Carlo connection, Pam had researched the story and produced the set of notes of which I had a copy. Any conversations that she had with Brinley and Sybil must of course have informed these, but more significantly I discovered that she had drawn on letters written by Alfred Jagger's second wife, Lucy. These letters had been written in the 1960s as part of Lucy's regular correspondence with her solicitors, the firm of Dunn Connell in Bradford, and they described what her husband Alfred had told her about events in Monte Carlo. Pam's summary of the contents of these letters in her notes provides vital evidence because these letters no longer exist – at her death, Lucy asked for all her papers to be destroyed and this was duly done.[13] However, the letters had been seen by Pam Hill, who had become a close and trusted member of the family. Joseph didn't record his adventure in Monte Carlo, but his son did through this conversation with his wife, transcribed in her letters and summarised by Pam. Pam's notes provide perhaps the most accurate account that exists of what happened in Monte Carlo. The contents of these notes have never been made public before.

Pam's notes intertwine several elements of family history as she surveys documents and articles and draws on personal observations as well as conversations with others. One of these conversations was with Ray Hammond, who researched the Monte Carlo story while working as a journalist for Channel 4 or ITV (she's not sure which). He told Pam that he had discovered that Joseph gave his sons £10,000 each after his Monte Carlo win. Surely this is too much of a coincidence. This reference must be to the huge sum that Joseph gave away, reportedly to his grandsons, and is proof that the family story was wrongly attributed by one generation to Brinley and Colin. It was to Alfred and Walter that Joseph made this enormous gift. It makes more sense that he would favour his only sons in this way rather than bestow such wealth upon only two of his many grandchildren. Proof could lie in the fact that, despite leaving each an equal share of his estate, Joseph's children were not equally wealthy.

Lucy's letters to her solicitors reveal what Alfred did with this gift. Before his father's death, Alfred was prospering in the wool trade and was married with two sons. His wife Louisa had been a teacher and was the daughter of William B. Lee, who founded his eponymously named wool business in 1874.[14] Marrying her in 1879 brought Alfred directly into a wealthy family but also a family business. Alfred and Louisa may have met because he was employed by her father, or they may have come across each other socially in Little Horton, where both of their families lived. Joseph was not to become rich until another few years after the wedding, and so the union represented quite a step up for Alfred.

William B. Lee was not, however, from the aristocracy or landed gentry. He was a self-made man who had worked as a wool sorter and then a foreman for a wool merchant.[15] Lee had built up his own business and a prosperous life for his family, but his origins were very much the same as Joseph's. Born within a year of each other, both men had worked their way up through the wool trade, but William had been luckier, just as Joseph's first partners, the Aykroyds had been. Now both men lived in Little Horton; one a bankrupt and the other at the helm of his own successful business. Lucy's letters reveal that Alfred invested £7000 in the firm of W. B. Lee & Co.[16] This would have been an enormous sum for him to find at that time, equating to almost £700,000 today. The most likely explanation is that Alfred used most of the money that his father had given him to invest in the firm and thereby set himself up financially for the rest of his life.

A second rearrangement of the family trust fund in 1913 illustrates just how much wealthier Alfred was than his siblings. All but one of Joseph's original trustees died within a few years of his wife Matilda. Their deaths prompted this reorganisation of the assets left in his will. With their father and mother dead, the Jagger children, led by Alfred, who was the only surviving trustee, changed the way that Joseph's trust fund operated. They applied to place all of their father's properties under the central management of an appointed solicitor, George Oscar Hindley, and then to redistribute them directly into their own ownership.[17] The property portfolio was divided up among them so that each could benefited from the rental income or sale of their own group of houses, but the value of the property division was not equal. Louisa Briggs took ownership of the plot of land in Little Horton which included six houses in Montague Street: Nos 42, 44, 46, 48, 50 and 52. Mary took the remaining four properties in Montague Street: Nos 18, 20, 22, 24.[18] Walter was given the Greaves Street houses: Nos 10 and 8 plus 6, his former home.[19] Alfred took the most valuable share of properties[20] and land, those in the Pasture Lane area of Clayton, near Bradford, and compensated his siblings for the difference.

Alfred Jagger should pay for Equality of partition the sums following namely to the said Walter Jagger the sum of three hundred and eighty-six pounds five shillings. To the said Louisa Briggs the sum of one hundred and fifty one pounds five shillings and to the said Mary Smith the sum of eleven pounds five shillings.

Alfred's share cost him the equivalent of approximately £50,000 today. This transaction highlights the money that he had at his disposal and how his life starkly contrasted with those of his siblings.

Louisa was sixty-two years old and living in Manchester Road, Bradford, when she became a property owner but she was never wealthy enough that her family could retire. She had been able to stop work after her father returned from Monte Carlo, but her husband Lister kept working until nearly the end of his life. He spent most of his career as a worsted and cotton warp twister, a fairly unskilled job, and only late on did he become a reed and heald mender. The reeds and healds are the parts of the loom which separate the warp threads which run lengthwise in the finished cloth and feed them through into the weaving sheds. This was a more technical job, the next step up in maintaining weaving machinery, but still fairly junior. There was an expectation that men doing this job would do it early in their career and then move on to something more skilful such as assisting or being apprenticed to an overlooker.[21] It's unlikely that Lister ever made this step as he was already in his fifties and dead at the age of sixty-seven.

Shortly after her husband died in 1920, Louisa had to face a devastating tragedy. Her only son, Walter, died the following January aged only forty-two, leaving two young daughters, Eileen and Dorothy, and a widow, Martha. They lived on the edge of Little Horton on Thornton Lane not too far from Louisa and her daughter Emily, whose home was very close to her mother's.[22] Emily had become a teacher, giving it up as all women had to when she married Charles Alfred Bulmer, a worsted spinner's manager in 1902, and gave birth to a daughter, Enid, two years later. The women must have rallied around to help the bereaved Martha cope with her girls, and Louisa was able to ensure that they had some financial security in the future.

At the end of her life Louisa moved back to 50 Montague St, one of the houses bought with the Monte Carlo winnings and which she now owned. Her sister Mary lived there with her and this shared home is where Louisa died in 1932, aged eighty-one.[23] She left an estate with a net value of £85 19d 6s (worth almost £5,500 today) which she split between her daughter Emily and her daughter-in-law Martha.[24] She left to her daughter 'all my furniture, jewellery, plate, plated goods, pictures, china, glass, linens and wearing apparel'. To Emily also passed ownership of four of the properties bought with the Monte Carlo winnings: Nos 42, 44, 46 and 48 Montague Street. Nos 50 (where Louisa died) and 52 were put into a trust fund with everything else that Louisa owned to be administered by her son-in-law Charles Bulmer, who was to make sure that it provided an income for Martha and her daughters. She decreed in her will that the properties should be rented out or sold, if Martha agreed, to ensure that her daughter-in-law and granddaughters had an income. After Martha's death or remarriage her share was to pass to her children Eileen and Dorothy Bulmer. For the time being Louisa's sister Mary continued to live at 50 Montague Street.

Mary, the youngest of Joseph and Matilda's daughters, had enjoyed financial security but a great deal of unhappiness in her personal life. After her father's return from Monte Carlo, Mary had not needed to work again, remaining in the family home with her parents until she married in 1883.[25] At this point, Joseph's foresight in granting his daughters sole ownership of their inheritance, independent of their husbands, proved to be a lifeline for Mary. Her marriage to Henry Smith failed. After the death of their young daughter Effie, there had been no further children and gradually the couple were estranged. When the census was taken in 1901 Mary was present at her sister Louisa's house. She was there again when the next census was taken in 1911. Surely it is too much of a coincidence to suggest that she just happened to be present on both census days, a decade apart? Surely this is proof that Mary and Henry were living separately? When he died in 1912 he bequeathed an estate valued at £25 (£2,252 today) to his brother and sister, and nothing to his independently wealthy wife. Mary, it seems, continued to live with her sister and after Louisa was widowed in 1920 they moved together into 50 Montague Street for the rest of Louisa's life.

Mary outlived her sister by six years, and at some point before her death moved into the home of her niece Emily and her husband Charles Alfred Bulmer. Charles played a key role among this family group of single women. With Louisa's son dead, Charles had stepped in as his mother-in-law's executor and now he took on the same role for her sister. Mary died at St Luke's Hospital in Bradford on 6 November 1938 aged eighty-two, leaving an estate of £886 (just over £50,000 today). In recognition of her care in the last days of her life, Mary left 'all of my furniture jewellery plate plated goods pictures china glass linen and wearing apparel' to her niece Emily. More importantly, she also gave Emily ownership of the four properties in Montague Street which her father had bought with the Monte Carlo winnings, giving the young woman ownership of all but two of the Montague Street properties that had passed to Joseph's daughters. Mary also continued the work that Louisa had done to make sure that the family of her dead son Walter was looked after by leaving his children (her grandnieces Eileen and Dorothy), as well as Emily and Charles's daughter Enid, a share in a trust that they would benefit from when they reached the age of twenty-one.

Mary was buried at Bethel Chapel. She joined her parents, her sister Louisa and her only child Effie in the family grave, indication perhaps of their closeness in life. Both sisters died women of assets as their father had wished. Joseph ensured the financial security of his family by giving away most of his winnings and setting up a trust, but Alfred's wealth and status was to eclipse them all.

19

A VICTORIAN GENTLEMAN

Alfred's marriage to Louisa Lee was the start of a solid and successful career in the wool trade which lasted over fifty years[1] and ended with him running his father-in-law's business.[2] Wool had continued to be the most important industry in Bradford, and the Wool Exchange, built in 1867, symbolised the wealth and importance that the city had gained as a result. The three-storey building with its impressive clock tower and rose windows still sits cathedral-like in the centre of the city. Portrait medallions decorate its exterior and commemorate the great inventors and entrepreneurs of the Industrial Revolution, including Titus Salt, James Watt and Richard Arkwright. Inside is a main hall with a hammer-beam roof with wrought-iron decoration.[3] Today it is home to a bookshop and café, but its original features survive and it's easy to imagine the scene during its Victorian heyday.

The trading floor in the centre of the hall was the hub of the Bradford wool industry. Here merchants came to buy and sell, trading verbally on price, quantity and delivery date. Only members were allowed on the floor and membership could only be awarded by the Wool Exchange's committee. To be in possession of a membership ticket was a mark not only of success but of huge status within the Bradford wool-trading community. Alfred was 'one of the older members of the Bradford Exchange' and part of this elite group.[4] Less privileged wool traders had to trade off-floor, restricted to the walk around the edge of the room, which was separated from the main hall by a colonnade of pillars. From here traders hoped to catch the eye of a member and begin the process of making a deal.

Alfred's fortunes altered dramatically in 1897 when Louisa died at the age of only forty-one, leaving her sons Brinley, ten, and Colin, four, to be brought up by their father. Perhaps Alfred found it difficult to cope with the challenges of earning money, running a household and raising two young sons alone, because soon after Louisa's death he moved his family into the home of her sister, Emily. Emily was married to Thomas Hayes, a grocer who had his own business and a comfortable home in Little Horton Lane where Emily was helped in the running of the house by her cook Edith Elliot and a servant named Nellie Appleby.[5] The couple had no children of their own and doted on their young nephews. It's likely that this relationship was a factor in Alfred's decision to move in with the Hayes so that his boys would get maternal love and affection from their aunt Emily. After all, he could have afforded nannies and servants to help him if he'd wanted. Perhaps Emily insisted, seeing her brother-in-law destroyed by grief and unable to cope.

This unusual family, together with their servants, eventually moved together out of Bradford and into a new home. Nab Lane climbs up a hill in Shipley, a leafy, more rural area outside the city where the air would have been fresher and the company more gentile. Just down the valley was Salt's Mill, the centre of Titus Salt's industrial empire, employing thousands while its model village of Saltaire housed them and provided healthcare, recreation and education. No. 5 Nab Lane was upwind of the mill and the noise and pollution that even a model factory could produce. It was a substantial house set in its own grounds in a wide and leafy road of equally large houses. These were the homes of the wealthy, men who had made their money in the textile trade and chose to live beyond the smoke and stink of their own factories. Unusually, though, 5 Nab Lane was owned by a woman. Emily Hayes held the deeds to it, not her husband.[6] Her father had died in January 1902 without a will, and so it was through probate that his entire estate, with a value of £5,565 (around £550,000 today), had been awarded to Emily's brother Fred; it seems likely that Fred gave funds to his sister at around this time to buy the house in Shipley.[7]

In November 1915, eighteen years after the death of his wife and at the age of sixty-one, Alfred decided to marry again.[8] The woman that he chose was Lucy Adeline Burgess, a thirty-one-year-old spinster only four years older than his son Brinley.[9] Unlike his first wife, Lucy was a working-class girl whose brothers were stuff warehousemen, office boys and steeplejacks. William, the closest to her in age, was a grocery assistant and perhaps that is how Alfred and Lucy met.[10] Alfred was still living with his brother-in-law Thomas Hayes, who owned his own grocery business in Bradford. Might William Burgess have been employed there, and that's how Alfred came to know his sister? Or perhaps Lucy's brother Edward, who was a stuff warehouseman, had been employed by Alfred at W. B. Lee & Co.? Britain was at war. Social conventions were changing, as was the role of women, and class barriers were breaking down. Alfred and Lucy may have been thrown together in circumstances under which they would not normally have met. She was certainly an interesting choice for a man who had cultivated all of the prerequisites to be a Victorian gentleman.

Alfred moved his new wife into the Hayes family home at 5 Nab Lane. Marrying a rich and successful businessman was change enough for Lucy, but moving into the rather grand house of his first wife's sister must have been daunting. Emily had been caring for Alfred, Brinley and Colin for nearly twenty years and may well have felt concern about this new woman in their lives. She may even have been jealous. However, everything suggests that Lucy's arrival was accommodated. The family continued to live together in Shipley and Emily and Thomas remained close to their nephews until her death in December 1923.

It wasn't until 1920 that Alfred bought Lucy a home of her own.[11] Alfred was now sixty-six years old, with a young wife and sons who were running the family business, and so perhaps he felt a desire to start the next phase of his life in a new place. He chose to move back into town to a relatively newly built house, 1 Laisterbridge Lane in Listerhills, part of the affluent Bradford suburb of Manningham, not far from Little Horton, where he had grown up.[12] Laisterbridge Lane is rather shabby now, but its semi-detached villas each have an imposing entrance with steps rising to an elaborately carved wooden porch and veranda. Some are painted today, suggesting how impressive they would have looked when Alfred and Lucy lived there. There are attic bedrooms and basement areas for servants, an essential part of the domestic world of these members of Bradford's middle class.

Bradford was still primarily a working-class town, with its wealthy industrialists living on its outskirts, but it was also home to a large and prosperous middle class populated by men like Alfred Jagger and a rapidly expanding group of professionals such as doctors, solicitors, teachers, accountants and engineers. Manningham, with its leafy streets and substantial villas, had always been attractive to those trying to escape the industrial centre.[13] Joseph Hobson Jagger had moved his family out to Manningham before his bankruptcy and Alfred had spent his early years there. Now, in later life, Alfred had chosen to move back to the area, probably for convenience because the house in Laisterbridge Lane was near to where his siblings lived and also to the places where he could indulge his personal interests. He was actively involved in civic life, and living closer to the centre would have facilitated this.

Alfred was a founder member of the Bradford Bowling Green Club and of the Bradford Chess Club in addition to being one of the oldest members of the Bradford Musical Union, but it was Freemasonry that occupied most of Alfred's leisure time now.[14] He joined the Prince of Wales Lodge in Bradford in September 1908 and remained a member for the rest of his life. Alfred achieved Master Mason status in March 1909 and then became Master of the Lodge in 1920, as well as serving as an officer in the Provincial Grand Lodge of West Yorkshire.[15] His role as Deacon in the Grand Lodge would have put Alfred at the very centre of ceremonial life. His job was to escort visitors and candidates and to act as messenger between the Master and the other officials. Having achieved senior office in his provincial lodge, Alfred was raised to some of the highest levels in several other orders of Freemasonry. He became a Mark Mason, a Knight's Templar and a Royal Arch Mason. He was a founder member of the Pudsey Lodge of Mark Master Masons, which was established in September 1915, and held senior positions at local and national level, including Overseer at the Mark Provincial Grand Lodge of West Yorkshire and Deacon of the Grand Lodge of Mark Master masons of England and Wales.[16]

Despite their thirty-year age gap, Alfred and Lucy lived together for nearly thirty years before he died in Laisterbridge Lane on 17 April 1941 at the age of eighty-seven. Mindful of his great age, Alfred wrote an obituary for himself just a few years before his death and it gives an insight into his personality and attitude to life. Alfred describes in it the achievements of which he was most proud:

> … was resident in Bradford for over 70 years. He was engaged with the wool trade for more than half a century and was one of the older members of the Bradford Exchange. He … took a keen interest in political, municipal and religious affairs, but was not attached to any party or politician/church! He was a staunch Free Mason … he filled the highest offices of several

other Degrees and Orders of Free Masonry, and contributed 'his bit' to the Masonic Charities and other good causes.[17]

This beautifully handwritten document, drafted by a man facing death, speaks clearly of Alfred's character. It shows no pride in his financial achievements, but huge satisfaction in the role he played in public life. Like his father, Alfred did not choose to live a life of conspicuous consumption in a grand house in the country but chose the comfortable home of his sister-in-law and then a house close to family and the area he knew from his childhood. He carried this simple and straightforward attitude to life through to his preparations for death, first in his will:

(in the interests of sanitary science) ... my corpse shall be cremated in the Crematorium at Scholemoor Cemetery Bradford ... and the ashes thereof scattered to the winds ... that there shall be no flowers and no mourning at my funeral and that everything in connection therewith shall be of the plainest character and done in the quietest possible manner.[18]

... and then in the death notice which he also drafted for himself:

on (insert date here), at No 1 Laisterbridge Lane, Bradford, Alfred the (query) husband [query then crossed through and replaced with 'dear'] of Lucy Adeline Jagger in his 88th year. Funeral service on Tuesday [crossed through and replaced with Saturday] next at 11.30am, in the Crematorium at Scholemoor Cemetery, prior to cremation. Relatives and Friends will please accept this, the only notification. No mourning and no flowers, by special request.[19]

Alfred leaves nothing to chance with Lucy. At first he allows her a space to decide how she would like to describe him and then changes his mind and takes the decision for her, adding 'dear husband' himself. Without fear or discomfort, Alfred also adds his best guess at the age at which he will die. Perhaps he was ill and knew that his death was coming and set about his preparations in an organised and efficient way. Alfred was pragmatic and unsentimental to the last. The draft obituary appeared only slightly abridged in the *Yorkshire Evening Post* on Friday 18 April 1941. Alfred was described as Lucy's dear husband.

Alfred was a millionaire in today's terms when he died, with a net estate worth £37,704 14s 1d, which equates to £1,715,000 today. Lucy was fifty-eight years old when she was widowed but was left well provided for, with an immediate payment of £200 (£9,000 today) and the rental income from the properties that Alfred owned at his death, which was to be paid into a Midland Bank account from which Lucy could draw interest and live comfortably for the rest of her life. The property portfolio and investments were to be managed by her stepsons Brinley and Colin. Lucy was also left all of the

> furniture, pictures, prints, books, linen, glass, china plate and other household chattels and effects and personal belongings whatsoever ... except the electric fittings gas fittings gas oven and gas boiler which I declare shall form part of my dwelling house Number 1 Laisterbridge Lane, Bradford.[20]

Brinley and Colin were left personal possessions which had significance to their father and their wider family and which illustrate vividly the wealth and status that Alfred had achieved. To Brinley, Alfred left 'my diamond scarf ring (which I have worn daily for over fifty years) and the gold watch bearing the initials "W.B.L" in monogram on the back of the case'. The W. B. L referred to is William B. Lee, Louisa's father, who gave the watch to his son-in-law Alfred, the man who had had invested in and helped to run the family business.[21] To Colin was left 'my gold sovereign case and its contents (four half sovereigns) my gold snuff box, my Maximillano Emperador (1866) mounted gold coin a spade guinea my gold rings my gold and silver watch guard my gold shirt studs and gold dress front studs and any other articles of jewellery worth possessing'. Alfred also returned his much-treasured Freemason clothing and regalia to the lodges to which they were linked to be used as his brother masons wished.

Alfred died a richer man that his bank-breaking father. He had inherited not only money from him but a chance to make something of himself, and an example that with hard work and ingenuity anything was possible. He didn't forget this, bequeathing £200 (£9,000 today) on trust to Bethel Chapel in Shelf, where his parents are buried, requesting the trustees to spend it as they think fit but 'I specially request such Trustees to maintain and preserve in a decent state of cleanliness and repair the grave in the grounds of such Chapel wherein rest the mortal remains of my Father and my Mother'.

There isn't a known photograph of Alfred in the family, but I imagine him to have been the most like his father of all of Joseph's children. He was a shrewd businessman, and used the advantages of a good marriage and the money that he inherited from his father to build a successful career and become a pillar of the Bradford establishment. For me, Alfred epitomises the promise of Victorian Bradford and the Industrial Revolution. Through hard work and good business sense he rose from the working classes to become a member of the new middle class, with a lifestyle befitting a gentleman.

There is evidence in Alfred's life of a level of wealth and social success that differed greatly from that of his sisters, proof perhaps then that Joseph did give his sons an enormous financial gift. But why would he give the equivalent of nearly £1 million each to Alfred and Walter and not to his daughters Louisa and Mary? What would have prompted him to give nearly a quarter of his total win to his sons during his lifetime and not do the same for his daughters? Well, I don't think that he did – or rather, he did give the money to Alfred, but not to Walter.

20

THE CLERKS

At the age of fifty-five, Walter was still employed full-time as an overlooker and his eldest sons had joined him to work in the mills; Arthur as a stuff warehouseman and Arnold as an invoice clerk.[1] Walter had neither been able to work for himself nor retire. When he and his siblings rearranged their father's trust fund in 1913, Walter received the Greaves Street houses, which represented the portfolio of property that was the smallest in value. However, in return he took the greatest payment from Alfred, the equivalent of £35,000 today, suggesting that a cash payment was worth more to Walter at that point than the promise of future rental income or property sales. He didn't choose to move in to any of his father's properties; instead he moved his family to 50 Marsh Street in the early 1920s, presumably purchasing the house with some of the money from his brother. Julia, his wife, died there in 1928 and his unmarried daughter Doris Vera moved in shortly afterwards to help him. Walter remained in the house with Doris for the rest of his life.

When he died in 1934, Walter left an estate with a net value of £261 18s 3d (worth approximately £17,000 today),[2] which he instructed to be converted into cash and divided equally between his children Emily, Arthur, Arnold, Edith and Doris. To Doris he also left 'the house situated at 50 Marsh Street … and all its contents'. The houses in Greaves Street that Walter inherited from his father, the first properties that Joseph had bought with his Monte Carlo money, are not mentioned specifically in his will. Walter almost certainly owned No. 6 right up to his death, though.[3] He'd allowed his son Arnold to move there, perhaps as early as 1913, when he took ownership of the property.

Arnold had married in 1912 and so it would have been of great help to the young couple, particularly as Arnold was away fighting for the entire course of the First World War. He joined up in 1914 and was a gunner with the Royal Garrison Artillery and Royal Engineers and was awarded not only a Long Service Medal but also a Distinguished Conduct Medal.[4] Certainly by the time that Arnold was discharged from the army in 1920 he and Annie had established 6 Greaves Street as their home, raising their children there and staying at least until her death in 1950.[5] Arnold may even have stayed until he remarried in 1962.

Presumably the ownership was transferred to Arnold at some point during this period, but there is a story that the house had to be sold because of financial difficulties. David Jagger, Arnold and Annie's son, grew up at 6 Greaves Street and remembers that his father rented it after either he or Walter had been forced to sell it. I feel certain that it was Arnold that faced this predicament. David remembers the house as being very much in need of modernisation, still lit by gas light and with no hot water supply. It seems that Arnold was reduced to renting a rather run-down property which he couldn't afford to renovate, despite his grandfather having once been a millionaire. No. 6 Greaves Street, the house bought with Monte Carlo winnings and which offered a home to the Jagger family for at least seventy years, deteriorated slowly and was eventually demolished.

Walter's life is not that of a man who had been given nearly £1 million by his father. So why was Alfred singled out among all of his siblings? His obvious business talents and lucky marriage do go a long way towards explaining his financial and social success, but the gift from his father certainly helped him along that path.

I have discovered the reason. There was a part of Alfred's life that he did not refer to in the list of his achievements that he left in his draft obituary, a series of events that would have surprised his fellow businessmen and his brother masons. It's a story that was left to his widow Lucy to tell many years after his death, and it's a story that has changed my whole understanding of what happened in Monte Carlo.

All of the accounts of what happened in the casino are clear that Joseph Hobson Jagger did not act alone. His theory – that wheels cannot spin true – required time to prove. He had to watch and record the numbers that the balls fell on to in several wheels until a bias was revealed, and he needed help to do this. The story goes that he employed clerks to record the numbers; Bethell said there were six clerks assisting him, and Derek and David Jagger always believed that Joseph Hobson Jagger went with his foreman. Employing clerks has always seemed a risky approach to me. They could so easily betray Joseph to the casino authorities, particularly after its security team were watching his every move to try to understand how he was winning. A betrayal at this point could have been very lucrative to the clerks if they'd offered the information to the casino in return for payment. Or what if they simply decided to play for themselves, using Joseph's own theory against him? How could he protest to the authorities?

An account written in the 1970s by a man who beat the casino in Nice by gambling with a team supports this concern that working with others is risky. Norman Leigh advertised for players to join him and at first found nobody he could trust among those who applied. He recognised that for a team approach to work he had to find people who were prepared to put in a lot of time to practise, people who had the stamina to play for long periods of time and the sort of personality that couldn't be distracted. And, of course, they had to be reliable.[6] Surely the cautious, meticulous Joseph would not have risked everything in this way. He must have known that his plan could only work if he took into his confidence men whom he trusted implicitly. Lucy's letters reveal that this is exactly what he did. The calculated risk-taker Joseph Hobson Jagger left nothing to chance when it came to his ingenious plan. Instead, he did the obvious thing: he relied on his family. The clerks were not employees or colleagues but his own sons.

Lucy was married to Alfred, so there seems no reason to doubt the veracity of her claim that he helped his father to break the bank at Monte Carlo. It is clear, too, I think, that the gift of £10,000 that Alfred received from his father and which he used to invest in business was given as thanks for his help in the casino. Alfred's role was common knowledge in his branch of the family, and Mollie Firth knew too, but why didn't he mention this incredible and unusual event in the obituary that he drafted for himself? Perhaps winning at roulette and using this money to buy into a business did not fit Alfred's image of himself as he had become in older life – a respectable and successful Victorian businessman.

Lucy's account does raise one point that seems incongruous. Walter was the grandfather of Derek and David Jagger, who have spent most of their adult lives researching the story of Joseph's win in Monte Carlo. If Walter had been to the casino with his father and brother then I find it hard to believe that his grandsons would not have heard about it. They have also always believed, based on their own financially tough childhood, that 'Alfred and his family benefitted, while Walter did not'.[7] Of course, it's possible that Walter never spoke of it in the same way that Joseph and Alfred seldom did. If Lucy's account is accurate, and Walter did go to Monte Carlo, then what happened to the £10,000 that he would have been given for his help in the casino by his grateful father? And why was the story of his part in the adventure not handed down in his branch of the family line as Alfred's role in the casino had been in his?

It is possible that the sale of 6 Greaves Street holds a clue. The family story has it that the sale was necessary in order to generate some money. It is also possible that Walter lost his £10,000 somehow or invested it unwisely but chose never to refer to it. This seems unlikely, however, as it appears to be his son Arnold who experienced the financial difficulties surrounding the property at Greaves Street. Walter Jagger was no fool. He was an overlooker, a job that required education and which entailed management and professional skills and came with a high degree of responsibly. His will shows a comfortably-off man who owned his own property. Mollie Firth, his granddaughter, knew him well and is categorical that Walter did not go with his father and his brother to Monte Carlo.[8]

The answer to this mystery, I feel sure, is that Alfred Jagger's widow Lucy, whose account of events in Monte Carlo was related to her by her husband at least twenty years before she recorded it in her letters, may have got the identity of the second 'clerk' wrong.[9] The wording of her account doesn't say that Joseph was assisted by Alfred and Walter; it says that he was accompanied by 'Alfred and his brother'. In her version of the story that her husband had told her, Lucy assumed that the second clerk was Alfred's brother. Perhaps the truth is that he was, in fact, another member of the family, close enough to be thought of as a son by Joseph Hobson Jagger and trusted so much that he asked for his help.

21

THE SECOND 'SON'

In all of the official documents relating to Joseph's life, one name that recurs often is that of his nephew Oates Jagger, the train driver. Oates was made a trustee of Joseph's will and consequently an executor of the numerous property transactions and investments that followed. Curiously, though, Oates is described on these documents as a gentleman, a status that seems incongruous with his background.[1] He was the son of an illiterate mother, started work as an eleven-year-old child in the mills of Bradford and went on to drive trains for a living. However, I discovered that his later life was rather extraordinary.

Oates was retired from work by the age of fifty-one, and he lived the rest of his life as a gentleman of means.[2] After his uncle Joseph Hobson Jagger returned from Monte Carlo a very wealthy man, Oates' financial position changed dramatically. When Joseph started to buy properties, Oates bought property too. He made purchases in Harewood Street, one of the houses becoming his family home for the rest of his life. He also invested in a property in Heath Street in 1899. When Oates Jagger died on 20 January 1910 at his house, 483 Harewood Street in Bradford, the gross value of his estate was £1,622, which equates to approximately £150,000 today, and nearly as much as his uncle Joseph had left.[3] Train drivers were not particularly well paid; the average wage was approximately 8 shillings a day, which equates to an annual wage of about £10,000 today, surely not enough to buy property and retire early to the leisurely life of a gentleman.[4] Most significantly, Oates became rich before his uncle died, and he was not a beneficiary of Joseph's will. If his money was not inherited from his uncle, then where had it come from?

Oates was a trustee and executor, and so perhaps his uncle gave him a financial gift, as he did other members of the family. Joseph had asked another nephew, Sidney Sowood, to lend him money when he wrote him the poem prior to his great adventure, and the two men clearly had a close and trusted relationship because Joseph made Sidney a trustee of his estate too. Joseph would of course have paid Sidney back, perhaps with interest, for his generosity at a desperate time. After his uncle's return to Bradford, Sidney had enough money to follow Joseph's example and buy property in Spicer Street in Little Horton.[5] The money to make these purchases must surely have come from Joseph, or it's possible that Joseph gave his nephew one of his own Spicer Street properties as a gift. It would not be unreasonable, then, to imagine that Oates benefitted in this way too, especially since he almost certainly helped his uncle plan his train route to Monte Carlo.

These financial gifts given before Joseph died were not of a life changing amount, however. We only have to look at Joseph and Matilda's own children to see this. Alfred was the exception because he had gone with his father to Monte Carlo, but the others continued to work for the rest of their lives. Sidney did too, despite his investment in property, and so this may not be an explanation for Oates' change of status. Nor did Oates inherit from his aunt Matilda. As a trustee and executor he must have been an enormous help to her in her widowhood, and as he outlived her by eight years he might have expected to be left money, but Matilda died with no real assets so it's extremely unlikely there was an inheritance from her. How could Oates Jagger, a train driver, have access to enough money to invest in property and retire early, and all before his bank-breaking millionaire uncle died?

The answer is obvious. I think that Oates Jagger is the other 'son' identified by Lucy as going with Joseph and Alfred to Monte Carlo. I think that he was one of the 'clerks' who helped Joseph to win by recording numbers and looking for sequences. Perhaps Oates and Alfred were involved in the formulation of the Monte Carlo plan itself. Both had experience of the wool trade, of spinning and the vagaries of the wheel. Perhaps they were sounding boards for Joseph's theory that an uneven spin could lead to riches in the casino. As a mark of gratitude, it was Oates and not Walter who was the recipient of the second £10,000 gift, the equivalent today of a staggering, life-changing sum close to £1 million.

Joseph was winning in Monte Carlo in 1881, and fortunately this was a census year. On the night that the census was taken, 3/4 April, both 'clerks' were at home, Alfred in Bradford and Oates in Keighley; Joseph was not. However, this does not rule them out of events. Monte Carlo was primarily a winter resort, December to April being the key months for gambling on the Riviera.[6] Joseph, Oates and Alfred could have been together in Monte Carlo during the first few months of 1881 (and November and December of the year before) watching the spin of the wheel, noting down the numbers and finally beginning to win. At this point, perhaps the younger men returned to Yorkshire, leaving Joseph behind in Monte Carlo. This is entirely consistent with the idea that Joseph stayed in Monte Carlo for protracted periods of time, and perhaps came and went over a period of years.

Oates' role does beg some key questions, however. If he was so integral to the story of Joseph's win in Monte Carlo, then why has neither David Jagger, Derek Jagger nor Mollie Firth heard of him? Derek had raised the question of who this wealthy man was in the notes that he left before he died:

> Because he had the surname Jagger it is likely he was a son of one of Joseph's brothers, or was he related in another way, possibly as a nephew. Obviously, he was a man of means, but from where did his inheritance come ...?[7]

Oates was my dad's great-uncle, and yet neither he nor I were aware of that or had ever heard of him. He was never mentioned in our family's version of the story. In truth, he has never been mentioned by anyone. Although his name crops up often in family archives, nobody has really thought to investigate Oates or just how integral he is to the Monte Carlo story. Perhaps Lucy Jagger, his sister and my great-grandmother hardly knew him. These were large families. Richard and Joseph were two of ten siblings and Richard had nineteen children to look after including Oates and Lucy. Despite all growing up in Bradford, it is possible that some of them didn't ever meet or at least hardly knew each other. Oates left home when he was young, and maybe he felt to Lucy and the others more like Joseph's son than Richard's.

More difficult to understand is why Lucy was left destitute only a few years after events in Monte Carlo. Her husband, James Milner, died of tuberculosis in 1889 at the age of only thirty-five, leaving Lucy alone with four children to support. Times were very hard for her, and she had to take in washing to survive.[8] Why didn't her wealthy brother Oates or her millionaire uncle Joseph help? When Lucy told the story of being given £5 from the Monte Carlo winnings she didn't say it was from her uncle, or from Joseph, she said it was from 'T'Monte Carlo man', which suggests distance, perhaps a relative whom she had never met before or hardly knew. Or perhaps those in the family who passed the story down gradually lost the name of the man who she referred to as

'T'Monte Carlo man' and assumed him to be Joseph. Maybe it was in fact Oates, the brother who'd become a gentleman, giving money to his widowed younger sister to help her and her children in very difficult times.

The Monte Carlo money proved to be divisive within a generation, perhaps not emotionally but socially. Whereas Joseph slotted unobtrusively back into his old life, both Alfred and Oates experienced a change in status with their newly acquired wealth. Alfred in particular chose to spend his time in a very different society to the rest of his siblings, and although he didn't live far away from them, contact was not as regular as it might have been before the win. Mollie Firth grew up knowing her grandfather Walter. They had Christmas lunch together every year after his wife died. But she only met Alfred, her great-uncle, once or twice despite his home being only a street away from hers. She recalls that he moved in much grander circles than she did. She didn't know his sons either. A friend once pointed Colin Jagger out to her at the symphony, but she never met him.[9]

It was perhaps the same with Oates. With a substantial home in a smarter area of Bradford, and living in well-funded retirement, it's quite possible that he didn't spend regular time with his siblings, perhaps not seeing them for long periods from one year to the next, perhaps until they were in extremis. When my grandmother died in 1967 my dad sold her house for £600 (approximately £10,000 in today's values); not unusual, I suppose, unless you know the level of poverty that my father grew up in.[10] It was a surprise to my mother to discover that Norah and Harry had owned their house at all. They had bought it after the death of Norah's mother, Lucy, she who had been left in dire need after the death of her husband. Lucy, whose brother was Oates Jagger. Is it possible that Oates gave her more than the £5 of family tradition? Did he give her the money to buy a house for her family and to pass on the investment to her daughter? If so, then she never talked of it. We may never know.

My father, Clifford Malcolm Fletcher, 1951. (Author's collection)

The photograph that Joseph Hobson Jagger sat for in Nice. (Author's collection)

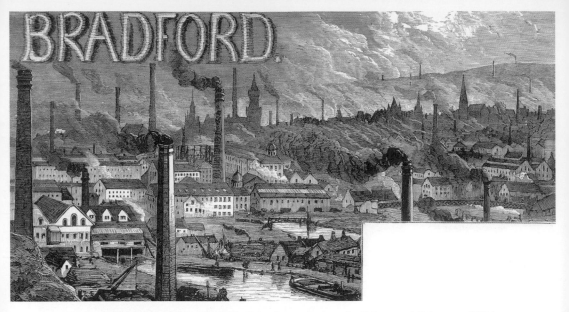

View of the industrial factories of Bradford in the week that the Prince and Princess of Wales (later Edward VII and Queen Alexandra) visited the town in 1882. This image was captioned 'the town is not supposed to be on fire'. (© Illustrated London News Ltd/Mary Evans)

Above: Ash Tree Farm, where Joseph's grandfather John Jagger was born in 1755. (© Anne Fletcher)

Left: St John the Baptist in Shelf, the church where many Jaggers were baptised, married and buried. (© Anne Fletcher)

Child labour at a wool mill. A girl spinning wool at Foster's mill, Bradford, 1902. (© Mary Evans Picture Library)

Wool sorters at work in a Bradford mill. My great-uncle Arthur Milner is on the extreme right. Like many wool sorters he contracted anthrax, but he recovered and lived until he was eighty-five. (Author's collection)

Workers in a Burnley cotton mill tend their looms c. 1904. (Courtesy of Lancashire County Council's Red Rose Collections)

The croupiers of the old Monegasque gambling tables watching for the arrival of players from a contemporary drawing. (From *Guide du Joueur* by Charles Limonsin, 1899)

Players in the Bad Homburg casino operated by the Blanc brothers.

The sea-facing facade of the casino as it appeared up to 1878, when Charles Garnier began the extension of the building. The section to the far right is the exterior of the *Salle Mauresque*.

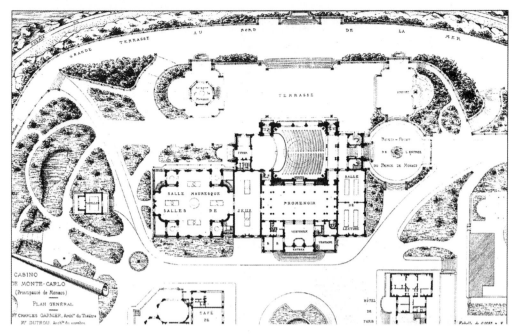

A general plan of the Monte Carlo casino, 1879, produced by the architect Charles Garnier.

The terraces at the casino showing a steamship departing after its passengers have disembarked *c.* 1920s. (© Mary Evans/Grenville Collins Postcard Collection)

My father with his parents and brother on a family holiday in Morecambe, 1935. Like many working-class holidaymakers of the time, they stayed in a boarding house where my grandmother did all of the cooking for her family and which only admitted them at certain times of day. They were forced to spend the rest of the time outside, even when it was raining. (Author's collection)

Conditions in the debtors' prison were tolerable for those with money or friends and family to support them. 'No. 4' engraving from 'Lancashire Insolvent Court' sketches of the debtors' prison at Lancaster Castle by a 'Briefless Barrister'. Designed and drawn on stone by E. Slack, 1836. (Courtesy of Lancashire County Council's Red Rose Collections)

Workers waiting for breakfast in Mr Chapman's courtyard in Mottram near Manchester during the Lancashire cotton famine, 1862. (© Illustrated London News Ltd/Mary Evans)

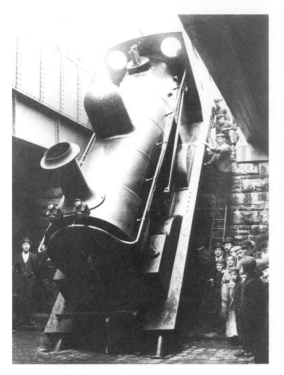

Above left: A train accident at Lonsdale Street Railway Bridge in Accrington, Lancashire, September 1899. A goods train hit the buffers and came down into the street between two sections of the bridge. The stoker jumped but the driver stayed with his engine and escaped uninjured. (Courtesy of Lancashire County Council's Red Rose Collections)

Above right: A souvenir postcard from Monte Carlo: 'I must focus or I will die!' The perils of playing on the roulette wheel at the Monte Carlo Casino, Monaco. (© Mary Evans/Grenville Collins Postcard Collection)

Below: The *Hôtel de Paris*. (© Anne Fletcher)

ROULETTE DE MONTE-CARLO

Manière de Miser sur le Tableau

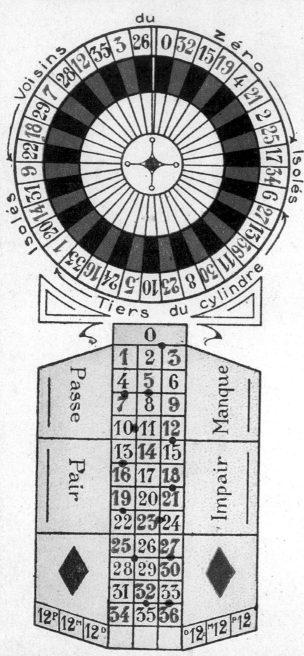

Edition C.A.BY, boulevard Carnot, 4 — Nice. *Déposé Reproduction interdite*

Pour le Tiers du Cylindre ●

Jeu indiqué par un point Rouge ●

Minimum 30 fr. Maximum 2160 fr.

Il faut 6 pièces

A Cheval 17 fois la mise

Pour les Voisins du Zéro ●

Jeu indiqué par un point Noire ●

Minimum 35 fr. Maximum 2520 fr.

Il faut 7 pièces

Transversale pleine	0—2—3	11 fois la mise
Carré	25—26—28—29	8 » »
A Cheval	....	17 » »

Instructions for a roulette game at Monte Carlo. (© Mary Evans Picture Library)

The key given to Joseph Hobson Jagger by his friends and admirers after he broke the bank. Proof of his great achievement. (© Anne Fletcher)

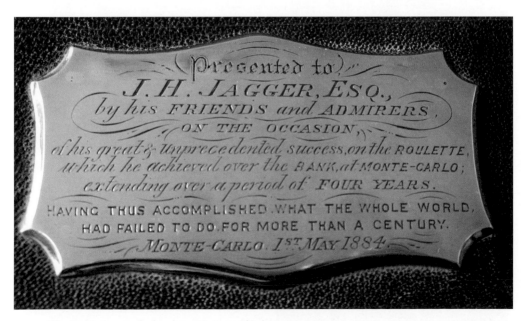

The inscription on the key box. (© Anne Fletcher)

Top: The facade of the casino facing the sea, the first view of the building for most Victorian travellers. (© Anne Fletcher)

Above: The facade of the casino from the *Place du Casino* and the entrance for those wishing to play. (© Anne Fletcher)

Left: Winter visitors to the casino strolling on its terraces.

Right: The entrance hall of the casino today, where Joseph would have collected his *carte du jour*. (© Anne Fletcher)

Below: The casino atrium today. The original casino was contained within this atrium. (© Anne Fletcher)

Bottom: Gamblers and visitors enjoying the *Salle Mauresque*. From an albumen print *c*. 1880. (Author's collection)

A souvenir postcard of the *Salle Mauresque*, the room where Joseph broke the bank. (Author's collection)

Left: Some of the houses in Spicer Street, Little Horton, Bradford, that Joseph purchased on his return from Monte Carlo. (© Anne Fletcher)

Below: 25 Greaves Street, Little Horton, the home that Joseph Hobson Jagger purchased with his Monte Carlo winnings and where he died. (© Anne Fletcher)

Above: Bethel Chapel, Shelf, where Joseph Hobson Jagger is buried. (© Anne Fletcher)

Below left: Joseph Hobson Jagger's grave at Bethel Chapel in Shelf, which he shares with his wife, two daughters and granddaughter Effie. (© Anne Fletcher)

Below right: The Wool Exchange in Bradford. Now a bookshop but once the focus of the wool trade where merchants like Alfred Jagger did business. (© Anne Fletcher)

The house in Shipley, 5 Nab Lane, that Alfred Jagger and his sons moved into following the death of his first wife. (© Anne Fletcher)

Port Elizabeth, South Africa. One of the ports that Brinley Jagger used when he travelled to the country to trade in wool for the family business. (Author's collection)

Above and below: Photocopies of the photographs that were kept with the key, showing Brinley and Sybil Jagger and other family members. (Author's collection)

An image of the house that I was told Joseph Hobson Jagger bought with his winnings, and the photo that revealed it to be Monk Barn, Brinley and Sybil's house. (Author's collection and © Anne Fletcher)

Above left: Lucy Milner, Joseph's niece and my great-grandmother, outside 12 Bottomley Street in Buttershaw, Bradford. Two generations of my family were born in the bedroom there, including my father. (Author's collection)

Above right: My father, his parents and his brother Sydney outside 2 Albion Street, Buttershaw, Bradford. (Author's collection)

22

TWO VERY RICH YOUNG MEN

Joseph's winnings are clearly traceable. He gave approximately one-third to Alfred and Oates in gratitude for their support before giving gifts to family and friends and investing in at least thirty-two properties. It is possible that he lost a sum to fraud as Mollie remembers, but I believe that he used most of his money to secure the financial future of his immediate family. Joseph invested the majority of his fortune to improve the lives of others.

The mystery of what happened to the money has grown over the years due to the modest circumstances of the family since Joseph's win. Generations of Jaggers and their Fletcher and Milner in-laws have lived inconspicuously, and in some instances in a fair degree of poverty. It does not look like a family that once had a member who broke the bank at Monte Carlo. In claims that nobody knew what happened to the money, that there was no will, previous accounts of Joseph's story have dangled a tantalising lure. They have implied that Joseph Hobson Jagger's fortune lies somewhere unclaimed, waiting to be discovered. This is not the case. However, although there are no lost millions to be found, there are lost millionaires, family members in distant branches of the family tree that many of us did not know.

This story says a great deal about how money can change the dynamic of a family, how divisive it can be. Over succeeding generations, the branches of Joseph's family began to grow away from each other, the more prosperous thriving in a different direction and losing contact with those whose lives seemed to return to how they might have been before had he never won at all. The roots of the prosperity lie with Alfred Jagger.

Alfred inherited the largest share of the Monte Carlo money and his investment of a lump sum of it into his father-in-law's firm, W. B. Lee & Co., transformed his life and that of his children. His sons, Brinley and Colin, were born into the privileged world created by the hard work and sound investments of their millionaire wool merchant father. They both worked in the family business, and it is through them that the final legacy of Joseph's win can be traced.

The company of W. B. Lee & Co., founded by their maternal grandfather, had begun as a general engineering company working for the textile industry and had quickly diversified into production and wool sales.[1] It was described in the early twentieth century as a 'wool, tops and noil merchant', and both Colin and Brinley described themselves as wool merchants.[2] 'Top' refers to the finest-quality, or 'top'-of-the-line, wool fibre. It is produced by combing and carding the wool to separate the long fibres from the shorter ones, called noils, and to ensure that all the fibres run parallel to each other. Worsted yarn is spun from these combed tops and so this fine-quality wool was essential to Bradford's worsted industry. When William B. Lee died in 1902, ownership of the company passed to his son Fred Lee, although it's likely that he and his brother-in-law Alfred Jagger had been running the company for some time as William was seventy-one or seventy-two at the time of his death.[3]

Fred had lived an unusual life for the son and heir of a textile magnate. He'd formed a relationship with Mary Mogen, the daughter of Reuben Mogen, a sergeant major who appears to have abandoned her and her mother when she was a child.[4] By the time they were in their early thirties, Fred and Mary were living together in his house in Eccleshill, a village to the north-east of Bradford. Although the census of 1891 says that they were man and wife, this was not the case. They did not marry until 1910, when they were both in their fifties,[5] and Mary was only to live for three years as Mrs Fred Lee before her death.[6] For most of this time the story locally was that they were brother and sister.[7]

Why they did not marry earlier, and why their living arrangements were apparently so unorthodox, we can only wonder. Perhaps his family did not approve. Mary was from the working class and poor, and her five younger brothers, all born in Ireland, worked at the very lowest levels of the social scale as hackle pin grinders and drillers in an ironworks.[8] Having Irish, possibly Catholic, brothers may not at the time have commended Mary as a suitable member of the Lee family. It had only been one generation since the Lees worked in the mills, but now as textile magnates there must have been high expectations on Fred, as the only son, to marry appropriately for their new social status. It seems that he had little choice but to hide his relationship with Mary away from disapproving comment.

Despite their long relationship, Mary and Fred had no children of their own. Fred did have an illegitimate daughter, described in his will as Mrs Frank Webster, his 'reputed daughter', and although he was able to leave a good sum in trust for her and her children, Fred did not leave his estate to her. Instead, when he died in June 1915, after some bequests to staff which reveal a touching affection for both the family firm and its employees, he left the residue in three equal shares to his sister Emily and their nephews Brinley and Colin.[9] From that point on the Jagger brothers both owned and ran the Lee family firm, reaping the full benefits of their father's investment of his Monte Carlo money into the company a quarter of a century before.[10]

In the years immediately before the First World War, the majority of the wool used in the textile trade in England came from countries that formed part of the British Empire.[11] For Brinley this meant the opportunity to travel the world. Australia provided nearly half of wool imports, followed by New Zealand and then South Africa. The British colonies, particularly Natal and the Orange Free State, were the main source in South Africa, producing wool almost exclusively for export.[12] In 1910 a treaty linked the Cape, Natal, Transvaal and Orange Free State into the Union of South Africa and trade boomed. A free trade policy in the Union, excellent railway links and a rise in the price of wool all contributed, as did the state's support of white farmers concentrating on commercial production while squeezing black farmers out of the market.[13] Between the wars, South Africa had one of the most buoyant economies in the world.[14] In contrast to the other Empire wool exporters, South African wool was in such demand that it sold before it had even left the country. Producers didn't have to pay to export their wool to London and Antwerp in order for it to be bought by merchants there – foreign wool merchants came to them.[15] From 1903 until the outbreak of the First World War Brinley took regular trips to South Africa to buy wool, journeys that coincided with great changes in that part of the world and also in the wool industry in Bradford.

East London, in the Eastern Cape Province, had established itself as the business centre of wool trade in South Africa in the 1890s. Buying and selling took place within this province, and also in nearby Durban, where auctioneer companies such as Reid & Acutt sold wool to buyers in their own auction houses.[16] Brinley used the fastest means of travel available at the time and that was the Union Castle Line of steamships, which offered a regular express mail service to South Africa. Every Thursday, promptly at four o'clock in the afternoon, a Union Castle ship left Southampton bound for Cape Town and at precisely the same time, another left Cape Town for Southampton. The fleet was distinctive. Each vessel had a lavender grey hull and red funnels topped with black.[17] Ocean liners of the fleet took four days to reach Las Palmas or Madeira and then sailed non-stop across the ocean, reaching Cape Town two weeks after leaving Southampton. Those travelling further could expect to reach Port Elizabeth on day seventeen, East London the day after that and Durban on day nineteen of the voyage.

Brinley took his first voyage in 1903, returning from Natal on 28 November that year. He travelled cabin class on the *Walmer Castle*, sharing dining areas, cabins and decks with miners, servants, mechanics, joiners, blacksmiths and train drivers. Perhaps this first trip was to give him a greater understanding of where the raw materials for the family business came from. The ship's manifest describes his status as 'clerk', which suggests that the sixteen-year-old Brinley was just starting out at W. B. Lee & Co. and to some degree working his way up to learn his trade. Whatever the trip's purpose, it must have been an extraordinary adventure for such a young man, travelling alone to the colonies for the first time.[18]

Durban on the Bay of Natal had been established in 1824 by twenty-five British settlers from the Cape Colony. Eleven years later the residents agreed to found a town and named it after the Governor of the Cape Colony, Sir Benjamin d'Urban.[19] The settlers established a sugar cane industry in the 1860s but struggled to attract the local Zulu population to work on the plantations, and so the indenture of Indian labour was begun.[20] The first steam train in South Africa made its first official journey in 1860, and electric light was introduced in 1896 (Bradford had only had electric lighting for seven years at this point). The town had suffered from dangerous anchorage in its port, but successful dredging resolved the problem in 1904 and by the time that Brinley was a regular visitor Durban was easier to access and had many of the comforts of home. The Royal Hotel and Marine Hotel provided excellent lodgings. Lily Langtry, the mistress of King Edward VII, performed at the Theatre Royal in 1906, and three years later the Electric Theatre opened as Durban's first permanent cinema. Gentlemen could travel on good roads to the race course or to The Durban Club to play chess or billiards.

The years following union may have been full of opportunity for men like Brinley but they also saw the early seeds of what would eventually lead to Apartheid in South Africa. Since his arrival in the country as a young lawyer in 1893, Mohandas (later Mahatma) Gandhi had been campaigning for political and social rights for Indians living in South Africa. He had experienced the appalling treatment of the immigrant workforce first hand when he was thrown off a train for refusing to leave a first-class carriage. The African National Congress was founded in 1912 in response to the impending changes to land ownership that became law the following year in the Natives Land Act. This Act limited the amount of land that could be owned by black South Africans and forbade black farmers to work on land owned by whites. This was the first piece of segregationist legislation to be passed in South Africa, leading eventually to full Apartheid.[21] Brinley would surely have noticed the Indian men pulling the rickshaws around Durban and the black servants and staff in the hotels and restaurants. Just how much he was concerned by the treatment of the non-white population we cannot know, although surely he must have seen it.

During this time of political and social turmoil, Brinley was not only a regular visitor to the new Union of South Africa but also stayed there for periods of time. From 1910 to 1915 he sailed to South Africa every year, travelling out usually in the autumn and returning to England the following spring.[22] In 1912 he arrived back at Southampton just eleven days before the *Titanic* left on its first and final voyage from the same port. In 1914 he left Durban on the *Galway Castle* in April; on board were, among others, two De Beers sisters on their way to school in England. In July 1915 Brinley travelled back to Plymouth from Durban, almost certainly to deal with the affairs of his uncle Fred, who had died in June.[23] There were only seventy fellow passengers in first class while third class was full of troops, an indication of a world at war.

These later journeys were different. Brinley was now a man in his twenties and he enjoyed all of the luxury that first class could offer. Wealthy passengers on the Union Castle line had the best cabins, private dining rooms and saloons to relax in as well as their own deck area. They remained separate from second-class, third-class and cabin/steerage-class passengers for the length of their voyage. It's likely that Brinley chose to travel this way because he was taking on more responsibility in the company and because he was now, together with his brother, its heir. The ship manifests describe him as a wool merchant and no longer just a clerk. If South Africa had become a principal source of wool for the W. B. Lee & Co. business, then it was important in the pre-war years for Brinley to get a good price.

In the early years of the twentieth century Bradford was experiencing a slump, especially in its export trade as competition grew in Europe, and because of yet another change in fashion. Edwardian women had begun wearing their dresses hobbled instead of full-skirted. This style was characterised by a skirt that was more form-fitting, giving more freedom of movement than the cumbersome Victorian styles with their hoops and petticoats. This new skirt, however, was to reduce the profits of manufacturers by a considerable degree: 'Before this freak of fashion got hold, we used to sell seven or eight yards for every dress, but during the last year we couldn't sell more than four'.[24]

But the outbreak of war in 1914 created a temporary boom.[25] Wool was a vital commodity, used to make uniforms, and 1916 was the busiest year that the wool-textile industry in Britain ever experienced.[26] The Wool Control Board was based in the city, ensuring that a steady supply of raw material was available at a very competitive price. This resulted in Bradford producing khaki and greatcoat cloth in enormous quantities, not only for the British Army but also for its allies in France, Belgium, Italy, Portugal, Russia and the Dominions. Hainsworth & Sons, a textile manufacturer established in Yorkshire in 1783 which still produces uniform cloth, provides a flavour of wartime demand in their company history:

> With the outbreak of war in 1914 the two mills had to adapt quickly to meet this unfortunate demand. Historically the various public services, railway companies, tramways, Post Offices etc. had all had their own specialised uniform cloth, but under war time restrictions only seventeen types were allowed. There was a change of emphasis from smarter costly cloths to cheaper utilitarian Serges for battledress and narrow flannel for shirts and hospital use. During the war years the War Office ordered 66 million yards of greatcoat cloth, 17 million yards of whipcord and a massive 231 million yards of narrow flannel.

By 1917 the textile towns of West Yorkshire were producing 250,000 yards of khaki cloth a week, and many mills were reserving all of their machinery and workforce for the War Office orders of strong, heavy fabrics like serge and whipcord.[27] These were manufactured into military jackets, trousers and greatcoats and stored in Leeds, in a new Army Clothing Depot that was built in 1915 to keep up with demand for khaki. When King George V and Queen Mary made a three-day visit to Yorkshire in 1918, their itinerary included a visit to a mill in Bradford and the depot in Leeds to recognise the contribution that the Yorkshire textile industry had made to the war.

Because of the role that woollen fabric played in the war effort, the wool trade was made a reserve occupation. This meant that these professions were regarded as being so essential to the success of the war that those employed within them were discouraged, and in some cases forbidden, from signing up for active service. Neither Brinley nor Colin fought in the war, despite being only in their twenties. Many men were not so fortunate. During the course of the war Lister & Co. saw 145 of its 1,200 men killed, 172 wounded and thirty-six taken prisoner. Few mills would have been unaffected.[28] Many joined the Bradford 'Pals' regiments which ensured that friends, relatives, neighbours and workmates could serve together by recruiting them all at the same time. While this boosted morale and enthusiasm, the effect on the communities that subsequently lost vast swathes of their young men was catastrophic.

On 1 July 1916, as part of the Somme offensive and on the bloodiest day in British military history, 2,000 Bradford pals were ordered to attack. Many were brought down by bullets and shrapnel before they'd even arrived at their positions. 1,770 of them were recorded as killed or wounded on that one day.[29] Brinley and Colin's cousin Arnold among other family members fought in the war; there would have been friends from school and business colleagues who signed up too, and undoubtedly they would have watched as many of their workforce departed for the front, many never to return. The brothers remained in Bradford, running W. B. Lee & Co. The contracts that they made during the war and the profits that they accrued from these orders secured the fortunes of the company and of both men, who became very, very wealthy indeed.[30]

The war proved to be a temporary, prosperous blip in what was in fact a gradual decline in the British wool trade. The boom lasted just long enough to create a false sense of security about the future which perhaps left many ill-prepared for what was to follow.[31] Manufacturers on the Continent were at first crippled by the war that was fought across their land, and their factories had fallen idle. Now post-war they were developing better technology and starting to beat the north of England in the textiles game.

Public taste was leaning towards lighter fabrics that were no longer expected to last forever, and France and Belgium became expert in making cheap, lightweight fabrics out of the cheaper stocks of wool.[32] Demand for Bradford's products slumped and prices and profits plummeted, forcing many out of business – particularly men like Brinley and Colin. As the middlemen, who found customers and bought goods from the manufacturers to sell on to them, the wool merchants were the first to feel the pinch. By the 1930s, most of the leading merchants in Bradford had gone out of business.

> Not only have all the big merchanting houses disappeared but a great many of the English firms too. Wool merchants, whose names seemed to us like the Bank of England. Not one or two of them, but dozens of them.[33]

The recession forced the textile industry to make radical changes. As firms went out of business, others merged or were taken over, consolidating formerly separate processes under one roof. Brinley and Colin chose this point of uncertainty and slump to leave the family business. In 1935 Bradford was clinging to its position as the world's leading worsted producer, but European and Japanese producers were snapping at its heels and would eventually bring the goliath to its knees.[34] Brinley and Colin, both in their forties, recognised this as the moment to sell their company and retire.[35] They lived for the rest of their lives as very rich men.

Their wealth came through the profits and eventual sale of W. B. Lee & Co., the company that their maternal grandfather had founded and into which their father had invested his share of the Monte Carlo winnings. Their bank accounts would also be added to over the years by a series of bequests. Their uncle Fred had inherited everything from his father William B. Lee, and because his wife was dead and he had no legitimate children, Fred left his nephews a third each of his estate, which had a gross value of just over £7 million in today's values. The remaining third went to Fred's sister Emily, Brinley and Colin's beloved aunt, who had no children of her own but had given a home to her nephews for nearly twenty years.

Emily left a small trust fund for her husband when she died in 1923 but the bulk of her estate, worth just over £2.5 million in today's terms, went in equal shares to Brinley and Colin.[36] She gave Brinley a satinwood bedroom suite and divided her brother Frank's china, oak furniture and paintings between Brinley and Colin. After the death of Emily's husband, her house, 5 Nab Lane, where she and her nephews had lived together, went to Colin. The boys' father, Alfred, died in 1941, leaving over £1 million in today's terms in a trust fund that the brothers managed on behalf of their stepmother. She was to outlive them both, and so neither benefitted from their father's money directly, but they didn't need to – they were by then very rich men in their own right.

23

MONK BARN

In 1935 both Brinley Lee Jagger and Colin Lee Jagger retired. Still in the prime of their lives, they were to enjoy nearly thirty years of leisure. They occupied a world far removed from that of their grandfather Joseph, who had chosen to eschew the trappings of wealth but whose desperate venture in Monte Carlo had in a large part funded the fine life lived by his grandsons. The brothers clearly enjoyed a certain status in the community, mixing in important circles and giving to charity. When new buildings were erected at Bradford Grammar School in 1938 it was decided to name buildings after donors. Brinley was a member of the appeal committee, and both he and Colin were old boys of the school. They donated £1,000 (the equivalent of nearly £59,000 today) to the building at the school of what became known as the Jagger Library.[1] Brinley also sponsored an award at the local Eldwick and Gilstead Horticultural Society show. The Brinley Jagger Trophy for tomatoes may be evidence of his interest in horticultural, or simply that Brinley and Sybil were a well-known and prominent couple in the area, where such gestures to the community were important.[2]

The Jaggers socialised and were on good terms with the family of Sir James Hill, one of the leading textile magnates of the period.[3] In 1891 Hill had founded a wool-importing and top-making business, rather like W. B. Lee & Co., which later became Sir James Hill and Sons Ltd. He became mayor of Bradford in 1908, a Liberal MP in 1916 and then a baronet. Sir James Hill and his sons joined a syndicate to buy Salt's Mill for £2 million in 1918 (the equivalent of almost £90 million today).[4] The Hills were among the elite of the Bradford textile industry and its social and political scene. It is reasonable to think that the Jaggers moved as part of this circle. They certainly had the wealth and the lifestyle to do so. Evidence of both their status and what this meant at the time can perhaps be seen in Colin's appalling driving record and its consequences.

In July 1935, around the time when he retired at the age of forty-two, Colin was fined £5 for driving without due care on a Doncaster race day. He drove abreast of traffic at a dangerous bend, crossing the line and only just missing a bus coming in the opposite direction.[5] His recklessness, or poor and inattentive driving, was to have fatal consequences. In 1952 Colin caused the death of a motorcyclist, a man aged only thirty-three. The report states that the victim was on the correct side of the road and yet Colin, with his previous record of driving without care and attention, had his charge of manslaughter reduced to one of dangerous driving, incurring a fine and a loss of his driving licence. The judge's verdict was that Colin was a steady and reliable man who had driven for forty years without mishap but had poor eyesight. There is no mention of Colin's previous conviction and the language suggests that his social status carried more weight in the decision than his driving record. Even the title of the article shows little interest in the man who lost his life: 'Good record broken by fatal crash.'[6]

In 1922, four years after he married Sybil, Brinley bought Monk Barn in Park Road, Bingley and the couple lived there until his death.⁷ To discover more about the house and their life there I followed up Brinley's link to the horticultural club and contacted the Eldwick Village Society. Local historian Allan Mirfield responded right away; he had just put the finishing touches to a presentation called *Houses of Distinction*, in which Monk Barn featured as one of the significant properties in the area. Allan emailed me a photo of the house and I recognised it immediately.

When Sybil passed the Monte Carlo key into the safe keeping of her Jagger relatives, it had come with a set of photographs. The originals have not survived, but the photocopies given to me by David Jagger show a home and a family. The house is very fine indeed, built of stone with a gabled end and on its facade and a generous number of stone mullioned windows with leaded lights. The grounds look extensive, well tended and clearly suited to a grand home. In one of the photographs there is a young man with a moustache wearing a bow tie, and in another his older self, leaning on a chair smoking a cigarette and holding a camera or possibly binoculars. There is a scene in the garden, presumably at the same big house, where there are beautiful trees behind a group of smiling men and women, one of whom has a child on his lap. There are also two seaside views; one depicting two couples strolling along a promenade and the other an older couple posing and smiling.

Finally, two photographs show a group of family or friends sitting on deck chairs outside a brick house with large windows. An elderly man with a walking stick and bowler hat forms part of this group and is also photographed alone outside the house. He appears to be the same man that is in the picture of the smiling couple at the seaside. David Jagger showed me these photographs originally and told me that this elderly couple were Joseph Hobson Jagger and his wife Matilda and that the grand house was the one in Pepper Hill that he had bought with his Monte Carlo winnings. I know now that Joseph did not build or buy a fancy house with his millions but returned to where he had lived before. The photo of the grand house that came with the key showed the same house that was in the photograph that Allan Mirfield sent to me. It was Monk Barn, Brinley and Sybil's home.

In the telling of the story over time, the ownership of the house in the photo had been misattributed by a couple of generations. Looking again at the photographs it was obvious. In them, all of the women's skirts are knee length and the younger woman in the group walking along the seaside promenade is wearing a cloche hat. These must be images from the 1920s onwards, by which time Joseph and Matilda were long dead. Brinley and Sybil had been guardians of the key, and it makes sense that these were their family photographs. I think they are the young couple walking on the promenade, and I think with them are Brinley's father Alfred and his wife Louisa. Alfred is very smartly dressed in a hat and an overcoat with a flower in its buttonhole. Frustratingly, the detail of his face has been obscured in the photocopying of these lost photographs. I think that the older couple which the family has long thought to be Joseph and Matilda are probably his son Walter and his wife. Nevertheless, here was final proof that Joseph did not invest in a palatial home and live a millionaire lifestyle. That was left to his grandson Brinley.

Monk Barn dates back to the mid-seventeenth century, and when Sybil and Brinley moved in it sat within grounds that included a pleasure garden with terrace and one of the earliest productive kitchen gardens in the area, planted with fruit trees.[8] Perhaps this was where Brinley enjoyed growing his famous tomatoes. There was also a paddock housing a stable and cart shed and somewhere to park the two cars that the Jaggers owned, a 1936 Alvis Firebird Saloon and a 1930 Sunbeam Saloon.[9] Life at Monk Barn was luxurious and comfortable. Sybil's great-niece Gillian Stretton remembers that it was very large and grand and had a stone-flagged kitchen with an Aga and a magnificent drawing room. The entrance hall was furnished with oak tables and seats and decorated with blue-and-white china, an oriental ginger jar, seventeen pewter plates, paintings and three framed maps.

The dining room where Sybil and Brinley liked to entertain was very grand, as Gillian remembers. At its centre was an expanding mahogany dining table. Two-branched candelabras and an array of cut glass ware adorned the table. An oriental carpet and velvet curtains completed the effect. A number of paintings were hung on the walls, mostly of landscapes and rivers, including two by English artist James Aumonier called *Woodland Scene* and *Figure and Landscape*. Mahogany and oak furniture and blue-and-white china and pewter decorated most of the ground-floor rooms. Some of these items were left to Brinley by his aunt Emily in her will and originally belonged to her brother Fred Lee: 'China, oak and pictures formerly belonging to my brother from [his house] Averingcliffe.'[10]

Most of Monk Barn's ground-floor rooms were wood panelled, with original fireplaces, as befits a house of the period.[11] In the study was a typewriter and sewing machine and in the lounge a Steinway Pianola Piano. The smoke room must have been a place to take tea or drinks and relax before or after dinner. Furnished with a three-piece suite and a small library of novels and reference books, here were drink decanters and tumblers, Lalique ashtrays and a silver tea set, cake stand and bonbon dish. The kitchen was large and modern and included a pantry, washhouse with sink, two larders and a wine cellar.[12] A staircase from the entrance hall led to the bedrooms. Sybil and Brinley's four bedrooms were furnished with oak or mahogany furniture, one had a satinwood bedroom suite, surely the one passed on to Brinley by his aunt Emily.[13] Also on the first floor was a dressing room, nursery, toilet and bathroom. A fifth bedroom was used by staff and was supplied with oak and painted furniture. It had its own bathroom and a box room, all reached by a back stair from the kitchen.[14] David Jagger recalls that there was a butler when he visited Monk Barn and Sybil retained both a housemaid and a cook.[15]

Some accounts of Joseph Hobson Jagger claim for him a life of unhappy luxury after his Monte Carlo win. I have found no evidence for this, but it may well have been his grandson Brinley's fate. David Wright describes him as an unhappy person, despite his great wealth. His own father told him that Brinley had 'been dying for thirty years because he was so miserable'. This unhappiness may have extended to how he felt about the Monte Carlo win as Pam, his surrogate daughter, recorded in her notes: 'Auntie Bid [Sybil] told me that Nunky [Brinley] didn't like to talk about it; he was apparently ashamed of the story! (That the money had gone, rather than been won, I think…).' Perhaps he didn't realise quite how much money his grandfather had brought home? Or perhaps Brinley was ashamed that his family fortune had been founded on the roulette tables of Monte Carlo?

Colin continued to live at 5 Nab Lane, the home left to him by his aunt Emily, until the last years of his life when he was cared for in a nursing home.[16] He did not marry and had no children and so when he died on 3 September 1961, aged sixty-seven, he named Brinley and Sybil as his executors and left his estate to his brother. A set of correspondence relating to the settlement of Colin's affairs reveals that he and his brother were still beneficiaries of the Emily Hayes trust and investments made by both William B. Lee and Fred Lee and that both brothers were continuing to manage the Alfred Jagger trust.[17] These inheritances and trusts, which comprised shares, bonds and property from both the Jagger and Lee sides of the family, now came in their entirety to Brinley or were put under his management. For a few months Brinley Jagger had sole control of the largest share of his grandfather's Monte Carlo legacy, but this was not to last. He died on 10 April 1962, leaving no will, and with no surviving children or siblings his entire estate went to his wife. He left a fortune of nearly £187,000, worth approximately £3.5 million today. Sybil was now a multimillionaire.

24

THE TWO WIDOWS

In the spring of 1962, the largest part of Joseph Hobson Jagger's Monte Carlo winnings was in the hands of two women, neither of them blood relations. Alfred, his son, who took a quarter share of Joseph's estate and a generous gift on top for his help in the casino, had the money that he accumulated split two ways. A share went to his two sons via the family business in which he had invested, and this all came to Sybil on Brinley's death. Alfred's widow Lucy inherited the rest – all of Alfred's personal holdings and wealth.

Close in age, these two women's lives had been intertwined for some time. Born three years apart, they had both married well – a son and his father. Alfred and Lucy wed first, moving into the home that he shared with Brinley. Brinley married Sybil three years later in 1918, and it's possible that they all lived together for a short while. After Alfred's death Brinley and Colin looked after their stepmother's business affairs, managing her trust fund for her. The two women outlived them all.

In 1962, Lucy was seventy-eight and had remained at Laisterbridge Lane in the house that Alfred had bought after they married.¹ Seventy-five-year-old Sybil stayed at Monk Barn, the house that had been her home for forty years. As well as the house, Alfred had left Lucy a trust fund and she had lived during the years after his death on the income from the investments within it. When Brinley and Colin died, the Alfred Jagger trust was left without trustees. Sybil was perhaps the more robust of the two women, both physically and emotionally, because it was to her rather than to Lucy that the trust's lawyers wrote. The letter suggested that both Sybil and Lucy should apply immediately to become the trustees. Alfred's accounts needed to be managed, and Lucy needed to be warned that she would be receiving less than she expected for her maintenance. The letter acknowledged that Lucy worried about money and so to avoid upsetting her, asked Sybil if she would make up the shortfall until matters were settled in order to give Lucy some peace of mind.²

Sybil and Lucy became trustees of the Alfred Jagger trust in August 1963.³ Despite being only three years younger than her stepmother-in-law, it seems that Sybil took on the management of Lucy's affairs after Brinley's death. Lucy lived another six years, dying at the Royal Infirmary in Bradford in January 1969 aged eighty-five.⁴ She had lived nearly thirty years as a widow, drawing all of the money that she needed from the trust that Alfred had left her. At his death in 1941 it was worth £37,704, the equivalent today of £1,715,000; by 1963 it had reduced to £5,513 (worth £105,900 today),⁵ and at Lucy's death there was just £3,052 (or £46,100 today) remaining.⁶ The value of her investments would have been impacted by the high rates of taxation payable on unearned income in this period.

During the Second World War, the highest rate of income tax hit an incredible 99.25 per cent, meaning that almost every penny of investment income (above certain thresholds) would have been gathered up by the Treasury. While this might have been justified in order to fund the war effort, income tax levels remained at historically high levels until well into the 1970s.

Indeed, shortly before Lucy's death the rate of tax on unearned income actually rose to above 100 per cent. During the sterling crisis of 1968, Chancellor of the Exchequer Roy Jenkins introduced taxes on unearned and investment income of up to 136 per cent, meaning that investors had to pay more income back to the Treasury than they had actually earned. Furthermore, this surcharge was levied retrospectively so there was no way for investors to avoid paying the sums due.[7] By marrying a much younger woman in 1915, a woman close in age to his two sons, both of whom she outlived, Alfred ensured that his share of the Monte Carlo winnings, which was by far the largest, was gradually spent. Lucy was able to live off it for nearly thirty years. She had borne no children and her nephews were dead, so she bequeathed this final rump of the fortune to a Bradford taxi proprietor, 'as a recognition of his many kindnesses to me'.[8]

Sybil lived on and remained a very wealthy woman, but within a couple of years of losing her husband and brother-in-law she also lost her two older sisters. Mary Isabel Hodgson died a month before Brinley.[9] Known as Isabel by the family, her great-nephew David Wright remembers her as being rather grand, like Queen Victoria. Mabel, who had married a wool merchant named Edward Athelstan Holroyd Wright, died on 30 March 1964. After Brinley's loss, the death of her two sisters must have affected Sybil profoundly. Isabel and Mabel lived within a mile of each other and Monk Barn was just up the road. The sisters were close and saw each other often.

One sister remained, however: Gladys Whitley Robertshaw. She was the youngest of the four girls and had never married. It's clear that her sisters looked after her from their positions of wealth and marital security. When their mother died in 1937, she left Gladys £8,800 (worth a little over £40,000 today) in her will. Gladys went to live with Isabel at her home, Deanroyd in Chellow Dene, Bradford, and was there from at least 1951.[10] Deanroyd was sold together with all of its furniture when Isabel died, and Gladys moved into Monk Barn with the recently widowed Sybil.[11]

By 1975, Sybil had sold Monk Barn. The great house must have been too much to manage. It is now divided into small homes and flats, and the gardens have been built on to a large extent, but the façade is as it was, and it's easy to imagine how it would have looked when the estate was intact. Sybil had tried to stipulate that the grounds of her much-loved home should never be built on, but to no avail.[12] The sisters moved together to 23 Petersgarth, Moorhead Lane in Shipley,[13] where they continued to live in Edwardian splendour, their day punctuated by the pouring of the sherry at eleven o'clock every morning by their daily help.[14] By 1978 Sybil and Gladys, aged ninety-one and eighty-seven respectively, needed more support and moved to a residential home nearby.[15] It was then that some of the Monte Carlo winnings were lost.

The proprietor, a rotund woman in her sixties, had established her home as a place to provide residential care. When the sisters moved in they were the only occupants. They were well looked after, maintaining the lifestyle that they were used to. Smoked salmon was a particular treat. The antiques that both women owned were given their own place in the house and their jewellery was locked securely away in the proprietor's safe. Sybil and Gladys's great-niece Gillian popped in regularly but became increasingly concerned after Sybil died. Gladys was happy, and chatted about how good everybody was to them but how it was getting expensive to look after her so well. Sybil had helped the proprietor out a little, and she really felt that she should do the same. Gladys had always been looked after by her own family, and Gillian was concerned that she could be naïve about money. Gladys's comments raised Gillian's suspicions, and perhaps she was right to feel this way.

Unbeknown to the family, both sisters had changed their wills. Within months of her arrival, Sybil had signed a codicil.[16]

Her original intentions laid out in her will, written before she entered the residential home, stated that the largest part of her estate was to be divided into four equal bequests to be given to Gladys (and after her death to be passed to Pam, whom Sybil had raised like her own daughter); Margaret Wright, the widow of her nephew Edward; Gillian Stretton (Edward's daughter); and David Wright (Gillian's half-brother). In addition, Sybil asked for a number of specific legacies to be made, including a payment of £8,000 (£42,000 now) to Gladys and the same sum to Pam, with other smaller amounts going to friends and charities. Sybil had a number of pieces of diamond jewellery, and took careful steps to leave these to members of the family and to friends:

> My platinum little finger ring with three large and eight small diamonds to my sister Gladys Whitley Robertshaw ... My ear-rings with five diamonds in each to ... Pamela Joan Hill ... [Sybil's adopted daughter] My platinum two-stone Diamond ring my Diamond Cluster Ear Studs mounted in Gold and my Platinum and Jade Drop Ear-rings to Gillian Stretton ... My Diamond Evening Watch Bracelet (eight sided) on black silk ribbon to my friend Mary Bilbrough ... My Black Onyx and Diamond Ear-rings (formerly belonging to the grandmother of the late Sir James Hill) to Lady Hill ... My Platinum Bar three-stone Diamond Brooch to Sylvia Adams ...My Diamond Crescent Brooch with Diamond Star in centre to Margaret Wright ... The Gold Cigarette Case formerly belonging to my late husband to my friend Denis Crosby Hill ...

All remaining jewellery, clothes and furs were to be divided between Pam, Gillian and Gladys. Any property still owned by Sybil at her death and all of the furniture was to be put at Gladys's disposal, keeping up the family practice of making sure that the unmarried sister was housed and well provided for. It's unlikely that Sybil owned any property at this point, and so according to the terms of the will £10,000 was to go to Pam instead as she would have inherited the property and furniture from Gladys. Sybil signed her will with a shaky hand.[17] Seven months later, Sybil authorised a codicil that bequeathed £2,000 to the proprietor. This was a considerable sum (worth almost £10,000 today), and after the specific legacies left to her sister and surrogate daughter, twice the size of any of the others listed in the will. Sybil's health must have deteriorated significantly as she did not sign the codicil but marked it instead with a cross.[18] She could only have known the proprietor for a matter of months.

Sybil was clear in her original will that all of her furniture and household articles were to be kept for Gladys's use and then passed on to Pam Hill. A paper in the family archive, however, shows that Sybil signed a document (or at least initialled it, as did Gladys), giving some of these items away to the proprietor:

> The following are gifts from Mrs. Jagger and Miss G. Robertshaw to [the proprietor]
> 3 Green Upholstered Chairs
> 2 Red Upholstered Chairs
> 1 Red Trolley
> 1 Oval Table
> 1 Chest of Drawers
> 1 Oak Court Cupboard
> 2 Kitchen Chairs
> 1 Kitchen Table
> China and Glassware
> 1 Canteen of Cutlery
> 2 Tapestry Stools
> 1 Standard lamp and Shade
> 1 Silver entrée dish (round)
> 3 Dining Room chairs.[19]

It's unlikely that any of these belonged to Gladys as the contents of the home that she shared with Isabel were sold off right down to the Hoover Dustette and condiment set.[20] The lounge at Monk Barn had been furnished with a tapestry covered three-piece suit and so it's likely that the tapestry stools and the other items are what remained of Sybil's furniture, intended in her will for the use of her relatives. This list was signed and witnessed but not in the presence of Sybil's solicitor, who was in touch regularly and was present for other matters relating to her estate.

Sybil died on 8 January 1979 and left an estate with a gross value of £141,999, worth approximately £650,000 today.[21] Only seventeen years before, she had been left the equivalent in today's terms of £3.5 million by Brinley. She had lived off this inheritance and probably supported Gladys a great deal, and she was in the habit of living well and spending quite a bit. Taxes, as we saw earlier, would also have taken a heavy toll but equally inflation may well have wiped out much of the value of the shares that she held. It had been in double figures throughout the 1970s and peaked at 25 per cent due to a rapid increase in oil prices, exacerbated by increases in wages negotiated by strong trade unions. However, the months that she spent in the residential home clearly had an effect on the size of her legacy too. The diamond jewellery that she had bequeathed to Gillian, Pam and others remained in the safe, the proprietor proving reluctant to let it go.

Gladys remained at the house for another nine months. During that time, she made two changes to her will. The version that she wrote in July 1964, when she was living at Monk Barn, stated just as Sybil's had that the main beneficiaries of her estate should be the family of her deceased nephew Edward Wright. His son David was to receive half (three-sixths), his mother Margaret two-sixths and his half-sister Gillian Stretton one-sixth. Gladys also made a few small cash bequests and took care to list her jewels and to whom they should be passed:

To [Florence] Margaret Wright … my large three-stone diamond ring [this may be the ring left to her by her mother]. To Gillian Margaret Stretton … my large opal and diamond brooch and opal and diamond ring. To Jeanne Edwards … my diamond watch bracelet. To Edith Doreen Oddy … my small diamond brooch. To Lena Shaw … my five stone diamond ring..[22]

In the months after Sybil's death, however, she made changes which gradually saw the proprietor and her friends benefitting from Gladys's generosity. A new will was produced in April 1979 which stated that the estate was now to be split equally between David and Gillian, leaving nothing to their mother Margaret.[23] The large diamond ring which had in the earlier will been designated as a gift for Margaret was now only to be used by her during her lifetime and then passed on to Gillian. The proprietor was to be given 'my fur coat and the sum of one thousand pounds'. Two weeks before her death this sum was increased to £3,000 in a codicil to the will which Gladys could no longer sign but marked with a cross. Perhaps most significant of all, a treasured keepsake left to her by her sister, 'my little finger ring', was to be put 'upon trust for the said [proprietor] during her life and upon her death I bequeath the said ring to Mrs Lessiter'. Gladys also bequeathed £250 (£1,100 today) to Mrs Lessiter (who lived next door), another £250 to Dr Groves and £100 (£450) to Linda, the maid at the residential home.[24]

These gifts of money and personal effects appear innocuous, perhaps typical of a spinster in the last months of her life who wishes to reward those who have cared for her. Gladys's family, however, did not think so. After she died on 18 October 1979 her relatives discovered the changes that had been made to her will. They did not understand why her sister-in-law Margaret had been taken out of the will and the legacies to the proprietor seemed to confirm Gillian's suspicions about her great-aunts having been taken advantage off. She received not only furniture from the two sisters in her care, but also a fur coat and Sybil's ring from Gladys, in total goods worth approximately £23,500 today. Gillian and David are convinced that the proprietor was running a 'classic old people's home con'.[25] Gladys in particular was easy prey to the appeals for a little financial help with expenses, and might well have felt obligated to help.

There is evidence that the proprietor extracted money where she could with dubious charges. For example, Mrs Lessiter was paid to look after Gladys while she was having an operation. The care went on for five weeks, at the end of which Gladys had paid £200 in addition to her normal charge of £70 per week. Sybil paid out £150 for Christmas 1978, presumably for a meal and accompanying festivities, and one week before she died was charged £100 for decorating, only a third of which was paid back.[26] These sums alone add up to nearly £4,500 in today's values. When the sisters changed their wills, their solicitors were present. Neither man had any suspicions about events leading up to these amendments, and Gladys's lawyer found her to be 'of sound mind and sober'.[27] The family believe that the proprietor coerced the sisters into inviting their solicitors to the house then left the room as the amendments were made so that no suspicions were raised. Her behaviour after Gladys's death adds further weight to the family's theory.

Gladys's furniture and jewellery were still in the house. The family decided that they could not rely on the solicitors for help and that they would have to claim their legacy themselves. Gillian and David knocked on the door and demanded, 'We've come to collect Miss Robertshaw's possessions!'[28] They were refused entry but entered anyway, reclaiming what furniture, cut glass and jewellery they could. The proprietor threatened to call the police but the family invited her to do as she pleased; perhaps knowing that she was in the wrong, she did nothing.

This, then, is what ultimately happened to the millions that Joseph Hobson Jagger brought home from Monte Carlo. He shared it equally between his children, only one of whose lives was truly transformed. Alfred's life as a millionaire was as much to do with his marriage and the family money that came to his own children as it was to the large sum that he received for helping his father in the casino. This, the largest share of the winnings, supported for the rest of their lives two women who were not blood relatives but had married into the family. Joseph had journeyed to Monte Carlo to save his family from bankruptcy and to ensure their financial future. Those recipients who managed the money well did transform their own lives. Others were able to make their lives more comfortable. What remained of the money was spent and diminished by the longevity of a wife, the vagaries of the stock market and perhaps by the pilfering of an unscrupulous woman.

25

THE LEGACY

We live at a time when recording every moment of our lives is the norm, where sharing even the most intimate detail is positively encouraged. It seems extraordinary, then, that the life of a man who did such an improbable and audacious thing could go undocumented. And yet the lives of so many men and women have been lost to history in this way. Evidence of Joseph's win against the casino has dwindled away until all that remains is a family story that has been told and retold through the generations. Even this has come to be disbelieved, regarded as perhaps only a figment of a writer's imagination, a story created to enliven an account of the gambling world of Monte Carlo. How could this story possibly be true when all that remains in the public domain about the details of Joseph's life, particularly his will, seems to contradict it? Of course, the family had the key and its inscription to encourage them in their search for proof, even though it evaded them. But the evidence is there. It has revealed itself only now through the reconstruction of Joseph's life brick by brick. There is a tangible legacy in stone and mortar, but its significance is only clear now that the whole edifice has been reassembled.

There is the house in Greaves Street, and those in nearby Spicer Street and Ida Street, which Joseph bought with his Monte Carlo winnings. These unassuming properties in central Bradford, although modest, represent the first steps in the building of a family trust that would not only lift his family out of poverty but support them for generations. W. B. Lee & Co. is still a thriving business in Bradford. It has diversified in recent years out of the textile business to support machinery in a wide range of sectors from printers to theme parks. It is still a mechanical engineering company, working from a traditional workshop with skilled staff using traditional turning, cutting and milling machines.[1] Its link with its founder and his Jagger relations has long since ended, but the company was a recipient of a large percentage of the Monte Carlo winnings in the form of the share that Alfred was given and chose to invest in the firm. At Bradford Grammar School, the Jagger Library was built using a sizeable donation from Joseph's grandsons, two men enriched by his success. Under its roof, alumni of the school such as David Hockney might well have studied. Monk Barn, the fine house in Bingley that Brinley bought, is further testament to the wealth that flowed down this branch of the family. Even the tomato trophy in Eldwick says something about how the status of this part of the family was transformed by its newly acquired wealth.

Joseph's greatest legacy, however, lies in the very real changes that his roulette success forced on the casino in Monte Carlo, in terms of both its gaming infrastructure and the way its staff operated. These changes were to be adopted by casinos all over the world. The casino had been forced to redesign its roulette wheels to defeat Joseph and this began a daily routine of not only changing the wheels from table to table every day but exchanging the component parts of each wheel daily too.[2] To ensure that the casino could never be beaten in the same way again, by a method that was frustratingly legal, the modifications went even further. In the casinos of France, Germany and Monaco, the practice had always been that after the croupier set the wheel spinning the ball was thrown in the direction of the spin. After Joseph's win, the Monte Carlo casino instructed its staff to throw the ball in the opposite direction in order to make its movement less predictable.[3] A new test was introduced to the daily preparation of the casino, too. It was ordered that between half past nine and ten o'clock every morning, before play started, each table should be examined and checked with a spirit level. Adolphe Smith witnessed one of these checks and recounts it in his book written in 1912:

> The most important part of the inspection is to make certain that the wheels are on a perfect level ... It was a strange experience, and reminded me of the search made at Westminster under the Houses of Parliament before the opening of a new session for fear there might be concealed somewhere a second edition of Guy Fawkes.[4]

These measures have all made it considerably more difficult to exploit a wheel bias today. Nevertheless, a search for 'Jagger's system' online will still list websites offering to sell Joseph's winning numbers for a fee. Unfortunately, using those numbers won't improve your roulette success today because Joseph's system was never about the numbers. His method relied solely on the biased mechanics of the roulette wheel itself, which have long since been improved. Following his 'system' today would give no advantage over the casino at all. Joseph did develop an infallible way of breaking the bank, but it only worked at that moment, on those particular wheels in Monte Carlo.

Despite the enormous odds, others have played to the wheel bias since and some have had success. It is reported on various casino and roulette websites that a Spanish record producer won a fortune in this way in the 1990s. According to these accounts, Garcia-Pelayo studied the individual wheels in the casinos in Madrid, watched thousands of spins and analysed the results using a computer. Like Joseph, he had trusted assistants: his five children. His observations identified that some wheels had a bias and that certain numbers were coming up more often than others. With this advantage over the bank he began winning. Once his method was known in Spain, Garcia-Pelayo moved on to Las Vegas and it is said that eventually, when he was too well known for his system to work, he retired with an estimated pot of $1.5 million. One account states that after suing him for the return of its money a casino was informed by the Supreme Court in Spain that Garcia-Pelayo had done nothing illegal. Like Joseph Hobson Jagger, he had simply been ingenious.[5]

Joseph's ingenuity in being the first to develop this completely legal way of beating the odds at roulette – and thereby forcing the casino to overhaul the way they operated in order to stop it happening again – makes him unique among the famous bank-breakers. The others relied on luck or on cheating, and nearly all lost everything they had won. Joseph's system was not only original, but he kept a fortune and never returned to the casino. Even more remarkable in this tale of beating the odds in an improbable way, Joseph devised his plan without ever having seen a roulette wheel before arriving in Monte Carlo and having never played. I think there is a case now not only to confirm Joseph Hobson Jagger's place in the list of those that have defeated the bank but for him to be considered as the person who can, with most justification, claim the title of 'the man who broke the bank at Monte Carlo'.

I'd like to think that Joseph's children were proud of him, that they admired this poor working-class man whose ingenuity had led him on to a great adventure and a remarkable achievement, but this may not have been the case. Alfred does not appear to have mentioned his role in events outside the immediate family, and it appears that his son Brinley was ashamed of the casino story. Perhaps they were too newly wealthy to welcome the truth that much of their status and money came from the roulette tables of Monte Carlo. It was left to later generations to feel proud of their ancestor Joseph. This pride came to be embodied in the key, an item treasured and handed down by his descendants. This, the most tangible element of Joseph's legacy, became the touchstone for his intangible legacy. Although never mentioned in any will, the key was passed on and kept safe, a reminder of the most remarkable event in the family's history. Matilda must have kept it and given it to her eldest son, Alfred, who had been in Monte Carlo with his father. Or perhaps Joseph gifted the key to his son in his lifetime. Alfred bequeathed it to his eldest son, Brinley, who died with no surviving children.

His widow, Sybil, decided to give it back to a direct descendant of Joseph Hobson Jagger. She chose the family of his second son Walter, giving it to his eldest child Arnold. Arnold was Brinley's cousin, and these two branches of Joseph's family seem to have had a good relationship. If the older gentleman in the photographs that have been kept with the key is Walter, then the images appear to depict him visiting Brinley and Sybil. David Jagger's childhood memories of going to Monk Barn with his father Arnold provide further evidence that these uncles, aunts and cousins did socialise with each other. From this point the custodianship of the key is certain: Arnold Jagger, Joseph's grandson, had it in his possession when he died in 1971. This is when it was almost lost.

Arnold Jagger married for the second time in 1962. His new wife, Elsie, had a difficult relationship with her grown-up stepsons (David Jagger and his brothers Derek, Peter and Kenneth), which eventually broke down completely after Arnold's death in 1971. Whether it was because of her animosity or simply because she wanted money, Elsie decided to sell their ancestor's key. She wrote to the casino in Monte Carlo describing the key's provenance and offering to sell it to them for £2,000 (over £24,000 in today's values), but she received no reply.

The key was instead offered in 1975 to Sotheby's, who agreed to include it in a sale later that year. Derek, the most ardent family historian at the time, sought advice from a solicitor and was distraught when he was told that the key was Elsie's to sell and that his only option was to go to the sale and try to outbid any potential buyer. As Derek prepared to do just this, surely concerned about just how much money he might have to spend to keep the key in the family, a telephone call told him that Elsie had died, just weeks before the sale was due. The solicitor dealing with her estate showed great astuteness and compassion when he declared that the Monte Carlo key was a Jagger heirloom and should be returned to Joseph Hobson Jagger's direct descendants. A relieved Derek took it home, and after his death in 1993 left it to his brother David, the great-grandson of the man for whom it was made.[6]

26

FAMILY PRIDE

My side of the family, the descendants of Joseph's brother Richard Jagger, knew nothing of the key, and my great-great-grandfather didn't live to see his brother have a much more successful gambling career than him. Hard times for Richard's family were made worse by his liking for the odd bet. His daughter Lucy told how on one occasion he lost his entire wage betting on a knurr match. With no money to buy food for the large family, Lucy was sent to the little local shop to ask if the shopkeeper would let her have some treacle on the tick (to be paid for at a later date). The shopkeeper knew full well that Richard had gambled his money away but relented and gave Lucy the treacle, either on the tick or as a gift; in any case, the family had bread and treacle for lunch that day. It could so easily have been just dry bread.[1]

After marrying James Milner, Lucy moved to Buttershaw, a village to the south-west of Bradford comprised of three steeply sloping streets that ran parallel to each other down the hill: Fleece Street, Orleans Street and Bottomley Street. It was a very insular community. Families lived close together, everybody knew everybody else's business and most lives revolved around the mill, owned by Henry Bottomley, which was at the centre of village life. Traditional Victorian Yorkshire back-to-back houses were built along these streets to accommodate the workers when the mill was established. Lucy and James came to Bottomley Street when it was newly built in March 1881 on the promise of work at the mill, which went on to employ virtually everyone in the village for decades.

Two generations of my family were born in the bedroom of this home, 12 Bottomley Street.[2] The house had been used for a short time as a club and had three storeys above ground: a living room on the ground floor, a bedroom on the first and a garret on the second where James kept canaries. There was no kitchen, and hot water came from a black-leaded boiler at the side of the fire. Toilet facilities were provided by a block of stone-built lavatories further up the street, one of which James and Lucy and their four children shared with their neighbours. James and Lucy already had a son when they moved in, and afterwards their three daughters appeared in quick succession, including my grandmother Norah in 1884.[3] This was my great-grandmother Lucy, left widowed in 1889 and forced to bring in washing, the woman who was given £5 by 'T'Monte Carlo man'.

My grandmother Norah Milner was eleven when she started work in the mill and her brother Arthur was possibly only nine.[4] She told my dad how terribly hard it was to work all morning and then try to study in the afternoon; she used to fall asleep and couldn't take anything in. At thirteen she started work full time. Despite the National Education Act, which was passed in 1870 and created schools financed from local rates, my grandmother and her brother and sisters all had to pay to attend the village school in Buttershaw. Many children would not have received even this basic education. It was not an education of any depth or duration either, as working-class children still had to work to contribute to the often meagre incomes of their families. When they were deemed to have reached a certain educational standard they could begin work as half-timers in the mills. My great-grandmother Lucy was completely illiterate. My dad remembers that she could write her name but that there was a great palaver involved, with somebody holding the table still while she painstakingly made the shapes of the letters, none of which made any sense to her individually.[5]

Lucy died in 1931, when she was eighty-three. Norah looked after her until then, only getting married to Harry Fletcher eight years before her mother died when she was thirty-nine. Their two children, Sydney and my dad Clifford, were both born at 12 Bottomley Street in 1925 and 1929 respectively, the second generation of my family to be born in the bedroom there. Norah was well into her forties at the time.[6] After Lucy died the Fletcher family moved just around the corner to 2 Albion Street, principally because this house had a small kitchen and its own toilet (albeit an outdoor one) and even a small handkerchief of garden at the front.[7] Behind the row of nine stone houses there was an enormous hen run, and my dad recalled being awoken too early every morning by the cockerel crowing and then enduring the clucking of one hundred hens throughout the day.[8] The house in Albion Street has a modern front door now and, like its neighbours, has signs of twenty-first-century life visible in its garden and through its windows; children's beach shoes drying on the line; cars parked outside and TV aerials on the roof. The hens are long gone. But the blackened stone walls of the house and the stone gate posts and surrounding wall around the front yard are just as they would have been when the Fletcher family lived there until Norah's death in 1967.

Just around the corner at the family's original home in Bottomley Street, No. 12 seems even less altered by time. Standing in front of it and touching the stone of the gate post, I could imagine my dad's hand slapping it as he ran down the path to play, and I could sense the swish of his grandma Lucy's skirt against it as she came in and out of the house over the years.

I have a photo of her standing next to it swathed in a shawl. Although only a little boy when she died, dad had known Lucy and had shared a bed with her when he was a baby. Lucy had slept with her grandson in a 'shut-up' bed or 'box-bed' at the side of the living room, a bed with wooden shutters that could be closed up during the day.[9] It is in tracing these degrees of separation that I have been able to come closest to Joseph Hobson Jagger; my dad knew Lucy, and Lucy was Joseph's niece. Perhaps this is where my dad's fascination with Joseph began. Mine certainly began with his.

Perhaps it was the poverty in which my family lived that made the story of a man who'd escaped and made his fortune so appealing. Joseph's tale might have piqued their interest because it engendered in them the hope that lives could be changed. Or perhaps it was the desire that many of us have to find a famous or extraordinary person in our family tree in whose reflected glory we can bask, and in doing so make our lives seem more exciting or meaningful. After all, if we share the same genes then maybe we are capable of such things too? Maybe for some members of the family it was the desire to find out what happened to the money that drove their interest, and the intoxicating prospect of lost millions waiting to be found. Whatever its impetus, this fascination and pride burned strong enough in three branches of our family that a much-loved oral history of our shared ancestor was kept alive for generations; sometimes only a snippet, sometimes a fact that wasn't quite accurate, but every detail was clutched, kept safe. All of the key threads of Joseph's story were in the family all along but they needed to be woven back together, like the worsted cloth that made Bradford so famous.

Joseph's story is testimony to how many ordinary lives have been lost to the past. Most of us have simply disappeared, with little more than an entry in a baptismal register or probate calendar to show that we were ever here. But Joseph Hobson Jagger was saved from this fate by a single extraordinary act.

By breaking the bank at Monte Carlo, he was rescued from obscurity. Perhaps it is more accurate to say that it was in the remembrance of this act and in the telling of its story that Joseph was really saved. His descendants have shown a tenacious desire not to lose sight of him and a determination not to allow him to slip from view beneath the weight of history. I'm proud to have played my part in resurrecting our 'man who broke the bank at Monte Carlo' and creating this record for all of us.

Appendix 1

PROPERTIES PURCHASED BY JOSEPH HOBSON JAGGER

Greaves Street, Little Horton
Number of houses purchased: Four
House numbers: 6, 8, 10 and 25
Date: 1881 (the freehold for No. 25 had been purchased by 1883 but the date is uncertain)
Joseph and Matilda remained at No. 25 for the rest of his life. Their daughter Louisa lived at No. 8 for a period (certainly between 1891 and 1908) and their son Walter moved into No. 6 when his parents moved out in the early 1880s and stayed there for at least twenty years.
All of the houses were inherited by Walter Jagger in 1913. No. 6 was home to his son Arnold from at least 1920 until at least 1950, possibly later. During this time the house was sold, and Arnold continued to rent it. No. 25 still stands but Nos 6, 8 and 10 were eventually demolished.

Ida Street and Spicer Street, Little Horton
Number of houses purchased: Not known, but could have been as many as eleven

House numbers: Not known
Date: Purchases were made in 1886 and in 1888
These properties are not mentioned in any of the later indentures which list the properties contained within the Jagger trust fund.

Pasture Lane, Clayton

Number of houses purchased: Nine
House numbers: 20 (Elm Terrace), 22, 24, 26, 28, 30, 32, 34 and 36
Date: Purchases were made in 1887 and in 1892
Joseph purchased a plot of land, with rights of way, in Clayton. Included in the transaction were nine properties on Pasture Lane (which included Elm Terrace). No. 20 (the property at Elm Terrace) was sold in 1908. The land and the remaining properties were inherited by Alfred Jagger in 1913.

Montague Street, Little Horton

Number of houses purchased: Eight
House numbers: 26, 28, 30, 32, 34, 36, 38 and 40 (later became 18, 20, 22, 24, 26, 28, 30 and 32)
Date: Purchases were made between 1886 and 1890
Joseph purchased a plot of land in the area which included Montague Street and the eight houses that stood on it. Later, Nos 42, 44, 46, 48, 50 and 52 were added to the property portfolio. This latter group is not mentioned until 1913, so it is likely that they were acquired after Joseph's death by his trustees and added to the trust as his will decreed. Louisa and her family were living at No. 32 in 1881, and this was possibly an impetus for the purchase by her father. In 1913 the Montague Street properties were split between Joseph's two daughters: Louisa inherited 42, 44, 46, 48, 50 and 52 and Mary inherited 18, 20, 22 and 24 (which had been numbered 26, 28, 30 and 32 when her father bought them). This suggests that four of the houses that Joseph originally bought (then Nos 34, 36, 38 and 40) had been sold off by that point.

Louisa lived at No. 50 at the end of her life and died there. She put it and No. 52 into a trust for her daughter-in-law Martha. The remaining properties (42, 44, 46 and 48) went to her daughter Emily, who also inherited her aunt Mary's properties, giving her ownership of all but two of the houses in Montague Street that her grandfather had purchased. The entire street is now demolished.

Appendix 2

NOTE REGARDING FINANCIAL TRANSLATIONS

Throughout this book, whenever historical financial amounts are translated into current (2017) values I have used the equivalent purchasing power as the basis for the calculation. This is more sophisticated than simply comparing relative values using straightforward retail price indices as the purchasing power indicator also takes into account relative levels of wages, outputs, etc. It therefore gives a better idea of the relative standard of living attributable to that amount of money when it was received or paid compared to the present day. However, this value might significantly *understate* the economic power and status that that amount of money conferred upon its owner at the time because certain measures of wealth have increased significantly faster than prices and wages in the intervening years – for example house prices, the value of gold, stock market investments.

For this reason, it is not unrealistic to estimate that Joseph Hobson Jagger's relative economic power from his £80,000 Monte Carlo win in *circa* 1881 was actually *eight or even sixteen times* greater than the £7.4 million stated elsewhere in this work. The *economic status* conferred by that amount of money – that is the status that sum of money might have given Jagger at that time in respect of average levels of earning and wealth – would have been around £60 million, while the economic *power* it would have granted him in terms of the influence it would have given him in relation to the state of the UK economy as a whole at that time would have been an extraordinary £124 million. To set this in a modern context, as recently as 2001 there were just over 200,000 millionaires in the UK. In 2017 there are estimated to be more than 700,000. So, in just sixteen years, the number of millionaires in the country has more than trebled and, therefore, the relative economic power of being a millionaire has declined commensurately. Put another way, using the economic power figure as our basis for comparison, Jagger's wealth in *circa* 1881 would have catapulted him into the top 900 richest people in the country at that time (as per comparative data from the *Sunday Times Rich List* for 2017).

All sterling calculations have been made using the measuringworth.com website, which also includes further (and no doubt better) explanations of the bases for their calculations.

Appendix 3

TIMELINE OF EVENTS DURING JOSEPH HOBSON JAGGER'S LIFE, 1830–1892

1830 Joseph Hobson Jagger is born in Bradford
William IV is King of England
July Revolution in Paris
The Liverpool–Manchester Railway opens
Delacroix paints *Liberty Leading the People*

1832 The first Reform Act extends the vote to some of the new middle classes

1833 The first British Factory Act makes it illegal to employ children under nine years of age

1834 Charles Babbage devises plans for a new kind of calculating machine, the Analytical Engine

1835 The first negative photograph is taken at Lacock Abbey by Fox Talbot

1837 Victoria becomes Queen of England
Charles Dickens begins publishing *Oliver Twist* in monthly instalments

1838   Gaming houses are abolished in France

1842   Thomas Cook arranges the first excursion (to Loughborough)

1845   The Great Famine in Ireland begins. It will kill around
        1 million people

1847   The Brontë sisters publish *Wuthering Heights* and *Jane
        Eyre* under pseudonyms

1848   Marx and Engels publish the *Communist Manifesto*
        Revolutions in Paris, Vienna, Venice, Berlin, Milan and
        Parma

1851   Joseph is working as a warehouseman; marries Matilda
        Townend; their first child, Louisa Jagger (later Briggs), is born

1853   The Crimean War begins
        Florence Nightingale saves lives by improving sanitation
        in military hospitals

1854   Alfred Jagger is born

1855   Mary Jagger (later Smith) is born

1858   Walter Jagger is born

1859   Joseph sets up in the cotton business in Manchester
        Charles Darwin publishes *On the Origin of Species by
        Natural Selection*

1860   Joseph's business fails amid recession in the cotton
        industry and he faces bankruptcy
        Abraham Lincoln is elected sixteenth President of the
        United States

1861   Famine in Lancashire caused by the collapse of the cotton
        industry
        Civil War breaks out in America; exports of cotton to
        Britain cease

1863   The Prince of Wales (later Edward VII) marries Princess
        Alexandra of Denmark
        François Blanc takes over the casino in Monte Carlo

1865   Lewis Carroll's *Alice's Adventures in Wonderland* is published
        Abraham Lincoln is assassinated
        The 13th Amendment abolishes slavery in America

1868   The railways reach Monte Carlo

1870   Joseph is working hand to mouth to support his family
Revolt in Paris and proclamation of the Third Republic

1876   Joseph is fundraising for his journey to the casino
Alexander Graham Bell makes the first telephone call

1877   The first tennis championship is held at Wimbledon

1878   Charles Garnier extends the casino at Monte Carlo

1880   Joseph Hobson Jagger breaks the bank at Monte Carlo
(*c.* 1880/81)
Inventor Joseph Swan begins installing lightbulbs at his
house, Underhill, in Gateshead (the first home in England
to be wired for electric lighting)

1887   Queen Victoria's Golden Jubilee

1888   Jack the Ripper murders five women in London
Kodak introduces the first commercially successful box
camera

1889   The Eiffel Tower is erected for the World's Fair in Paris

1891   Charles Wells breaks the bank at Monte Carlo twice
(and again in 1892)

1892   (25 April) Joseph Hobson Jagger dies at home in Bradford
The song 'The Man Who Broke the Bank at Monte Carlo'
is performed for the first time

NOTES

Prologue & 1 Bradford

1. Victoria & Albert Museum website History of fashion 1840-1900 (www.vam.ac.uk) and Laver, James, *Costume and fashion: a concise history* (London: Thames and Hudson, 1995).

2. *Notes on the life of Joseph Hobson Jagger of Pepperhill, Shelf, 1830-1892* [c. 1991], West Yorkshire Archive Service, Bradford. Document reference 50D94/3.

3. Paterson, Mike, *A brief history of life in Victorian Britain: a social history of Queen Victoria's reign* (London: Robinson, 2008).

4. Wright, D. G. and Jowitt, J. A., *Victorian Bradford: essays in honour of Jack Reynolds* (Bradford: City of Bradford Metropolitan Council, Libraries Division, 1982, c. 1981).

5. Cudworth, William, *Worstedopolis. A sketch history of the town and trade of Bradford, the metropolis of the Worsted industry* (Bradford: printed by W. Byles and Sons, 1888).

6. Wright and Jowitt, *Victorian Bradford*.

7. A letter from a *Morning Chronicle* reporter quoted in the *Bradford Observer* on 13 December 1849.

8. Wright and Jowitt, *Victorian Bradford*.

9. Crape is the anglicised version of the French word crêpe and it refers to a crimped fabric with a finely ridged surface which was often dyed black and used to make mourning clothes.

10. Wright and Jowitt, *Victorian Bradford*.

11. Ibid.

12. From Angus Reach's article in the *Morning Chronicle*, 1849. Source: The British Newspaper Archive (www.britishnewspaperarchive.co.uk).

13. Bellerby, Rachel, *Chasing the sixpence: the lives of Bradford mill folk (*Ayr: Fort Publishing, 2005).

14. Quoted in the annual report of the joint director of public health (Bradford and Airedale) 2011/12 NHS Airedale, Bradford and Leeds City of Bradford Metropolitan District Council. I believe that this is an extract from a sanitary report made about 1837 by Mr Smith of Deanston.

15. I continued this tradition, without having realised then that it existed, by giving both of my sons my maiden name of Fletcher as a middle name.

16. According to the 1841 census.

17. Jeremiah married his second wife Sarah Binns at the church on 27 December 1779. He was buried there on 5 December 1802. Sarah was baptised there in 1751. Jeremiah's son John married Lydia Longbottom at the church on 5 April 1779. Thank you to Ben Stables for assisting with Jagger research in Shelf.

18. Jeremiah Jagger's burial record of 1802 records his status as 'Shelf Weaver.' John Jagger's marriage record of 5 April 1779 lists his as a 'Weaver' and Abraham Jagger's marriage certificate from 1810 describes him as a 'Weaver.'

19. Cudworth, William, *Rambles round Horton: historical, topographical, and descriptive* (Bradford: Thos. Brear & Co., 1886).

20. From the annual report of the joint director of public health (Bradford and Airedale) 2011/12 NHS Airedale, Bradford and Leeds City of Bradford Metropolitan District Council.

21. LETTER XV [Thursday, Dec. 6, 1849] *Supplement to the Morning Chronicle*, 22 Jan 1850. Source: The British Newspaper Archive (www.britishnewspaperarchive.co.uk).

22. Bellerby, *Chasing the sixpence*.

23. Ibid.

24. *The Representation of the People Act, 1832* (or first *Reform Act*) broadened the franchise's property qualification in the counties, to include men who were small landowners, tenant farmers, and shopkeepers and in the boroughs, giving the vote to all male householders who paid a yearly rental of £10 or more and some lodgers. *The Third Reform Act*, 1884 enfranchised all male householders but it wasn't until 1918 that there was universal male suffrage. Women were not allowed to vote until 1918 and then only if they were over thirty years of age. In 1928 *The Equal Franchise Act* finally gave equal voting rights to men and women aged over twenty-one.

2 Monte Carlo

1. Only the Vatican at 0.44km² is smaller than Monaco.

2. Schwartz, David G., *Roll the Bones: the history of Gambling* (New York; London: Gotham, 2006). The information about Rimmel's violet crop comes from Smith, Adolphe, *Monaco and Monte Carlo* ([S.I.]: Richards, 1912).

3. The town of Homburg had the prefix 'Bad' or 'bath' added after it developed as a spa town. I have used the name of Bad Homburg for the town throughout for simplicity.

4. Schwartz, *Roll the Bones*.

5. Braude, Mark, *Making Monte Carlo, a history of speculation and spectacle* (New York: Simon & Schuster, 2016).

6. Smith, Adolphe, *Monaco and Monte Carlo* ([S.I.]: Richards, 1912).

7. Ibid.

8. This story is told in Ring, Jim, *Riviera: The Rise and Rise of the Côte D'Azur* (London: Faber & Faber, 2011) and also in Quinn, Robin, *The man who broke the bank at Monte Carlo: Charles Deville Wells, Gambler and Fraudster Extraordinaire* (Stroud: The History Press, 2016).

9. Smith, *Monaco and Monte Carlo.*

10. Ibid.

11. Braude, *Making Monte Carlo.*

12. Ibid.

13. Smith, *Monaco and Monte Carlo.*

14. Braude, *Making Monte Carlo.*

15. Quinn, Robin, *The man who broke the bank at Monte Carlo.*

16. Braude, *Making Monte Carlo.*

17. Schwartz, *Roll the Bones.*

18. Ibid.

19. Ring, *Riviera.*

20. Ibid.

21. Schwartz, *Roll the Bones.*

22. Quoted in Ring, *Riviera* and Quinn, *The man who broke the bank at Monte Carlo.* An article in *The New European* 20-26 January 2017 gives the date when the country stopped collecting income tax as 1896.

23. Schwartz, *Roll the Bones.*

24. This comes from the leaflet *The History of Monte Carlo Casino* (leaflet given to casino visitors) and confirmed by the archivist of the Société des Bains de Mer. The room was completely rebuilt in 1898 by Henri Schmidt, redecorated in the Baroque style and renamed the *Salon Schmidt.* This is the décor that visitors see today although the room is now called *La Salle Europe.*

25. *Cook's Handbook to the Health Resorts of the South of France and Northern Coast of the Mediterranean* (London:

Thomas Cook & Son: Simpkin, Marshall & Co.,1881-82 [1881].

26. Sennett, Chris, *All About Monte Carlo and Roulette by O. Plucky, B. Careful & C. Wisdom etc.* (London: Edmund Seale, 1913).

27. *Cook's Handbook to the Health Resorts of the South of France and Northern Coast of the Mediterranean.*

28. *The Spectator*, 18 February 1928.

29. This is now the Café de Paris.

30. Bethell, Victor, *Monte Carlo Anecdotes and Systems of Play* (London: William Heinemann, 1901).

31. Braude, *Making Monte Carlo.*

32. Graves, Charles, *The Big Gamble. The story of Monte Carlo* (London: Hutchinson & Co., 1951).

33. Bethell, *Monte Carlo Anecdotes and Systems of Play.*

34. The steamship was named *Charles III* after the Prince of Monaco from Graves, *The Big Gamble.*

35. Braude, *Making Monte Carlo.*

36. Schwartz, *Roll the Bones.*

37. Ring, *Riviera.*

38. Article in *The Guardian* by Leo Benedictus Friday 17 November 2006.

39. *Cook's Handbook to the Health Resorts of the South of France and Northern Coast of the Mediterranean.*

40. Sennett, *All About Monte Carlo and Roulette by O. Plucky, B. Careful & C. Wisdom etc.*

41. Graves, *The Big Gamble.* These rules still apply today. Gamblers must be appropriately dressed and cannot be admitted without showing identification, although there is a charge to enter now. Monegasques, that is residents of Monaco, are still not permitted to enter the gaming rooms.

42. Schwartz, *Roll the Bones.*

43. Braude, *Making Monte Carlo.*

44. Ibid.

45. Bethell, *Monte Carlo Anecdotes and Systems of Play.*
46. Schwartz, *Roll the Bones.*
47. The majority of Monaco's government income now comes from financial services and tourism. In 2013 an estimated 86% of the population was employed in services (from *The World Factbook* on www.cia.gov).
48. Ring, *Riviera.*
49. Ibid.
50. Graves, *The Big Gamble.*

3 *The Rise of the Non-conformists*

1. From *The pattern of Religion in Victorian Bradford* in Wright, D. G. and Jowitt, J. A., *Victorian Bradford: essays in honour of Jack Reynolds* (Bradford: City of Bradford Metropolitan Council, Libraries Division, 1982, *c.* 1981).
2. The *Non-Conformist and Non-Parochial Registers 1567-1970* (source: *Ancestry.co.uk*) list Hannah as being baptised in 1781, Abraham in 1784, Squire in 1786 and Samuel in 1803. I cannot find William and Jeremiah in the records but assume they would have been baptised as their siblings.
3. Marriage registration of Abraham Jagger and Sarah Hobson 30 December 1810. Abraham's wife and father and mother could not sign their names.
4. Detail from the 1841 census.
5. *Electoral Register 1832, Halifax Parish, Shelf township* (source: Ancestry) lists Abraham Jagger and no other eligible voter in Pepper Hill.
6. All financial translations have been calculated using www.measuringworth.com (see Appendix 2).
7. *Electoral Register 1832, Halifax Parish, Shelf township* (source: Ancestry) shows ownership by Abraham Jagger of a Freehold House 'in his own occupation.' This doesn't quite tally with the Land Tax Records (source: *Ancestry.*

co.uk) which show Abraham as renting various properties in the period 1830 until 1842 when he is listed as owning a cottage in Pepper Hill. He was certainly qualified to vote in 1832 but it's not certain therefore if it was as a property owner or tenant.

8. 2 November 1834.

9. 1841 census shows the family living in Cock Hill.

10. 1851 census records that William (16) is a mechanic apprentice, Joseph (13) is a power loom weaver/worsted and Oates (11) is a spinner/worsted.

11. 1851 census.

12. Certainly, this is the case by the census of 1881.

13. Sarah Jagger is aged one year in the 1841 census.

14. The 1851 census shows that the Sowoods are living at 17 Pepper Hill and Abraham is at 38 Pepper Hill.

15. Martha Jagger married Joseph Oates on 2 March 1835.

16. 1841 census.

17. 1851 census

18. Recorded in *Lund's Trades Directory, 1856*.

19. Census 1851

20. Bellerby, Rachel, *Chasing the sixpence: the lives of Bradford mill folk (Ayr: Fort Publishing, 2005)*.

21. From *The pattern of Religion in Victorian Bradford* in Wright, D. G. and Jowitt, J. A., *Victorian Bradford: essays in honour of Jack Reynolds* (Bradford: City of Bradford Metropolitan Council, Libraries Division, 1982, c. 1981).

22. Recorded in *The Gazette (London Gazette)*, issue 22374, 6 April 1860.

23. Ibid.

24. From information provided by Liz McIvor, Curator, Social History and Technology, Bradford Museums & Galleries.

25. Recorded in *The Gazette (London Gazette)*, issue 22374, 6 April 1860.

26. Ibid.

4 *An Upwardly Mobile Community*

1. From the 1851 census.
2. Cobblers repaired shoes, whilst cordwainers made them.
3. In the 1851 census, Jemima was registered in her mother's name of Townend.
4. Taylor, Simon and Gibson, Kathryn, *Manningham, Character and diversity in a Bradford suburb* (Swindon: English Heritage, 2010).
5. Ibid.
6. Ibid.
7. From an article in the *Bradford Antiquary*, the journal of the Bradford Historical and Antiquarian Society, by George Sheeran, *Back-to-back houses in Bradford* (third series vol 2 1986).
8. Taylor and Gibson, *Manningham*.
9. Ibid.
10. 1861 census.
11. This information all comes from the 1851 census.

5 *Going to Monte Carlo*

1. Bethell, Victor, *Monte Carlo Anecdotes and Systems of Play* (London: William Heinemann, 1901).
2. Detail here is from the Thomas Cook Company website.
3. Graves, Charles, *The Big Gamble. The story of Monte Carlo* (London: Hutchinson & Co., 1951).
4. Sennett, Chris, *All About Monte Carlo and Roulette by O. Plucky, B. Careful & C. Wisdom etc.* (London: Edmund Seale, 1913).
5. *Bradshaw's Continental Railway Guide, 1913* says play started at 11.30am. Chris Sennett's *All About Monte Carlo and Roulette by O. Plucky, B. Careful & C. Wisdom etc.* says 10.00am as does an illustration in Charles Graves' *The Big Gamble* (page 49) called 'The rush in the '80s at 10.00am when The Casino doors opened.' Adolphe Smith also says

in his book *Monaco and Monte Carlo* that an inspection of the gaming rooms took place between 9.30am and 10.00am, before they opened to the public.

6. Sennett, *All About Monte Carlo and Roulette by O. Plucky, B. Careful & C. Wisdom etc.*

7. Polovtsoff, General Pierre, *Monte Carlo Casino* (London: Stanley Paul & Co. 1937).

8. Schwartz, David G., *Roll the Bones: the history of Gambling* (New York; London: Gotham, 2006)

9. From an article in *GQ Magazine* called *The Wagers of Sin* by Nick Foulkes, June 2010.

10. Graves, *The Big Gamble*.

11. Angus Reach writing in the *Morning Chronicle*, 1849, about Oldham. Source: The British Newspaper Archive (www.britishnewspaperarchive.co.uk).

12. From the unpublished memoir by my father, Dr Clifford Malcolm Fletcher, called *Some notes on my ancestry*, written in December 1998 (source: author's collection).

13. Bellerby, Rachel, *Chasing the sixpence: the lives of Bradford mill folk (Ayr: Fort Publishing, 2005).*

14. Wright, D. G. and Jowitt, J. A., *Victorian Bradford: essays in honour of Jack Reynolds* (Bradford: City of Bradford Metropolitan Council, Libraries Division, 1982, *c.* 1981).

15. Ibid.

6 A Desperate Adventure

1. © Historic England [2017]. The National Heritage List Text Entries contained in this material were obtained on 14 November 2017. The most publicly available up to date National Heritage List Text Entries can be obtained from http://www.historicengland.org.uk/listing/the-list.

2. Quinn, Robin, *The man who broke the bank at Monte Carlo: Charles Deville Wells, Gambler and Fraudster Extraordinaire* (Stroud: The History Press, 2016).

3. Kelly's *Directory*, 1893.
4. Recorded in *The Gazette* (*London Gazette*), issue 22374, 6 April 1860.
5. Information comes from The National Archives resources on line (www.nationalarchives.gov.uk).
6. '*The Diary of John Grano*', MS. Rawl. D 34, Rawlinson Manuscripts, Bodleian Libraries, University of Oxford.
7. *The Insolvent Debtor: A Lay of Lancaster Castle*, Anon. 1861.

7 Manchester

1. Recorded in *The Gazette* (*London Gazette*), issue 22374, 6 April 1860.
2. The 1861 census records Joseph as a cotton and stuff agent.
3. The first canal not to follow an established water course and the model for those that followed (source: British Waterways).
4. Greater Manchester Museum of Transport.
5. Museum of Science and Industry website lists exchanges opening in London and in Manchester in 1879, there is debate as to which opened first.
6. *Spinning the Web*: The story of the cotton industry (Manchester City Council).
7. Recorded in *The Gazette* (*London Gazette*), issue 22374, 6 April 1860.
8. Angus Reach writing in the *Morning Chronicle*, 1849, about Manchester. Source: The British Newspaper Archive (www.britishnewspaperarchive.co.uk).
9. *Spinning the Web*: The story of the cotton industry (Manchester City Council).
10. Ibid.
11. This exact and that above are inscribed on the plinth of the statue of Abraham Lincoln that stands in Manchester.
12. Quoted in *The Illustrated London News*, 29 November 1862. Text reproduced courtesy of The Illustrated London News/ Mary Evans Picture Library.

13. Baillie, Rev. John, *What I saw in Lancashire ... A plea for the distressed operative* (London: John Nisbet, 1862).

14. *Spinning the Web.*

15. Act for the Relief of Insolvent Debtors, 1842.

16. From the National Archives website, research guide to bankrupts and insolvent debtors (www.nationalarchives.gov.uk).

17. Recorded in *The Gazette* (*London Gazette*), issue 22382, 4 May 1860.

18. Lancaster Castle do not retain any records of those incarcerated for debt and Lancashire Archives only hold details of insolvent debtors up to 1824. It is possible that the National Archives, who now hold the archive of the Court for the Relief of Insolvent Debtors, may turn up further information.

19. Letter sent by Joseph Hobson Jagger to Sidney Sowood, 5 Nov. 1875 (author's collection)..

20. Abraham died on 3 December 1860 and his will was not proved until 28 April 1862. Joseph was Executor and possibly the probate was delayed by his bankruptcy proceedings.

21. His father's will, proved on 28 April 1862, states that Joseph was still living at Girlington Road. The 1871 census shows him at 6 Greaves Street with his family.

22. Letter from F. D. Jagger to Hield Bros (author's collection).

23. Thomas Cook company archive.

24. Source is www.wirksworth.org.uk. Nominal annual earnings for an adult male, skilled in textiles, in 1881.

25. Sennett, Chris, *All About Monte Carlo and Roulette by O. Plucky, B. Careful & C. Wisdom etc.* (London: Edmund Seale, 1913).

26. Calculated using www.historicalstatistics.org/Currencyconverter.

27. *Cook's Handbook to the Health Resorts of the South of France and Northern Coast of the Mediterranean* (London: Thomas Cook & Son: Simpkin, Marshall & Co.,1881-82 [1881].

8 The Railwayman

1. From an article in the *Bradford Antiquary* by John Thornhill, *'All Change' Bradford's through railway schemes* (First published in 1986 in volume 2, pp. 35-46, of the third series of *The Bradford Antiquary*, the journal of the Bradford Historical and Antiquarian Society).

2. From an article in *History Extra* 14 September 2010 by Becky Hoskins, *Where History Happened: The Birth of the Railways*. These details are quoted in the article by railway historian Christian Wolmar.

3. Ibid.

4. These details come from a report by Lieut-Col C. S. Hutchinson, The Secretary, (Railway Department) Board of Trade, submitted 16 March 1871. The Board of Trade was the first government department to assume responsibility for the railways (source: www.railwaysarchive.co.uk).

5. Report by Lieut-Col C. S. Hutchinson, The Secretary, (Railway Department) Board of Trade, Whitehall, 12 November 1872 (source: www.railwaysarchive.co.uk).

6. Accident Returns: Extract for Accident at Staplehurst on 9 June 1865 from Railways Archive (www.railwaysarchive.co.uk).

7. From a letter written by Charles Dickens to his old school friend Thomas Mitton on 13 June 1865. Source is House, Madeline and Storey, Graham: general editors, *The Letters of Charles Dickens* (Oxford: Clarendon, 1965-2002) vol. 11, page 56.

8. From the introduction to the *Railway Employment Records 1833-1963* an online partnership between Ancestry & The National Archives).

9. From the Thomas Cook Company Archive

10. Ring, Jim, *Riviera: the rise and rise of the Côte D'Azur* (London: Faber & Faber, 2011).

11. *Cook's Handbook to the Health Resorts of the South of France and Northern Coast of the Mediterranean* (London: Thomas Cook & Son: Simpkin, Marshall & Co.,1881-82 [1881].

12. Ibid.

13. From the Thomas Cook Company Archive

14. They married on 2 November 1834.

15. Marriage record 2 November 1834.

16. Oates Jagger's birth certificate 1839.

17. 1851 census.

18. Church of England *Marriages and Banns, Bradford* (source: Ancestry) show that Richard married Rachel on 12 January 1856. His first wife Mary had been alive at the time of the 1851 census so must have died between 1851 and 1856.

19. By the time of the 1861 census Oates is resident at Girlington Road, but he may have moved there earlier.

20. The 1861 census shows Sarah Ann Bairstow aged twenty-two living as a lodger in Bowling with her 4-month-old daughter.

21. See the 1881 census. Mary married John Ogden 14 October 1883.

22. Reported in the *Bradford Observer*, 28 June 1866 (the marriage took place on 26 June). The baptism records for Bingley record Sarah Ann's birth as 24 December 1867 and her baptism as 12 April 1868.

23. Marriage record, 5 November 1870.

24. The 1861 census records that Oates is an Assistant Engine Man. Research from Peter Witt, Midland Railway Society shows that he could have walked easily from Girlington Road to Bradford Forster Square station.

25. Cudworth, William, *Manningham, Heaton, and Allerton, townships of Bradford, treated historically and topographically* (Bradford: W. Cudworth, 1896).

26. Sara Ann's baptism record in April 1868 says that Oates is an engine driver.

27. From the introduction to the *Railway Employment Records 1833-1963* online (partnership between Ancestry.com & The National Archives).

28. From the 1871 census.
29. Information from Peter Witts, Midland Railway Society.
30. From the 1881 census.
31. Information from Peter Witts, Midland Railway Society.
32. The Midland Railway ran the line from 1853.

9 *Sin, Scandal and Suicide*

1. Graves, Charles, *The Big Gamble. The story of Monte Carlo* (London: Hutchinson & Co., 1951).
2. *The Graphic (London)* 23 Feb 1895.
3. Société des Bains de Mer, *The History of Monte Carlo Casino*.
4. Ibid.
5. Sennett, Chris, *All About Monte Carlo and Roulette by O. Plucky, B. Careful & C. Wisdom etc.* (London: Edmund Seale, 1913).
6. Graves, *The Big Gamble*.
7. Pastoral address by the Bishop of Gibraltar.
8. Graves, *The Big Gamble*.
9. *Aberdeen Journal 1885*.
10. Le Queux, William, *The Secrets of Monte Carlo* (London: George Newnes, 1911).
11. Quinn, Robin, *The man who broke the bank at Monte Carlo: Charles Deville Wells, Gambler and Fraudster Extraordinaire* (Stroud: The History Press, 2016).
12. Sennett, *All About Monte Carlo and Roulette by O. Plucky, B. Careful & C. Wisdom etc..*
13. Smith, Adolphe, *Monaco and Monte Carlo* ([S.I.]: Richards, 1912).
14. Graves, *The Big Gamble*.
15. Smith, *Monaco and Monte Carlo*.
16. Bradshaw, George, *Continental Railway Guide and General Handbook*, 1913 (Botley, Oxford: Old House Books & Maps, 2012. Facsimile of 1913 edition).

17. *Cook's Handbook to the Health Resorts of the South of France and Northern Coast of the Mediterranean*, Thomas Cook, 1881-2.
18. Ibid.

10 *Systems and Players*

1. Schwartz, David G., *Roll the Bones: the history of Gambling* (New York; London: Gotham, 2006)
2. Ibid.
3. Braude, Mark, *Making Monte Carlo, a history of speculation and spectacle* (New York: Simon & Schuster, 2016).
4. Smith, Adolphe, *Monaco and Monte Carlo* ([S.I.]: Richards, 1912).
5. Letter from Dr. Arbuthnot to Lady Suffolk, July 6, 1731.
6. Schwartz, *Roll the Bones*.
7. Smith, *Monaco and Monte Carlo*.
8. Graves, Charles, *The Big Gamble. The story of Monte Carlo* (London: Hutchinson & Co., 1951).
9. Ibid.
10. Schwartz, *Roll the Bones*.
11. Quinn, Robin, *The man who broke the bank at Monte Carlo: Charles Deville Wells, Gambler and Fraudster Extraordinaire* (Stroud: The History Press, 2016).
12. Ibid.
13. Schwartz, *Roll the Bones*.
14. Smith, *Monaco and Monte Carlo*.
15. Braude, *Making Monte Carlo*.
16. I am grateful to Robin Quinn for this anecdote.
17. Bethell, Victor, *Monte Carlo Anecdotes and Systems of Play* (London: William Heinemann, 1901).
18. Sennett, Chris, *All About Monte Carlo and Roulette by O. Plucky, B. Careful & C. Wisdom etc.* (London: Edmund Seale, 1913).
19. Schwartz, *Roll the Bones*.

20. *Dundee Courier*, 12 April 1898.
21. Bethell, Victor, *Monte Carlo Anecdotes and Systems of Play* (London: William Heinemann, 1901).
22. Polovtsoff, General Pierre, *Monte Carlo Casino* (London: Stanley Paul & Co. 1937).
23. *Manchester Evening News*, 26 January 1893.
24. Polovtsoff, *Monte Carlo Casino*.
25. Bethell, *Monte Carlo Anecdotes and Systems of Play*.

11 The Key

1. Quinn, Robin, *The man who broke the bank at Monte Carlo: Charles Deville Wells, Gambler and Fraudster Extraordinaire* (Stroud: The History Press, 2016).

12 Breaking the Bank

1. *Cook's Handbook to the Health Resorts of the South of France and Northern Coast of the Mediterranean* (London: Thomas Cook & Son: Simpkin, Marshall & Co.,1881-82 [1881].
2. *Dundee Courier*, 12 April 1898.
3. Sennett, Chris, *All About Monte Carlo and Roulette by O. Plucky, B. Careful & C. Wisdom etc.* (London: Edmund Seale, 1913).
4. The leaflet issued by the casino *The History of Monte-Carlo Casino* states that the Moorish décor was introduced in 1878 by Charles Garnier. Adolphe Smith says that this transformation happened earlier (p307 suggests around 1872). However, by the time that Joseph was there, the *Salle Mauresque* transformation had happened and Cook's Handbook confirms this in its description of the main gaming room.
5. *Cook's Handbook to the Health Resorts of the South of France and Northern Coast of the Mediterranean* (London: Thomas Cook & Son: Simpkin, Marshall & Co.,1881-82 [1881].
6. Sennett, *All About Monte Carlo and Roulette by O. Plucky, B. Careful & C. Wisdom etc.*

13 A Prolonged Adventure

1. Schwartz, David G., *Roll the Bones: the history of Gambling* (New York; London: Gotham, 2006)

2. Leigh, Norman, *Thirteen against the Bank* (Harmondsworth: Penguin, 1978).

3. From an article in the *Illustrated Sporting and Dramatic News*, 6 August 1927. Text reproduced courtesy of The Illustrated London News/Mary Evans Picture Library.

4. *Western Daily Press*, 18 April 1913.

5. Bethell, Victor, *Monte Carlo Anecdotes and Systems of Play* (London: William Heinemann, 1901) p63.

6. Ibid.

7. According to two accounts, the roulette wheels used in Monte Carlo are made in Paris (Chris Sennett says 'the roulette wheel or cylinder is made in Paris' p39 and Charles Graves,' Paris manufacturers' p 77). Adolph Smith concurs but states that they were previously made in Strasbourg p365. Because I am uncertain of the dates here, I have used Paris in my account.

8. Bethell, *Monte Carlo Anecdotes and Systems of Play*, p65-6.

9. Ibid.

10. Quinn, Robin, *The man who broke the bank at Monte Carlo: Charles Deville Wells, Gambler and Fraudster Extraordinaire* (Stroud: The History Press, 2016).

11. Schwartz, *Roll the Bones*.

12. *The Tatler*, 25 April 1956.

13. From an article in the *Illustrated London News*, 22 May 1937. Text reproduced courtesy of The Illustrated London News/Mary Evans Picture Library.

14. Polovtsoff, General Pierre, *Monte Carlo Casino* (London: Stanley Paul & Co. 1937) p173

15. Graves, Charles, *The Big Gamble. The story of Monte Carlo* (London: Hutchinson & Co., 1951) p76.

16. Ibid.

17. Ibid., p77.
18. Charles Garnier's *Monte Carlo Casino General Plan, 1879* shows four tables and Adolphe Smith says there were five (p308).
19. Graves, *The Big Gamble*, p77.
20. Bethell, *Monte Carlo Anecdotes and Systems of Play*, p63.
21. Graves, *The Big Gamble*, p76.
22. From an article in the *Telegraph and Argus, 25 June 1960* by my father Dr Clifford M Fletcher.
23. Last Will and Testament of Joseph Hobson Jagger, 7 October 1881.
24. Information from Ron Cosens www.cartedevisite.co.uk.
25. From the trade directories of *Alpes-Maritimes*, list of photographers based in Nice in 1875. The *Archives départementales des Alpes-Maritimes* has an incomplete collection of trade directories for the years 1879 to 1884.

14 The Return

1. Marriage certificate of Mary Jagger and Henry Smith 21 November 1883.
2. Quinn, Robin, *The man who broke the bank at Monte Carlo: Charles Deville Wells, Gambler and Fraudster Extraordinaire* (Stroud: The History Press, 2016).
3. *Reynolds's Newspaper*, 22 January 1893.
4. Smith, Adolphe, *Monaco and Monte Carlo* ([S.I.]: Richards, 1912).
5. Graves, Charles, *The Big Gamble. The story of Monte Carlo* (London: Hutchinson & Co., 1951).

15 Building a Future

1. Berenson, Bernard, *My Dear BB – The Letters of Bernard Berenson and Kenneth Clark, 1925-1959* (New Haven: Yale University Press, 2015) p. 11.
2. From an Indenture between Thomas Ellis of Horton and Joseph Hobson Jagger of 6 Greaves Street, Horton dated

16 August 1881 (source: West Yorkshire Archive Service, Wakefield ref. 1881 vol. 859/p.669/no.793).

3. From deeds dated ref. 1886 vol. 25/p65/no 37 and ref. 1888 vol. 22/p.493/no.279 (source: West Yorkshire Archive Service, Wakefield). Derek Jagger's notes on reviewing the deeds state 'probably 11 properties.' (source: author's collection).

4. The purchases in Montague Street are listed in deed ref. 1886 vol.25/p.64/no.36 and deed ref. 1890 vol.2/p.493/no.265 (source: West Yorkshire Archive Service, Wakefield). (See Appendix 2.)

5. An Indenture of Partition dated 28 March 1913 summarises the property that Joseph bought in Pasture Lane as being numbers 20,22, 24, 26, 28, 30, 32, 34 and 36 (source: West Yorkshire Archive Service, Wakefield ref. 1913 vol. 14/p.800/no.280). Number 20 was sold in 1908.

6. Electoral Register 1888 (source: Ancestry)

7. Marriage certificate for Mary and Henry Smith 21 November 1883.

8. 1891 census

9. 1881 census

10. Ibid.

11. 1891 census

12. Ibid. and Indenture of Conveyance 25 January 1908 ref.1908 vol.4/p.990/no.407 (source: West Yorkshire Archive Service, Wakefield).

13. 1881 census

14. Bellerby, Rachel, *Chasing the sixpence: the lives of Bradford mill folk (Ayr: Fort Publishing, 2005).*

15. 1891 census onwards.

16. Bellerby, *Chasing the sixpence.*

17. The Indenture of Conveyance, 25 January 1908 ref.1908 vol.4/p.990/no.407 (source: West Yorkshire Archive Service, Wakefield) records Walter Jagger as living at 6 Greaves Street. By 1911 he had moved to 568 Little Horton Lane (1911 census).

18. 1881 census.
19. Marriage certificate of Mary and Henry Smith 21 November 1883.
20. Ibid.
21. 1891 census.
22. 1871 census.
23. 1891 census.
24. These details come from the inscription on Joseph Hobson Jagger's grave monument at Bethel Chapel where Effie is also buried.

16 A Quiet Achievement

1. Clifford M Fletcher published in the *Telegraph and Argus* 25 June 1960. The details of this story were picked up in later newspaper articles.
2. The 1891 census doesn't list any resident domestic help.
3. Graves, Charles, *The Big Gamble. The story of Monte Carlo* (London: Hutchinson & Co., 1951). p55
4. *The man who broke the bank at Monte Carlo: Charles Deville Wells, Fraudster and Gambler Extraordinaire*, Robin Quinn, 2016.
5. Braude, Mark, *Making Monte Carlo, a history of speculation and spectacle* (New York: Simon & Schuster, 2016).
6. Ring, Jim, *Riviera: the rise and rise of the Côte D'Azur* (London: Faber & Faber, 2011).
7. Smith, Adolphe, *Monaco and Monte Carlo* ([S.I.]: Richards, 1912).

17 Lost Millions

1. The Last Will and Testament of Joseph Hobson Jagger, 7 October 1881 (source: The National Archives www.nationalarchives.gov.uk)
2. Ibid.

3. According to the Indenture, 5 February 1896 ref.1896 vol.7/ p.336/ no. 160 (source: West Yorkshire Archive Service, Wakefield) Alfred was at 105 Horton Lane, Louisa at 8 Greaves Street, Walter at No. 6 Greaves Street and Mary at 20 Reginald Terrace

4. Marriage Certificate of Samuel Raistrick and Matilda Jagger, 8 February 1896.

5. The Last Will and Testament of Joseph Hobson Jagger, 7 October 1881 (source: The National Archives www. nationalarchives.gov.uk).

6. Indenture, 5 February 1896 ref.1896 vol.7/ p.336/ no. 160 (source: West Yorkshire Archive Service, Wakefield)

7. Indenture of Partition dated 28 March 1913 ref. 1913 vol. 14/p.800/no.280 (source: West Yorkshire Archive Service, Wakefield).

8. Last Will and Testament of Samuel Raistrick 28 November 1896.

9. She was certainly there in 1901 according to the census taken that year.

10. Death certificate of Matilda Raistrick 17 October 1902. It states that Mary was present at her death. The house belonged to Louisa and I presume she would have been present too.

11. Marriage Certificate of Samuel Raistrick and Matilda Jagger, 8 February 1896.

12. Page from the *Bradford Almanack* date unknown from West Yorkshire Archive (Bradford) file on Joseph Hobson Jagger.

13. Indenture of Partition dated 28 March 1913 ref. 1913 vol. 14/p.800/no.280 (source: West Yorkshire Archive Service, Wakefield).

14. The Last Will and Testament of Joseph Hobson Jagger, 7 October 1881 (source: The National Archives www. nationalarchives.gov.uk).

18 A Generous Gift

1. Information from www.nationalarchives.gov.uk guide to death duties 1796-1903.
2. From the author's conversation with Mollie Firth, 24 October 2016. The older relatives were the wives of her cousins Derek Jagger and Denis Holdsworth.
3. From BBC History www.historyextra.com.
4. Ibid.
5. Information from the Sadleir family website.
6. Reported to Clifford M Fletcher and recorded in his unpublished manuscript, *Some notes on my ancestry*, December 1998.
7. Reported to me by David Jagger.
8. Marriage Register Jan-March 1918 (source: Ancestry).
9. Gladys' birth certificate 1891 says he's a Master Butcher. The 1901 census records Job as a butcher too as does his marriage certificate 21 April 1880. His wife Mary's death certificate (1935) describes him as a worsted manufacturer.
10. The Last Will and Testament of Sybil Marion Jagger, 4 April 1978. Probate 7 February 1979 (source: Ancestry).
11. Dennis William Lee Jagger was born on 29 June 1921 (birth certificate dated 10 August).
12. Told to me by David Wright
13. At least I assume that Lucy's papers were destroyed as Read Dunn Connell confirmed to me that they no longer hold any records concerning Lucy or Alfred Jagger (in a letter dated 18 February 2011).
14. From an article in the *Bradford Telegraph & Argus* by Chris Holland published on 7 May 2014.
15. 1861 and 1871 census.
16. Letter from Lucy Jagger 1962 in the Dunn Connell papers as recorded in Pam Hill's research.

17. Indenture of Partition dated 28 March 1913 ref. 1913 vol. 14/p.800/no.280 (source: West Yorkshire Archive Service, Wakefield).

18. The houses were numbered differently when Joseph purchased them (numbers 26,28,30 and 32).

19. The 1911 census shows he was living at 568 Little Horton Lane.

20. The remaining properties in Pasture Lane and Beaconsfield Road, Clayton together with two plots of land. The land and properties that Joseph Hobson Jagger bought here in 1892 and 1887 were largely sold off by his executors and children in 1908 (Indenture of Conveyance 25 January 1908 ref.1908 vol.4/p.990/no.407 source: West Yorkshire Archive Service, Wakefield).

21. Information supplied by Liz McIvor, Curator (Social history & Technology), Bradford Museums and Galleries.

22. In 1911 Louisa was in Manchester Road and Emily in Parkside Road according to the census that year.

23. Details from the burial records for Bethel Chapel (book entry 3978 grave W3). Supplied by Christine Firth, Bethel Chapel.

24. Last Will and Testament of Louisa Briggs, 8 June 1923.

25. Marriage certificate of Mary Jagger and Henry Smith, November 1883 (source: Ancestry).

19 A Victorian Gentleman

1. Alfred Jagger's handwritten draft of his own obituary dated 30 March 1937 (source: author's collection).

2. According to Pam Hill's notes this was recorded in a letter written by Lucy Jagger in 1962 (part of the Dunn Connell papers seen by Pam Hill but now destroyed).

3. These details come from Historic England's database of protected historic buildings (list entry Number: 1132985) © Historic England [2017]. The National Heritage List Text Entries contained in this material were obtained on 14 November 2017. The most publicly available up to date

National Heritage List Text Entries can be obtained from http://www.historicengland.org.uk/listing/the-list.

4. Alfred Jagger's handwritten draft of his own obituary dated 30 March 1937 (source: author's collection).

5. 1901 census

6. The Last Will and Testament of Emily Hayes, 20 March 1921. The use of 5 Nab Lane is left to her husband Thomas.

7. I'm assuming they moved around 1902/3. They were certainly there in 1911.

8. Pam Hill's notes say 1902/3 when Lucy was nineteen and Alfred was forty-nine but the 1911 census shows they were not married then.

9. 1911 census.

10. Ibid.

11. Registry of Deeds ref: 1920 vol. 88/p113/no.42 (source: West Yorkshire Archive Service, Wakefield)

12. Laisterbridge Lane does not exist in the 1911 census so my assumption is that it was built close to the time when Alfred bought it.

13. Taylor, Simon and Gibson, Kathryn, *Manningham, Character and diversity in a Bradford suburb* (Swindon: English Heritage, 2010).

14. Alfred Jagger's handwritten draft of his own obituary dated 30 March 1937 (source: author's collection).

15. Records of Library and Museum of Freemasonry.

16. Alfred's obituary and records of Grand Lodge of Master Mark Masons London.

17. Alfred Jagger's handwritten draft of his own obituary dated 30 March 1937 (source: author's collection).

18. The Last Will and Testament of Alfred Jagger 14 October 1940 (source: Ancestry).

19. Alfred Jagger's handwritten draft of his own death notice dated 30 March 1937 (source: author's collection).

20. The Last Will and Testament of Alfred Jagger 14 October 1940 (source: Ancestry).
21. From Pam Hill's notes. She says that Alfred ran the business and had £7,000 invested in it. Her source was a letter written by Lucy Jagger in 1962, part of the Dunn Connell papers seen by Pam Hill but now destroyed (source: author's collection).

20 *The Clerks*

1. 1911 census.
2. The Last Will and Testament of Walter Jagger 10 May 1934 (source: Ancestry).
3. Mollie Firth recalls that her grandfather Walter Jagger owned the house and let her uncle Arnold live there. She was born in 1916 so presumably her awareness of this must come from the early 1930s. Walter died in 1934 (source: author's conversation with Mollie Firth 24 October 2016).
4. British Army Medal Index Cards 1914-1920 (source: www. findmypast.co.uk. Archive reference WO372/10)
5. British Army Medal Index Cards 1914-1920 (source: www. findmypast.co.uk. Archive reference WO372/10) lists Arnold B Jagger as being discharged in 1920. From 1921 to 1931 Arnold is listed as living at 6 Greaves Street on the electoral register. Annie's probate record in 1950 lists her as resident there (source: Ancestry).
6. Leigh, Norman, *Thirteen against the Bank* (Harmondsworth: Penguin, 1978).
7. Notes left by Derek Jagger
8. From the author's conversation with Mollie Firth, 24 October 2016.
9. The letters were written in the early 1960s and Alfred died in 1941. He could have told his story to Lucy some years before this.

21 *The Second 'Son'*

1. For example, in Indenture, 5 February 1896 ref.1896 vol.7/ p.336/ no. 160 and Indenture of Conveyance, 25 January 1908 ref.1908 vol.4/p.990/no.407 (source: West Yorkshire Archive Service, Wakefield).

2. 1891 census.

3. The Last Will and Testament of Oates Jagger, 4 January 1910. Probate recorded 14 March 1910 (source: Ancestry).

4. From the introduction to the *Railway Employment Records 1833-1963* an online partnership between Ancestry & The National Archives.

5. Deed ref. 1889 vol. 28/p. 553/ no. 290 and deed ref. 1888 vol. 28/ p.471/ no. 253 (source: West Yorkshire Archive Service, Wakefield).

6. Sennett, Chris, *All About Monte Carlo and Roulette by O. Plucky, B. Careful & C. Wisdom etc.* (London: Edmund Seale, 1913).

7. *Notes on the life of Joseph Hobson Jagger of Pepperhill, Shelf, 1830-1892 [c. 1991]* West Yorkshire Archive Service, Bradford. Document reference 50D94/3.

8. From the unpublished memoir by my father, Dr Clifford Malcolm Fletcher, called *Some notes on my ancestry,* written in December 1998 (source: author's collection).

9. From the author's conversation with Mollie Firth, 24 October 2016.

10. Last year the same house sold for £56,500 which gives some idea of what Joseph Hobson Jagger's property portfolio might be worth in today's market.

22 *Two Very Rich Young Men*

1. An article in the *Bradford Telegraph & Argus* by Chris Holland published on 7 May 2014 refers to the company in this way as does *White's Directory 1894* ('Engineers – mechanical').

2. *Kelly's* Directories for 1901 and 1912.

3. 1901 census lists him as 71 years old.

4. From the marriage certificate for Fred Lee and Mary Moger 4 July 1910. In the census of 1871, 17-year-old Mary and her five younger siblings are listed as living with their mother, but no father is resident. This is still the case in 1881.

5. The census of 1891 records Mary Moger as 'Mary Lee, wife' but the marriage certificate for Fred Lee and Mary Moger shows that they did not marry until 4 July 1910.

6. A new trustee was appointed for Fred Lee's estate in 1946 after the death of one of his original appointees and the *Deed of Appointment of a New Trustee of the Will* dated 15 October 1946 states that his wife Mary had died on 15 November 1913.

7. This story was related to me by members of the Eccleshill Local History Group.

8. As listed in the 1881 census.

9. Fred remembered a great many employees in his will, giving them cash bequests including 'my work-people commonly known by the names of Horace, Charley ...Frances, Sweeney, Harrison and Wood.' He left money also to his coachman, his servant and his two office boys.

10. This tallies with Pam Hill's notes which say that during the period 1914-1918 Brinley and Colin Lee Jagger jointly owned the company of W. B. Lee & Co. This was recorded in a letter written by Lucy Jagger in 1962 (part of the Dunn Connell papers seen by Pam Hill but now destroyed).

11. In the years 1909-1913, the Empire was the main source of wool. Nearly 50% came from Australia, the next biggest supplier was New Zealand and then South Africa. From Rose, John Holland et al, *Cambridge History of the British Empire Vol. 1* (Cambridge: Cambridge University Press, 1929).

12. Rose, John Holland et al, *Cambridge History of the British Empire Vol. 1* (Cambridge: Cambridge University Press, 1929).

13. Martin, William G., *South Africa and the World Economy: remaking race, state and region* (Rochester, NY: University of Rochester Press, 2013).

14. Aldcroft, Derek H., *From Versailles to Wall Street, 1919-1929* (London: Allen Lane, 1977).

15. Information provided by John Deare from the Natal Inland Family History Society, Natal Midlands branch of SA Genealogical Society.

16. Ibid.

17. Cox, Martin, *A brief Company history (*available on the *Maritime Matters* website).

18. This information is extracted from the *Names and Descriptions of Passenger*s list compiled for the voyage by the Union-Castle line ship the *Walmer Castle* from Natal to Southampton on 28 November 1903 (source: Ancestry).

19. From the web site *South African History Online* (SAHO), an open access digital archive which has the objective of redressing the imbalance in the presentation of the history of South Africa which has resulted from segregation.

20. *South African History Online.*

21. This comes from a report produced by the Research Unit, Parliament of the Republic of South Africa in 1913 called *Reflections on the impact of the Natives' Land Act, 1913 on local government in South Africa (*sourced from the *South African History Online* website*).*

22. The *Names and Descriptions of Passenger*s lists from the Union-Castle line show that Brinley Jagger sailed to South Africa on their ships each year between 1910 and 1915, returning to England in the spring. On 9 April 1910 he arrived back in Southampton on board the *Norman* after boarding at Port Elizabeth. The 1911 census (taken on 2 April) shows that Brinley was not in the country. In 1912 he returned from Durban on the *Edinburgh Castle* arriving in Southampton on

30 March. He boarded in Cape Town for his journey home on the RMS *Saxon* in 1913, arriving on 29 March. The *Galway Castle* brought him home from Durban in 1914, arriving on 16 April and in 1915 he sailed on the *Dunvegan Castle* from Durban to Plymouth arriving home on 16 July.

23. Fred Lee died on 14 June 1915 and his will cleared probate on 25 February 1916. Brinley Lee Jagger was one of two executors of the will.

24. Speech by John Maddox, Chairman of the Bradford Manufacturing Company at the company AGM in 1912, quoted in Keighley, Mark, *Wool city: A history of the Bradford textile industry in the 20th century* (Ilkley: G. Whitaker & Company Ltd., 2007).

25. Taylor, Simon and Gibson, Kathryn, *Manningham, Character and diversity in a Bradford suburb* (Swindon: English Heritage, 2010).

26. Keighley, Mark, *Wool city: A history of the Bradford textile industry in the 20th century* (Ilkley: G. Whitaker & Company Ltd., 2007).

27. Ibid.

28. Ibid.

29. Ibid.

30. This information comes from David Wright who was told that Brinley and Colin made a fortune as a result of the contracts made during the First World War.

31. Taylor, Simon and Gibson, Kathryn, *Manningham, Character and diversity in a Bradford suburb* (Swindon: English Heritage, 2010).

32. Keighley, Mark, *Wool city: A history of the Bradford textile industry in the 20th century* (Ilkley: G. Whitaker & Company Ltd., 2007).

33. J. B. Priestley quoted in Taylor, Simon and Gibson, Kathryn, *Manningham, Character and diversity in a Bradford suburb* (Swindon: English Heritage, 2010).

34. Keighley, Mark, *Wool city: A history of the Bradford textile industry in the 20th century* (Ilkley: G. Whitaker & Company Ltd., 2007).

35. From an article in the *Yorkshire Post and Leeds Intelligencer*, 13 May 1938 which refers to Brinley and Colin's retirement three years ago. This date is supported by Pam Hill's notes.

36. Last Will and Testament of Emily Hayes, 20 March 1921 and National Probate Calendar (source: Ancestry).

23 *Monk Barn*

1. From an article in *The Yorkshire Post* on Friday 13 May 1938 about the building of the school. The information about the size of the Jagger donation comes from Pam Hill's notes.

2. The *Eldwick Village Society Newsletter* issue 346 September 2007 is evidence that the trophy was still being awarded.

3. Evidence of a close relationship can be found in Sybil Jagger's will signed by her on 4 April 1978. She left her black onyx and diamond earrings to Lady Hill as they had formerly belonged to the late Sir James Hill's grandmother.

4. Keighley, Mark, *Wool city: A history of the Bradford textile industry in the 20th century* (Ilkley: G. Whitaker & Company Ltd., 2007).

5. From a report in the *Yorkshire Post and Leeds Intelligencer* on 19 November 1952.

6. From a report in the *Yorkshire Post and Leeds Intelligencer* on 1 July 1935.

7. Brinley and Sybil Jagger referred to their home as Monk Barn in advertisements for staff, in their correspondence and in Sybil's will. The name plate on the post at the entrance uses this name. However, when the property was listed on 9 August 1966 as a Grade II protected building, it was

registered as Monks Barn. Historic England's database still
has it listed under this name (list entry Number:1300878 as
at 14 November 2017 www.historicengland.org.uk/listing/the-
list). As this listing happened after the Jaggers sold the house I
have decided to use their name for their home, Monk Barn.

8. From Historic England's database of protected historic
   buildings (list entry Number:1300878 as at 14 November 2017
   www.historicengland.org.uk/listing/the-list).

9. These details are given in a property for sale advertisement
   placed in the *Yorkshire Post and Leeds Intelligencer* on
   Saturday 9 September 1922 for Monk Barn, Park Road,
   Bingley.

10. The Last Will and Testament of Emily Hayes witnessed
    20 March 1921 (source: Ancestry).

11. Details from a property for sale advertisement placed
    in the *Yorkshire Post and Leeds Intelligencer* on Saturday
    9 September 1922 and from Historic England's database of
    protected historic buildings (list entry Number:1300878)
    © Historic England [2017]. The National Heritage List
    Text Entries contained in this material were obtained on
    14 November 2017. The most publicly available up to date
    National Heritage List Text Entries can be obtained from
    http://www.historicengland.org.uk/listing/the-list.

12. *In the matter of Brinley Lee Jagger deceased. Valuation for
    Probate.* Produced by Gaunt, Fosters & Bottomley Solicitors,
    Bradford and John H. Raby & Son, Valuers, Bradford,
    18 May 1962 (from the family archive of David Wright).

13. Last Will and Testament of Emily Hayes witnessed
    20 March 1921.

14. From the property for sale advertisement in the *Yorkshire
    Post and Leeds Intelligencer,* Saturday 9 September 1922.

15. Sybil Jagger placed adverts for staff in the *Yorkshire Post
    and Leeds Intelligencer.* On 24 April 1928, 23 April 1932
    and 10 March 1932 she was seeking a capable cook and
    stated that a housemaid was kept. On 2 December 1939 and

23 December 1940 she was looking for a young housemaid-waitress, presumably to help at Christmas and New Year.

16. Telephone directories and Colin's will written in 1954 show that he was at Nab Lane at that time. His probate record from November 1961 shows that he was resident in a care home at his death (source: Ancestry).

17. From letters exchanged between Sybil Jagger (as executor) and Dunn, Connell & Co solicitors 19 March and 22 July 1963 and a summary of the financial balance of Colin Jagger's estate dated 30 June 1963. According to the latter, Colin's estate was virtually worthless by the time that duties and debts had been paid (from the family archive of David Wright).

24 *The Two Widows*

1. The Last Will and Testament of Lucy Adeline Jagger, 30 May 1962.

2. Letter from Dunn Connell & Co to Sybil Jagger dated 19 March 1963 (from the family archive of David Wright).

3. Probate record 15 August 1963 to revise Alfred Jagger's estate (source: Ancestry).

4. Probate record 14 April 1969 for Lucy Adeline Jagger (source: Ancestry).

5. Probate record 15 August 1963 to revise Alfred Jagger's estate (source: Ancestry).

6. Probate record 14 April 1969 for Lucy Adeline Jagger.

7. David Wright knows that this happened to Colin Jagger, so it is reasonable to expect it happened to Lucy too. Source is www.income-tax.co.uk/history of income tax and *Daily Telegraph*, 21 June 2003.

8. The Last Will and Testament of Lucy Adeline Jagger, 30 May 1962.

9. 18 March 1962

10. The address is stated in the insurance renewal notice for a diamond ring sent by the County Fire Office, Limited to Gladys Robertshaw on 6 December 1951 (from the family archive of David Wright).

11. Record of the items for sale on 20 September 1962, produced by John H. Raby & Son, Auctioneers, valuers, estate agents for Gladys Robertshaw (from the family archive of David Wright). Gladys's will dated 3 July 1964, gives her address as Monk Barn.

12. This story was recounted to me by David Wright.

13. First codicil to the will of Miss G. W. Robertshaw, 24 March 1975 gives 23 Petersgarth as Gladys's address. Sybil's will dated 4 April 1978 also gives this address (from the family archive of David Wright).

14. This detail was told to me by David Wright who was a regular visitor.

15. Sybil's will, 4 April 1978, shows her residence as 23 Petersgarth. The codicil dated 7 November 1978 shows that she has moved to the residential home (from the family archive of David Wright).

16. Codicil to the will of Sybil Marion Jagger, 7 November 1978 (from the family archive of David Wright).

17. Last Will & Testament of Sybil Marion Jagger, 4 April 1978.

18. Codicil to the will of Sybil Marion Jagger, 7 November 1978 (from the family archive of David Wright).

19. This is a type written list signed by Gladys Robertshaw and initialled by Sybil Jagger and witnessed by Kathleen Anderson and L. Smith (from the family archive of David Wright).

20. Record of the items for sale on 20 September 1962, produced by John H. Raby & Son, Auctioneers, valuers, estate agents for Gladys Robertshaw (from the family archive of David Wright).

21. Probate register 7 February 1979 (source: Ancestry).

22. Last Will and Testament of Gladys Whitley Robertshaw, 3 July 1964.

23. Last Will and Testament of Gladys Whitley Robertshaw, 6 April 1979.
24. Codicil to the Will of Gladys Whitley Robertshaw, 5 October 1979 (from the family archive of David Wright).
25. This is David Wright's interpretation of events, told to me when we met.
26. From a handwritten set of notes (from the family archive of David Wright).
27. David Wright's account of his conversation with Edward Green, Gladys's solicitor.
28. Events recounted by David Wright who was present.

25 *The Legacy*

1. From an article in the *Bradford Telegraph & Argus* by Chris Holland published on 7 May 2014.
2. Polovtsoff, General Pierre, *Monte Carlo Casino* (London: Stanley Paul & Co. 1937).
3. Graves, Charles, *The Big Gamble. The story of Monte Carlo* (London: Hutchinson & Co., 1951) page 77.
4. Smith, Adolphe, *Monaco and Monte Carlo* ([S.I.]: Richards, 1912). Charles Graves states that the daily checking of the wheel with a spirit level was instituted after Joseph's win (*The Big Gamble. The story of Monte Carlo* page 77). David Schwartz confirms this (*Roll the Bones: the history of Gambling* page 314).
5. This story is told on a number of web sites including www.casinoroulettesecrets.com and the Casino Las Vegas blog. The details vary and there is some uncertainty about the legal consequences and how much money Garcia-Pelayo retained but the consistent element of the story is that he exploited the bias as Joseph had done.
6. David Jagger's account of events.

26 *Family Pride*

1. From the unpublished memoir by my father, Dr Clifford Malcolm Fletcher, called *Some notes on my ancestry,* written in December 1998 (source: author's collection).
2. Ibid. Susan (1882), Ruth (1887) and Norah (1884) and Norah's two sons Sydney (1925) and Clifford (1929).
3. Ibid.
4. Labour certificate for Norah Milner 27 September 1895 (source: author's collection).
5. From the unpublished memoir by my father, Dr Clifford Malcolm Fletcher, called *Some notes on my ancestry,* written in December 1998 (source: author's collection).
6. Ibid.
7. Ibid.
8. Ibid.
9. Ibid.

SOURCES

Books

Aldcroft, Derek H., *From Versailles to Wall Street, 1919-1929* (London: Allen Lane, 1977)

Baillie, Revd John, *What I saw in Lancashire ... A plea for the distressed operative* (London: John Nisbet, 1862)

Bellerby, Rachel, *Chasing the sixpence: the lives of Bradford mill folk* (Ayr: Fort Publishing, 2005)

Bethell, Victor, *Monte Carlo Anecdotes and Systems of Play* (London: William Heinemann, 1901)

Bradshaw, George, *Continental Railway Guide and General Handbook 1913* (Botley, Oxford: Old House Books & Maps, 2012; facsimile of 1913 edition)

Braude, Mark, *Making Monte Carlo: a history of speculation and spectacle* (New York: Simon & Schuster, 2016)

Butterworth, Michael, *The man who broke the bank at Monte Carlo* (Bath: Chivers, 1985, c. 1983)

Cook's Handbook to the Health Resorts of the South of France and Northern Coast of the Mediterranean (London: Thomas Cook & Son: Simpkin, Marshall & Co.,1881-82 [1881]).

Cudworth, William, *Manningham, Heaton, and Allerton, townships of Bradford, treated historically and topographically* (Bradford: W. Cudworth, 1896)

Cudworth, William, *Rambles round Horton: historical, topographical, and descriptive* (Bradford: Thos. Brear & Co., 1886

Cudworth, William, *Worstedopolis: A sketch history of the town and trade of Bradford, the metropolis of the Worsted industry* (Bradford: W. Byles and Sons, 1888)

Firth, Gary, *J. B. Priestley's Bradford* (Stroud: Tempus, 2006)

Graves, Charles, *The Big Gamble. The story of Monte Carlo* (London: Hutchinson & Co., 1951)

House, Madeline and Storey, Graham (eds), *The Letters of Charles Dickens* (Oxford: Clarendon, 1965-2002)

Jones, J. Philip, *Gambling yesterday and today: a complete history* (Newton Abbot: David and Charles, 1973)

Keighley, Mark, *Wool city: A history of the Bradford textile industry in the 20th century* (Ilkley: G. Whitaker & Company Ltd., 2007)

Laver, James, *Costume and fashion: a concise history* (London: Thames and Hudson, 1995)

Leigh, Norman, *Thirteen against the Bank* (Harmondsworth: Penguin, 1978)

Le Queux, William, *The Secrets of Monte Carlo* (London: George Newnes, 1911)

Martin, William G., *South Africa and the World Economy: remaking race, state and region* (Rochester, NY: University of Rochester Press, 2013)

Paterson, Mike, *A brief history of life in Victorian Britain: a social history of Queen Victoria's reign* (London: Robinson, 2008)

Polovtsoff, General Pierre, *Monte Carlo Casino* (London: Stanley Paul & Co., 1937)

Quinn, Robin, *The man who broke the bank at Monte Carlo: Charles Deville Wells, Gambler and Fraudster Extraordinaire* (Stroud: The History Press, 2016).

Ring, Jim, *Riviera: the rise and rise of the Côte D'Azur* (London: Faber & Faber, 2011)

Rolt, L. T. C., *George & Robert Stephenson: the railway revolution* (London: Longmans, 1960)

Rose, John Holland *et al.*, *Cambridge History of the British Empire Vol. 1* (Cambridge: Cambridge University Press, 1929)

Schwartz, David G., *Roll the Bones: the history of Gambling* (New York; London: Gotham, 2006)

Sennett, Chris, *All About Monte Carlo and Roulette by O. Plucky, B. Careful & C. Wisdom etc.* (London: Edmund Seale, 1913)

Smith, Adolphe, *Monaco and Monte Carlo* ([S.I.]: Richards, 1912)

Taylor, Simon and Gibson, Kathryn, *Manningham: Character and diversity in a Bradford suburb* (Swindon: English Heritage, 2010)

Wright, D. G. and Jowitt, J. A., *Victorian Bradford: essays in honour of Jack Reynolds* (Bradford: City of Bradford Metropolitan Council, Libraries Division, 1982, *c.* 1981)

Other Published Sources

Bingley Conservation Area Assessment, City of Bradford Metropolitan District Council, 2004

'The Diary of John Grano', MS. Rawl. D 34, Rawlinson Manuscripts, Bodleian Libraries, University of Oxford

Reflections on the impact of the Natives' Land Act, 1913 on local government in South Africa, Research Unit, Parliament of the Republic of South Africa, 1913

Société des Bains de Mer, *The History of Monte Carlo Casino* (leaflet given to casino visitors)

Online Archives and Resources

Ancestry (ancestry.co.uk)

The British Newspaper Archive (www.britishnewspaperarchive.co.uk)

The Charles Dickens Letters Project (www.dickensletters.com)

The Gazette (www.thegazette.co.uk)
The National Archives (www.nationalarchives.gov.uk)
Parliament.co.uk
Railways Archive (www.railwaysarchive.co.uk)
Spinning the Web, the story of the cotton industry, Manchester
  City Council (www.spinningtheweb.org.uk)
South African History Online (www.sashistory.org.za)
Victoria & Albert Museum, history of fashion 1840-1900 (www.
  vam.ac.uk)

Archives and Collections of Libraries, Societies and Museums

Archives départementales des Alpes-Maritimes
Bethel Chapel (Christine Firth)
Bingley Local History Society (Allan Mirfield)
The Bodleian Library, Oxford
Bradford Family History Society
Bradford Grammar School (Lesley Purcell)
Bradford Historical and Antiquarian Society
Bradford Museums & Galleries (Liz McIvor, Curator, Social
  History and Technology)
City of Bradford Metropolitan District Council
Eccleshill Local History Group
Exeter Local History Society (Dick Passmore)
Freemasons' Hall
Grand Lodge of Master Mark Masons London
Greater Manchester County Record Office
Halifax Antiquarian Society (David C Glover and Ben Stables)
Lancashire County Council (Paul Hatch)
Lancashire Record Office
Lancaster Castle (Christine Goodier)
Library and Museum of Freemasonry
Local Studies at Bradford Central library
London Illustrated News

Manchester City Council Archives
Mary Evans Picture Library
Natal Inland Family History Society (John Deare)
Natal Midlands branch of SA Genealogical Society
National Library of Scotland.
Société des Bains de Mer (Charlotte Loubert)
Society of Genealogists
Sotheby's
Thomas Cook UK archive (Paul Smith)
West Yorkshire Archive Service, Bradford
West Yorkshire Archive Service, Wakefield

ACKNOWLEDGEMENTS

I have many people to thank for this book. There would not be one at all if Amy Licence, through a Twitter conversation about women who write history, hadn't spotted the potential in the story. At Amberley Books, I am enormously grateful to Jonathan Jackson for taking me on and to Shaun Barrington and particularly Alex Bennett and Hazel Kayes for their skill and patience in steering me and the book through to production and launch.

For the story I must of course thank my father Dr Clifford Malcolm Fletcher for telling it to me and igniting in me the desire to record it for all of us. I embarked on this project to complete the work that he started and as a tribute to him. This book is dedicated to your memory, Dad. David and Joyce Jagger, among all of my newfound family, have supported me the most, sharing information and meeting with me over the years. But I'd also like to thank Mollie Firth and David Wright for their invaluable contributions. Robin Quinn, my fellow bank-breaker historian, in doubting Joseph's existence gave me the impetus to prove that he really did go to Monte Carlo. His support has extended to providing me with a truly excellent index. My brother Dr David Fletcher supplied map research and helped me to find our family photos while my mother, Pauline Fletcher, provided many useful family anecdotes and most importantly told me how proud my dad would be.

My research would have been impossible, and Joseph's story left untold, if it wasn't for the many local historians, societies, libraries, collections and museums who have generously shared information with me. Some are run by volunteers and some are under-resourced but all are indispensable repositories of research and knowledge. Without these men and women and their passion and commitment, so many of our ancestors and their histories would be lost. I have listed those who have helped but I'd like to thank in particular Peter Witts from the Midland Railway Society, who helped me unravel my family's connections with the early railways; Allan Mirfield from the Bingley Local History Society, who solved the mystery of the 'big house bought with the winnings' by showing me Monk Barn; and Dick Passmore and his colleagues at the Exeter Local History Society, who, unbeknownst to them, unearthed the reason for Joseph's journey to Monte Carlo.

Mary Drysdale and Jenny Warbrick, my fellow biographers, have kept me going with our regular writing sessions, and this book has taken shape through their insightful critique over many years. My thanks too to Jo Neville for reading the entire manuscript and giving me invaluable feedback. Jane Manson, my research partner, has travelled with me to Bradford and to Monte Carlo, never tiring of discussing the story and always inspiring me with her enthusiasm for it. Dr Tracy Borman gave me advice at the very start of this project which has guided the organisation of both my research and my writing, and for this I'm very grateful.

Last and not least I must thank the three most important men in my life. My husband Jon has not only given me the space and time to write this book, but has never failed in his encouragement, helping me with constructive comment and creative ideas when I was flagging and always reassuring me that I could do it. Thank you, JJ. To my lovely boys Joseph (who was named after Joseph Hobson Jagger) and Matthew, thank you for sharing me for so long with your famous ancestor. This account is for you. I hope that it will show you that with courage, creativity and imagination, you can achieve anything.

INDEX

Note: For the purposes of this index 'Joseph Hobson Jagger' is abbreviated to JHJ